WE SPEAK FOR OURSELVES

We Speak for Ourselves

THE EXPERIENCES OF GAY MEN AND LESBIANS

Jack Babuscio

First published in Great Britain 1976
This revised edition first published 1988
SPCK
Holy Trinity Church
Marylebone Road
London NW1 4DU

British Library Cataloguing in Publication Data

Babuscio, Jack
    We speak for ourselves: the experiences
    of gay men and lesbians. – Rev. ed.
    1. Homosexuality – For counselling
    I. Title
    306.7′66′024362
    ISBN 0-281-04349-3

Typeset by Acorn Bookwork, Salisbury, Wiltshire
Printed in Great Britain by
St Edmundsbury Press Ltd., Bury St Edmunds, Suffolk

To Richard Minta Dunn

Acknowledgements

Thanks are due to the following for permission to quote from copyright sources:

American Journal of Psychotherapy: 'Psychotherapy Today or Where Do We Go From Here?' by Carl R. Rogers, in the *American Journal of Psychotherapy*, January 1963

Angus & Robertson (U.K.) Ltd and Outerbridge & Lazard, Inc: *Homosexual: Oppression and Liberation by* Dennis Altman

The Campaign for Homosexual Equality: *Comments on Manifesto 7*, a Report prepared by the London West End Group of the Campaign for Homosexual Equality

The Gay Academics Union, Inc.: 'Coming Out' by Howard J. Brown, in *The Universities and the Gay Experience: A Conference Sponsored by the Men and Women of the Gay Academics Union, 23 and 24 November 1973*

RT Collective (*RT: A Journal of Radical Therapy*): 'Surviving Psychotherapy' by Christopher Z. Hobson, in *Rough Times*, ed. Jerome Agel

St Martin's Press, Inc: *Society and the Healthy Homosexual* by George Weinberg

Chapter 3, 'Passing through Oppression', is based on an article entitled 'Passing for Straight: The Politics of the Closet', which originally appeared in *Gay News*, No. 62. The author is grateful to *Gay News* for permission to use this material.

Contents

Preface to the First Edition

The title of this book speaks for a new generation of homosexuals, one concerned with probing the creative possibilities of being gay in the present rather than locating the causes of homosexuality in the past.

It has never been my aim in writing *We Speak for Ourselves* to pursue any particular counselling theory or to suggest interviewing techniques for use in counselling situations. Such information can readily be found elsewhere. But it has been my wish to allow gay men and women to explore the personal and social implications of their own situations and in their own words. Such an approach, I believe, will serve the purpose of widening the reader's understanding of what it means to be gay by demonstrating through example the ways in which attitudes to sexuality can affect gay relationships and influence aspirations towards a fuller and happier life.

In reading this book, the reader will bear in mind that no one homosexual or group of homosexuals can speak for all homosexuals, any more than one heterosexual or group of heterosexuals can speak for all heterosexuals. Each individual represented in these pages speaks for him or her self alone. No one claims to be, or is presented as, a representative of a type.

One thing most contributors do have in common, however, is a deep awareness of the important place that homosexuality has had in their lives. This consciousness is evident in much of what they say, and it reflects, at least in part, the individual and group counselling situations in which most have been involved.

The material in this book, reproduced here with the full consent of all contributors, consists primarily of edited transcriptions of tape-recordings, but also of letters and personal statements submitted to me at my request. Names, places, and minor details have been altered in every instance, with the exception of those few accounts which have already been published elsewhere. This determination to protect the anonymity of individuals, I would add, reflects my own wish to respect the privacy of all those concerned.

JACK BABUSCIO
London 1976

Preface to the Second Edition

For the second edition of *We Speak for Ourselves*, I have expanded the discussion in several chapters to take account of changes over the last decade in areas such as legislation, anti-gay discrimination, shifting church views on homosexuality, etc. There is also a greatly expanded Critical Bibliography and a completely rewritten Guide to Organizations Giving Advice and Help.

I have left the original organization of the book intact, but have included two additional chapters on the subject of AIDS. AIDS is a public health problem with important implications for everyone, but a problem which, at the present moment in time, is of greatest concern to gay men, who currently represent the highest risk group in Britain (and with whom these additional chapters are principally concerned, unlike the rest of the text where attention is equally divided between lesbians and gay men). It would be difficult to underestimate the human consequences of AIDS, the appearance of which has had a devastating impact upon the entire gay community. Not only has it caused great suffering to those afflicted with the disease, along with their partners, friends and families, it has also led to homosexuality being further stigmatized, thus exacerbating the difficulties associated with, for example, self-acceptance as gay, coming out, and the forging of a homosexual identity and community. The repercussions of AIDS are many and complex, and it is hoped that this revised edition of *We Speak for Ourselves* will be of assistance in focusing attention on at least some of the principal areas of present concern.

JACK BABUSCIO
London 1988

1
What are the Problems?

We only become what we are by the radical and deep-seated refusal of
that which others have made of us.

Jean-Paul Sartre,
preface to Frantz Fanon's *The Wretched of the Earth* (1961)

An Urgent Word to the Reader

This book is intended for all those who counsel others and who care
about the quality of that counselling. It is for the professional and
the non-professional alike—for anyone, in short, who gives help to
those who seek understanding and assistance in living their lives.
Counsellors are, in this broad sense, help-givers. They are parents
and friends, teachers and clergy, nurses and psychologists, you and
I. People, in other words, to whom others feel they can come and
talk.

But counselling involves more than simply listening. Those who
help others are also agents of change, modifying the feelings and
attitudes of individuals, as well as their social situations. Often, such
people feel inadequate to their task when confronted with a
homosexual. At such times they bemoan their inadequate knowledge
or their lack of qualifications in psychology, deciding, in the end, to
refer this 'problem' to a 'specialist' in the field, or, failing that, to
someone who has earned a reputation for being 'good with such
people'. These counsellors, in particular, will find this book useful,
for it has been my intention throughout to share with the reader
what I have found to be most helpful and practical in my own
counselling experience with lesbians and gay men.

As the reader is already aware, the past two decades have been
marked by a growing wave of public attention to all the varieties of
human sexual behaviour. Unfortunately, most of the growth has
been in volume rather than quality. As far as homosexuality is
concerned, the present AIDS epidemic and the tendency of many to

regard the disease as essentially linked to gay sex has resulted in a health crisis being used to enliven perennial charges that homosexuality is sick and unnatural. The gay label attached to this epidemic has done much to shape the public's perception of AIDS and of homosexuals, which in turn has had the most profound consequences for the gay community. What is most needed, at a time like this, is a book that can objectively set the record straight and also provide information and advice on a variety of problems arising out of homosexual adaptations.

It is important, when we speak of homosexuality, to remember that we are dealing with very substantial numbers of men and women from all social groups. Using the Kinsey Institute statistics[1] and the cross-cultural studies of Martin Weinberg and Colin Williams of the (Indiana) Institute for Sex Research,[2] we find that, on average, ten per cent of the entire adult population is predominantly homosexual. Even those who reject such high figures as these are confronted with the fact that no source estimates the incidence of homosexuality as being less than one in twenty—five per cent of the total population. Opting for the very lowest figure available, this means that, in terms of numbers, there are some two million adults in the UK who are predominantly attracted to their own sex. If we are to include the even greater number of people who have at least some personal involvement in homosexuality, or who are attracted to both sexes, the figures will be very much higher.

Taking into account the social context in which the homosexual lives, many of these more than two million gay people will be confused and troubled by their sexual orientation. With the advent of AIDS there is now even less genuine acceptance of homosexuality as a valid sexual and social lifestyle than there was in the 1970s, a decade which saw a great upsurge in publicity and discussion on the subject. As a man in his early twenties remarked to a journalist who had accompanied a Gay Pride march through the centre of London: 'Try wearing a 'Glad to be Gay' button for a day or so, and see for yourself just how accepting people really are.'

Indeed, in some respects our less inhibited references to homosexuality appear to have actually intensified fears and prejudices. Inhibitions and feelings of guilt are often exacerbated in those very people who have been awakened to their true sexual identity by the recent storm of publicity. In its relentless exposure of everything that departs from the statistical norm, the media have made voyeurs of us all; they have not necessarily made us more accepting of the legitimacy of the sexual variations which they describe in such graphic detail.

All the same, public concern about AIDS, combined with increasing publicity on behalf of sexual minorities, has important implications for the counsellor. Today's help-givers find themselves confronted with ever-increasing numbers of people who are able to identify their homosexual component. Not all these people, though, can cope with their discovery. 'The love that dare not speak its name' may have found its tongue, but self-acceptance is more difficult to come by. The journey from the 'closet' to the 'street' is often long and painful, and the counsellor must understand the special nature of the problems that the traveller faces. It is not enough to be an unbiased and sympathetic listener, important though this is. Counsellors need to know, as best they can, what it is like to be 'different', to bear a stigma, in an increasingly hostile world.

Those of us who care to help people in distress should be alarmed, then, by the swelling number of cases of discrimination and violence against homosexuals. The equation of AIDS and homosexuality has led many to blame gay men for the epidemic, with all other sufferers of the disease being regarded as 'innocent victims'. Many gays have been very deeply affected by this unfair conceptualization of AIDS, with feelings of guilt adding to the pain of rebuke against the gay lifestyle currently predominating in the media. Though neither guilt nor blame are useful responses to an epidemic, their prevalence underlines the seriousness of the situation which homosexuals are now facing.

The need is therefore obvious, and *urgent*. Counsellors are required who can and will be of help to the large numbers of gay people who are coming of age, or who are grown up but troubled, in this era of AIDS. For all too many, the pain of loneliness and social isolation is even more acute than ever, and these burdens are scarcely made lighter when some sections of the community to whom we traditionally turn for help in our emotional and spiritual lives show only apathy, want of knowledge or even, and most regrettably, hostility, when understanding, acceptance and compassion are required.

But first the counsellor needs to be aware of his or her own position with regard to homosexuality. We are dealing here with a

3

psychosexual orientation which rouses strong and often contradic-
tory feelings in people. It is imperative, if we have the interest of
those we would help at heart, that we carefully examine our conscience to ascertain the extent to which the available evidence may
have coloured our attitude. So much of the published literature on
the subject has tended, until very recently, to regard homosexuality
per se as a problem. This is as true of the subjective-confessional
autobiographies of homosexuals as it is of the sensationalist fiction
that purports to explore the so-called 'tragic twilight world' of the
homosexual. But it is even more true of both the descriptive and
analytical accounts which view homosexuality from the position of
the outsider and the quasi-hysterical outpourings of certain sections
of the media which stigmatize gay men as carriers of a 'plague'.
These historical, psychiatric, sociological, legal, theological, medical
and journalistic accounts are usually concerned with the aetiology or
social impact of what their authors regard as socially or physically
destructive, neurotic, deviant, criminal, sinful or sick behaviour.

This book grows out of a disillusionment with such works, the
theory and discussion of which is rarely grounded in the problems
and situations of real people. And it is this fact, more than any other,
that has led me to write a guide for counsellors who work, or who
will in future work, with homosexuals. I have therefore attempted in
these chapters to present a world that will be recognizable to those
who live in it, rather than those who briefly tour it; and to demonstrate that such problems as do exist for the homosexual—and it is
my intention to allow gay people to define these problems for
themselves, and in their own words—spring from negative societal
reaction to homosexuality rather than from anything inherent in the
homosexual orientation itself. (Discussion of AIDS and the
tremendous impact it has had on the homosexual community has
been largely left until Chapter 8.) In short, my aim throughout is to
provide as many insights as possible into the multifarious ways in
which gay people view their status as citizens of a world whose
institutions are designed to meet not their needs, but those of the
heterosexual majority.

The Problem of Identity

Because attention has been focused almost exclusively on the *causes*
of homosexuality, the *creative* aspects of this sexual variation have

been largely ignored. This, of course, is understandable. So long as homosexuality is regarded as a sexual orientation in need of alteration or 'cure', there can be little concern for the creative process of self-actualization—the growth towards psychological maturity, the realization of individual potential, and the development of fulfilling relationships.

No matter how compassionate or well-intentioned the researcher, it is none the less a fact that any investigation into the aetiology of homosexuality will be biased from the outset unless the search is broadened to encompass the whole field of human sexuality. In other words, to consider only the question 'What causes homosexuality?' without also asking the parallel question 'What causes heterosexuality?' is to make a value judgement in favour of the latter. Heterosexual behaviour is thus taken to be the norm—an unquestioned assumption which determines the selection of evidence, colours the interpretation of facts, and ensures a conclusion that does scant justice to gay people.

It is as a direct result of society's failure to accept homosexuality as a legitimate variation of the sexual drive that the gay person's principal problem becomes one of finding an acceptable identity within a hostile environment. Yet this search for a satisfying self-image is often thwarted by a barrier of demeaning myths and stereotypes which still surround the issue of homosexuality. Consider, for example, the story of **Claude**, thirty-eight, who, as a young man, consulted the literature of homosexuality—'analytical, fictional, and confessional'—in the hope of finding some acceptable sense of self-as-homosexual:

You can't name a book that I didn't consult. And in each of them the message rang out loud and clear: you're a criminal, and your crime is against God, nature, society, yourself.

As I talk to you I wonder what on earth made me persevere. I think, perhaps, because one *must* know *who* one is, and *why* one is different. And as homosexuality was not, in those days, something you dared discuss in polite conversation, one consulted the 'experts'. And this is what I did. I read everything I could get my hands on. But the literature was uniformly negative. How well I remember those *thousands* of case studies shrouded in gloom and doom, all written in plaintive tones of guilt and self-hatred. I wanted to cry aloud after reading them. The unhappy homosex-

ual! Sentenced to 'life' for the crime of being gay. How ironic that word, 'gay', seemed to me then. . . .
I began to look upon the straight world with envy and sorrow. The heterosexual inhabited a kind of golden world from which I was for ever excluded. I felt very much an alien. It's rather like the title of that book, *Invisible Man*. That's how I felt, like an invisible man.

It is very difficult to feel good about oneself when so little of a positive nature is said about one's own kind. Since the sense of self is in large part determined by an individual's perception of his or her social role, popular stereotypes and social expectations are liable to count for a great deal in the development of the gay person's self-concept. This can be seen in the story of **Martin**, twenty-four:

The problem I was faced with years ago, when I first realized I was gay, was learning to like myself. This isn't easy when people think of you as sick or immature.
Before I even knew I was homosexual, I remember my school friends talking about the 'pooves'. When finally I realized I was '*one of them*', you can imagine how I felt. . . .
I fought my homosexuality for a long time. I'd persuade myself that I couldn't be *entirely* gay since I didn't behave like the stereotyped gays they joke about on telly, or that you see in films.
Eventually, though, I couldn't deny it any longer. That is, I couldn't deny it *to myself*. I still laughed along with the others when 'queer jokes' were told. I hated myself afterwards, and also felt disloyal. And, of course, all this only aggravated my feelings of guilt.
And yet, I felt it was wiser to say nothing because if all the others felt this way about homosexuals, there must be some good reason. And I *didn't* want to lose my friends. . . .There were *so many* risks in being open. So I kept my homosexuality a secret for as long as I could.

As this story suggests, the self-admitted homosexual is not necessarily a self-accepting one. In fact, at some point or other in their lives many gays have tried, like Martin, to deny their gayness, and with fairly predictable results.
As Christopher Z. Hobson has said, in an essay entitled 'Surviving Psychotherapy':[3]

In my teens I tried actively not to be homosexual. Even when I stopped trying, at twenty-two, I didn't accept being gay—I merely decided to express it until something changed, because I realized that in trying not to love men, I was losing the ability to love at all. Not until I was twenty-five did I begin to see homosexuality as something that shouldn't be despised, and not until I was twenty-eight—only one year ago—did I 'come out' in the sense of beginning to live openly as a homosexual. Only then, moreover, did I actively step into gay life and begin to meet other gay people. During those fourteen years I had almost no sexual contacts and was, naturally, unhappy, frustrated, and confused.

The Stigma of Homosexuality

So long as significant numbers of people refuse to accept homosexuality as a legitimate variety of sexual expression, many gays will continue to fear the consequences of being open. The counsellor must therefore not be surprised to learn that even in this 'permissive' age there still exist homosexuals who, like Martin, and Christopher Hobson, refuse to put at risk their friendships, reputation, or general well-being by 'coming out', or being open, to their family and friends. After all, our society is one in which everyone is assumed to be heterosexual until proved otherwise, and the reaction of those who discover the homosexuality of a relative, friend, or colleague is often one of surprise or pain, anger or resentment, and only rarely one of genuine acceptance. 'The tune is called by the heterosexual male', David Blamires has observed; 'it is a world in which . . . his sexual preferences, his fantasies, even, permeate almost every aspect of life.'[4]

Gay people are thus at risk of feeling inferior *not* because of what they do, but, rather, because of the threat which they represent. To summarize briefly this curious logic: homosexual activity is labelled 'deviant'; deviance is perceived as failure-to-conform; nonconformist behaviour is socially proscribed; and the ensuing penalties are rationalized by a philosophy that explains the 'threat' which sexual minorities represent. Thus, homosexuality is, for some, a sin; for others it is 'against nature'; still others regard it as an illness; and, under the law, it may constitute a crime.

There can be few homosexuals who have not believed at some time or other in their lives the validity of one or more of these damaging stereotypes: sinful, unnatural, sick, criminal: **Tina**, for example, is a young, recently divorced mother of a seven-year-old son who once lived 'in constant fear of succumbing, some day, to the temptation of loving another woman':

I don't know that my religious upbringing was any more strict than that of most girls my age. I took a keen interest in church affairs, though. All of the social events in our village that I was permitted to attend were church affairs.

My most vivid recollections of these gatherings is that they seemed to be dress rehearsals for marriage—learning how to be wives and mothers, or husbands and fathers. Perhaps that's unfair, but that's how I remember them. . . .

Then, of course, Mother would always speak of my future in terms of a home and family. 'Now, when you're married, dear', she'd say, or, 'When you have children', or 'Your husband' this, and 'Your husband' that. . . . It made me think of the family as part of some grand design and I felt, who am I to upset everyone's plans for me? Yet I couldn't generate even the slightest enthusiasm for the prospect of one day being a wife, mother, homemaker. . . . I was very confused by my attitude. I seemed, to myself, unique.

When I was about fifteen I began to experience 'feelings' for other girls. I felt very guilty about this. It was quite bad enough thinking about *boys* in that way. It was positively *evil* to have these feelings for girls. Still, two and two didn't yet add up to 'lesbian'. I was learning, though, what it means to be different, and to feel isolated.

One night I remember I couldn't sleep because a close friend, someone towards whom I felt very close, for whom I had very warm feelings (and who, I think, felt the same way about me), suddenly moved up north. I was despondent! I wanted to die, I felt so suddenly alone.

At about two o'clock in the morning, I was still awake. I put my robe on and started down to the kitchen. But when I came into the hall I saw the light was on in my parents' room. I could hear them talking in hushed voices. It was something to do with this girl who had 'disgraced' herself with a woman who was lodging in her parents' home. I heard my mother say, in the voice she generally reserved for sinners, 'There's a special place in hell for *those* women. . . .' Our parish priest apparently agreed, because on the following Sunday his sermon was full of oblique references to the affair, and these were 'spiced' with quotations from the Scriptures. Leviticus, I think. . . .

I suppose the more sophisticated knew precisely what the old fellow was on about, but I was much too naïve. A friend later explained it to me: '*Lesbians*', she said. And that was all.

The next day I went to the library and checked the dictionaries. After reading the entry for 'lesbian', I was in a panic. I imagined all of hell's devils pointing at me. I was in no doubt now. My feelings had branded me a sinner.

It is very easy to minimize the extent of suffering experienced by individuals who imagine their faith to be in conflict with their homosexuality. Counsellors should keep Tina's story in mind, then. For although Tina is today convinced that Christianity and homosexuality are compatible, it was not so long ago that feelings of guilt and shame, based on the conviction of being a sinner, were, for her, a source of considerable anguish. Counsellors concerned to help those with this particular conflict are advised to look carefully at Chapter 5.

An even more frequently encountered charge than 'sinner' is one which says that homosexuality is 'against the laws of nature'. **Derek**, nineteen, still regards his gayness as a form of perversion:

It's unnatural, isn't it? Nature never intended two blokes to have sex, did it? . . . It would be a right old world if everyone was like us. There wouldn't be anybody left! The world would die off. . . . It's just not natural! What about kids? Why were we made the way we are, different sexes, if it weren't natural, you know, to have kids? . . .

I don't know. I wish I was wrong. I really do, because . . . most of the time, I feel like a freak inside . . . and I guess that's what I am, too: a freak. . . .

Although the argument that homosexuality is 'unnatural' has no rational standing, it is none the less a seductive one to the popular imagination. Hardly surprising, then, that some gays, like Derek, have successfully internalized its surface plausibility and regard themselves as 'freaks'. My advice to counsellors who attempt to deal with this 'nature argument' is to be first quite certain that they understand it themselves. Generally speaking, people who claim that homosexuality is 'unnatural' are, in effect, asserting that: (a) nature did not intend two men or two women to enjoy sex together, as the function of sex is reproduction; (b) the structure and function of the sexual organs are determined by nature and must not be 'perverted' by man.

Let us briefly consider these assertions, each of which assumes that a law of nature embodies observable and repeatable phenomena acting in a certain way and under a specific set of conditions. Two examples of such 'natural laws' would be: (1) humans cannot fly, and (2) there is pain during childbirth. Now to say that something is against the laws of nature means that the laws of nature must not be altered. Yet in both examples given above man has, in fact, modified the 'laws' of nature. Hence, the law which says that humans cannot fly has been bypassed by the laws of aerodynamics. As far as birth pains are concerned, we should not forget that less than a century ago people passionately argued either (a) that nature had not intended to make childbirth painless, or (b) that God intended women to suffer pain in childbirth because of Eve's sin: 'In sorrow thou shalt bring forth children' (Gen. 3.16). Yet how many among to-day's clergy would protest against the administration of sedatives for use by expectant mothers on the grounds that this is an obvious subversion of the 'laws' of nature? I believe that few, if any, would do this.

In short, there is nothing within nature itself that can possibly serve as a criterion for the modification of its 'laws'. Man is a *creative* being, constantly correcting his ethical insights and altering his universe into something better that will give added meaning to his life. Nature cannot be the guide for man's actions; it is man who must impose upon nature his own dreams and values.

As for Derek's assertion that the race would become extinct if homosexuality were the norm ('The world would die off. . . .'), even this is no longer (if ever it was) a tenable contribution to our argument. It assumes, first, that the only valid function of sex is procreation and, second, that those who do not choose to procreate are socially irresponsible. If this were so, we would then need to consider such questions as: 'Is celibacy unnatural?' 'What would happen if we all took the vow of chastity, as many clergy do?' 'Is it unnatural to have sex purely for pleasure, rather than for procreation?' 'Must women remain celibate after their menopause?' 'Should we advise heterosexuals who cannot have children to abstain from sex?'

What the counsellor needs to emphasize is that sex for pleasure is neither undesirable nor 'unnatural'. Sex reaches into the total texture of our lives, and for this reason alone it must be valued as a road to loving relationships. This is the point to stress, and though it may not put an immediate end to all anxieties and doubts, it can be an important first step along the road to self-acceptance for gays like Derek.

Another stereotype used to discredit gays is that which says: homosexuals are sick and therefore deserve our pity. **Peter**, a post-graduate student, speaks here of his rejection of the 'sick' label during the course of his two years of psychotherapy:

It's very strange that if gays are, as they say, 'psychologically sick', then it's always traced back to the fact of their being homosexual. But if heterosexuals are 'sick' in this way, it can be attributed to unknown factors; no one says to them, 'You're sick because you're heterosexual.'

Funnily enough, it was my therapist who made me realize that being gay didn't automatically mean 'being sick'. I'm sure this wasn't his intention, but several things he said started me to think. At one of our sessions, he expressed an opinion that confirmed bachelors were 'disturbed' because they 'feared' marriage and women. Later, at another session, he remarked that some psychiatrists, himself included, firmly held to the opinion that a belief in God was a symptom of autistic behaviour, 'a dangerous absorption in fantasy'. In effect he was saying that prayer is a form of magic, and that those who pray are unable to face reality—they're 'disturbed'.

This shattered me, and I asked him at another session if he meant what he said. He was obviously a bit bothered with himself for having said *anything*. He also seemed a bit concerned by my interpretation, but he stood by all he said.

By his logic, then, I was sick for being homosexual and unmarried, but healthy because I'm an agnostic. It was then that I asked myself who exactly is it that says I'm sick? Who determines how you define normal, healthy behaviour? It's a legitimate question because standards differ. Take the Soviet Union, for example, where political nonconformity is often defined as mental illness

. . . It's difficult to avoid the conclusion that mental health is measured according to how well you conform to what the majority think and do.

It is a rather daunting task to consider the crimes committed throughout history in the interests of protecting the 'health' of the individual and of society. As far as homosexuality is concerned, those who think of gays as ill are, as Peter implies, positing heterosexuality as the norm. Yet most informed opinion of recent origin has rejected this assumption. Indeed, in 1974, the members of the American Psychiatric Association, after assessing the matter in the most rigorous diagnostic and statistical terms, overwhelmingly concluded that homosexuality could not be considered a form of personality disturbance or mental breakdown, i.e. that homosexuality, of itself, does not regularly cause subjective distress, nor is it regularly associated with any generalized impairment in social effectiveness. Regrettably, the current wave of panic over AIDS threatens to obliterate the voice of reason and to reinforce the notion that homosexuality is a disease.

Many of us, awed by science, sometimes forget that psychological theories about the nature of man are not universally accepted truths but, rather, *partial* versions of the truth put forward by people whose ideas are often diametrically opposed. Facts do not 'speak for themselves'; they are interpreted by human beings. And human beings are not in total agreement about what constitutes illness. In fact, there is considerable disagreement on this point within the therapeutic profession itself. As Professor Carl Rogers, the founder of the client-centred approach to psychotherapy, has said:[5]

Our differences as therapists do not lie simply in attaching different levels to the same phenomenon. . . . We differ at the most basic levels of our personal experience. . . . We are not agreed on whether the goal is removal of symptoms, reorganization of personality, curing of disease, or adjustment. . . . A one-sentence summary would be: The field of psychotherapy is in a mess. Therapists are not in agreement as to their goals or aims. . . . They are in deep disagreement as to the theoretical structure which contains their work. They cannot agree as to whether a given experience for a client is healing or destructive, growth-producing or damaging. They cannot agree as to what constitutes failure. They diverge sharply in their views as to the promising

directions for the future. It seems as though the field is completely chaotic and divided.

In addition to the labels 'sin', 'unnatural', and 'sick', certain
sexual acts performed by homosexuals, legal in the case of heterosexuals, are regarded by the law as 'criminal'. This particular form of
discrimination will be considered at some length in Chapter 3. For
the time being it is sufficient to point out that serious problems can
arise from the fact that the age of consent for homosexuals is
twenty-one, whereas heterosexuals are considered adults (for the
purposes of sexual activity) by the age of sixteen.

Mike, nineteen, talks about what he regards as the principal
problem of being labelled 'criminal' in consequence of one's sexual
preferences:

> Let's say that you're straight and between the ages of sixteen and
> twenty-one. If you're having relationship problems with the
> opposite sex, you can go to people and talk about it. Books and
> films tell you how to behave, what you should do in certain
> situations, where you can go when you need help. Now if you're
> gay, there's nothing of the kind. In the first place, you're sup-
> posed to be celibate till the age of twenty-one. And if you're not,
> you had better keep it quiet. Another thing is that people are
> afraid of giving advice. They are afraid of running foul of the law.
> You can't advertise social activities for under-twenty-ones, be-
> cause this can put you in trouble with the law, too—it may be
> thought an incitement to criminal activity. . . .
> All this limits your opportunities for meeting other gays of your
> own age. It means you're slow to develop gay relationships. And
> the longer it takes, the more difficult it becomes. It's not easy to
> get a good relationship going if you've had so little practice doing
> it.
> The law says no sex till you're twenty-one! Can you imagine
> making that demand on hets? They wouldn't stand for it! I'd say
> this attitude on the part of the law has made me fairly cynical of
> our system of justice.
> Speaking for myself, though, I can't say that the law has inhibited
> me in any noticeable way. Perhaps you feel a bit more 'brave' at
> university. And then, too, there's Gay Soc. . . . No, I'd say I
> don't ever *think* of the law as far as sex is concerned.
> But that's not true for everyone I know. I know guys of my own

age who literally cut themselves off. They're afraid to get close to someone else . . . and I know that this springs, at least in part, from the legal situation. Inside, you know you're a lawless person. This is bound to affect your outward behaviour.

Mike's point about the way in which relationships are inhibited by the internal knowledge of one's lawlessness suggests another way in which society's negative attitudes restrict the growth of personality. When gays are discouraged from expressing their feelings of tenderness and affection—feelings regarded as healthy when directed towards the opposite sex—then progress towards positive self-identification is once again thwarted. Thus, for Peter Wildeblood, author of *Against the Law*, it proved impossible to be a self-accepting homosexual while living a conventional life in English society. The internal knowledge of being a lawless person was, in fact, the start of a split existence, the double lifestyle of the 'passing' homosexual:[6]

> I was forced to be deceitful, living one life during my working hours and another when I was free. I had two sets of friends; almost, one might say, two faces. At the back of my mind there was always a nagging fear that my two worlds might suddenly collide . . . it was necessary to watch every word I spoke, and every gesture that I made in case I gave myself away.

The Human Consequences of Social Pressures

The stereotypes outlined above will only matter if gays accept them as being true to themselves. 'It is thus with most of us,' says Eric Hoffer, 'we are what other people say we are. We know ourselves chiefly by hearsay.'[7] Once the labels 'sinner', 'unnatural', 'sick', and 'criminal' are internalized, feelings of guilt and shame are thus the inevitable result. Such feelings can then adversely affect all of one's relationships, particularly with regard to one's parents. Mothers and fathers often sense the existence of a 'problem', yet remain silent, and then are hurt that their children should not trust them sufficiently to share their worries. **Ralph**, twenty, is a case in point:

> My parents knew something was wrong when I dropped out of university. They couldn't understand this as my grades had always been well above average. . . .
> At university I worked hard at fighting my homosexuality. In

14

time, I became very tense. I found I couldn't concentrate on my studies. Finally, in mid-term, I dropped everything.

I returned to Nottingham, made plans to get a job and save some money, then maybe go to Canada.

My parents were really confused. But they thought, well, he's got this problem that he wants to keep to himself; okay, let's see how it goes, 'but stay with us, you can save more money that way, then make up your mind later'.

Weeks and then months went by, and they noticed that I was becoming more and more distant with people, *and* with them. The truth is that their presence made me feel uneasy. There was this unspoken thing between us, so that we couldn't be in a room together without an argument.

There was frustration on all sides. . . . Maybe theirs was in some ways worse. I don't know. My father becomes angry when he can't express his feelings in words. He's never had much of an education himself, and he's always wanted me to have a good one. . . . Sometimes they'd try and guess what was bothering me. They'd say, 'Is it a girl? Let us know if it's a girl, because we'll try and understand. Please trust us.' And I'd probably snap back something like, 'No, it's *not* a girl, now please leave me alone.' And this, you know, would only make my father more upset, while my mother would go on about her being 'of no use whatsoever'. . . .

All of which had the effect of making me want to crawl into a deep hole, cover myself up with dirt, and just stay underground for ever.

When people like Ralph are unable to find constructive outlets for their feelings of guilt and shame, there is always the possibility that eventually they may project such feelings on to others like themselves. And this is one of the principal reasons why some gays have such difficulty in developing relationships beyond the casual stage, a problem discussed at greater length in Chapter 7.

The social isolation which Ralph and others have described is, in fact, one of the most frequently encountered causes of unhappiness and suffering for homosexuals who seek the help of a counsellor. Many, having successfully insulated themselves for years against all but the most superficial contacts, will find it extremely difficult, if not impossible, to relate to other gays in an undefended way. Such a legacy of repression is particularly hard to overcome in the case of older homosexuals. The guilt and inhibitions which lead to early social withdrawal may take a high toll in terms of a person's psychological well-being. The present older generation, having been conditioned to be shy and secretive, does not have the freedom of approach currently enjoyed by many younger gays. **Phil**, sixty-seven, has just moved into a local authority home. He attempts here to define some of the problems confronting older gays:

> The older homosexuals were forced to lie. There wasn't much of a choice. Lie and survive: that's the story. And now we're paying the penalty.
>
> Some of the younger ones don't like to hear this. They haven't lived through the sort of days people like me did. They don't understand. They expect you to be always positive about things, to be brave and militant. They don't want to be depressed by your sad stories of days-gone-by. . . .
>
> Yes, I am bitter. People think your need for love dies, at latest, by the age of sixty. There's a greater need for companionship at my age. . . . I would like to be in touch with other homosexuals of my age group. But there are problems when you're older—distances, for example, or time and costs.
>
> Older people are often much more stable and loyal than the young. I wish more people could understand.

The process of ageing can be stressful and problematic for all people, regardless of sexual orientation. But as gay relationships involve none of the legal supports that keep heterosexual marriages intact, older homosexuals are often depicted as lonely, isolated, and unable to maintain active social involvement with other gays. Thus, the 'folk view' often portrays the ageing homosexual as, in the words of one commentator, 'so desperately lonely and frightened . . . that he frantically beats the walls in his anguish'.[8]

It would help the counsellor to balance this traditional perception of the older homosexual's psychological problems with that of more recent studies on the subject. Data collected by Weinberg and Williams, for example, strenuously contradict the folk view outlined above. 'We find', say the authors,[9]

> no age-related differences in self-acceptance, anxiety, depression, or loneliness. In fact, our data suggest that in some respects our

older homosexuals have greater well-being than our younger homosexuals.

Why this wide discrepancy between the two views? The most likely answer, it seems to me, is that many commentators will impute to older gays their own perspectives and expectations, thus concluding that the social situation of the older homosexual is unenviable. What such commentators fail to perceive, however, is that people can, and *do*, adapt in a positive manner to the realistic possibilities of their socio-sexual situation.

This is not to suggest, of course, that the situation of older gays is without problems. Some aspects of the 'folk view' can certainly be supported, as Phil's story suggests. Thus, older homosexuals tend to have fewer social contacts within the gay scene; they visit pubs and clubs less frequently; they are far more likely to be living alone; they may be faced with socio-legal problems such as inheritance, taxation, and insurance.

On the other hand, there are tentative steps being taken to alleviate the isolation and loneliness of elderly gays such as Phil. As far as providing social contacts is concerned, gay groups are now arranging meetings in a new sort of atmosphere, one largely free of the tension and sexual barter so characteristic of the commercial pub, club, and disco scene. These meetings are providing opportunities for homosexual men and women of all ages to meet socially without the usual automatic sexual motives being read into simple acts of friendliness and concern. (A list of such gay groups can be found on pp. 179–91.)

Much more can still be done, of course, and CHE's 'Comments on *Manifesto 7*', which deals with the emotional needs of the retired and elderly gay, makes two constructive suggestions:[10]

Local Authorities and others who run old people's homes must seriously consider the needs of the homosexuals who may be admitted to their establishments. The problems of the older homosexual differ in kind, though not in degree, from those of heterosexuals and must attract different solutions. At the moment these problems are dealt with inside a heterosexual framework. . . .

Finally, we should all realize that although . . . we have referred to the problem of the elderly homosexual, it would be truer to say that it is the problem of *our* attitude to him or her that needs to be considered. Although it is proper to initiate research and carry out practical aid programmes, it must be borne in mind that ultimately our reaction as individuals to the elderly homosexuals that we meet is of greater importance.

Summary

In this chapter I have defined the counsellor as an agent of social change, as well as someone offering help to those seeking understanding and assistance in the conduct of their lives.

Most homosexuals lead quite happy and satisfied lives. However, there are those who do require help from outside their immediate circle of family and friends. It is here that the counsellor can be of use in helping to alleviate the loneliness and isolation which, for all too many, remain as acute as ever.

Finding an acceptable identity has been isolated as the principal problem confronting the homosexual (**Claude, Martin**). This problem is a direct result of society's failure to accept homosexuality as a legitimate variation of the sexual drive. The gay person's search for an acceptable self-image is, in turn, thwarted by a barrier of stereotypes: 'sinner' (**Tina**), 'unnatural' (**Derek**), 'sick' (**Peter**), and 'criminal' (**Mike**). These stereotypes can, if successfully internalized, result in feelings of guilt and shame that will adversely affect one's relationships (**Ralph**).

Those who have isolated themselves from others in this way may, in time, find it extremely difficult to relate to other gays in an undefended way. The legacy of repression is particularly difficult to overcome in the case of older gays (**Phil**). However, counsellors are advised to balance the traditional folk view of the ageing homosexual with that of more recent research which suggests that in some respects older gays have greater well-being than younger homosexuals.

2

On Being Different

To be nobody-but-myself—in a world which is doing its best, night and day, to make you everybody else—means to fight the hardest battle which any human being can fight, and never stop fighting.

e. e. cummings,
quoted in Charles Norman's *The Magic-Maker* (1958)

Most people find it difficult to justify their aggressive behaviour or intolerant attitudes unless they are first able, in some way or other, to dehumanize their victims. 'Every society', Nietzsche once observed, 'has a tendency to reduce its "opponents" to caricatures.'[1] Hence, blacks are 'niggers'; the police are 'pigs'; politicians of a right-wing hue are 'fascists'; students are 'hippies'; judges speak of certain categories of defendant as 'monsters'; gays are labelled 'sinner', 'unnatural', 'sick', and 'AIDS carriers'. Such stereotypes, because they are dismissive of individual differences within particular groups, are not only cruelly unfair and potentially destructive of self-esteem; they can, in addition, be self-fulfilling prophecies.

One means of reversing this process of intolerance and dehumanization is through empathy—the capacity to participate in another person's feelings or ideas. This basic *human* skill is of great importance to the counsellor, particularly to the *non-gay* counsellor, for it helps one to respond to others as *people*, rather than as *problems*. Unless we are able to place ourselves in someone else's shoes, it may well be impossible to understand the thoughts and emotions of others whose experiences and lifestyles are sometimes very different from our own.

This empathetic quality doesn't necessarily lead to attraction, of course. In other words, I may feel I understand you, yet still not care to have you as a friend. But empathy should facilitate mutual understanding and help to eliminate any feelings of intolerance which, try as we may, some of us still find difficult to purge. In this chapter, then, I am asking the reader to consider the question:

19

'What is it like to be a member of a sexual minority?', and, by way of assistance in reaching an answer, I shall supply the views of those who describe themselves as homosexual, bisexual, paedophile, transvestite, and transsexual.

Sexual Labels

Sexuality remains, even today, a subject shrouded in mystery, controversy, and ignorance. Adding to the general confusion are the use of labels to compartmentalize sexual behaviour for the purpose of immediate identification. I shall not dwell here on the ethics of labelling except to say that if labels must be used, they should at least be used with as much caution and precision as possible. For we can never assume, thanks to the popular mythology surrounding sexuality, that another person's understanding of a label or term will even approximately correlate with that of our own.

Take for example, the term 'homosexual'. Definitions abound, and some of these will be the subject of further exploration below. For now, it is enough to stress the importance of the gay person's definition. It is absolutely essential that counsellors know the way or ways in which homosexuals perceive themselves. One reason for laying such emphasis on this might be illustrated by reference to a recent conversation of mine with Andrew, a boy of fifteen who phoned my office to seek advice on whether or not he was homosexual. Having never met him before, I asked Andrew if *he* thought he was homosexual. 'Yes', he said, he did. I asked why. 'Because', he answered, 'one of my mates says I look like a "bird".' The logic of the remaining part of our conversation goes something like this: if you look like a woman, then you can't be a 'man'; you must, therefore, be a 'homosexual'.

On the basis of this and, I regret to say, countless other folk interpretations of sexual behaviour, I feel that to discuss the subject of homosexuality with any degree of clarity, we must first define our terms. This, of course, is easier said than done. Take, for example, the term 'homosexual'. The homosexual, some say, is one who engages in sexual activity with someone of his or her own sex. Nothing, it might appear, could be less controversial than that. Yet such a *behavioural* definition is woefully incomplete, for it says, in effect, that homosexuals only differ from heterosexuals in the use they make of their sexual organs.

20

If we pause for a moment to reflect on this definition, we soon realize its inadequacy. Emotions are, in the total make-up of gays, every bit as important as genital manipulation. If we are to accept a purely behavioural definition of homosexuality, then what is to become of those whose desires and preferences for their own sex are repressed or unfulfilled? Or those who engage in heterosexual activities without being, in any 'technical' sense, heterosexual? Or those who engage in homosexual activities without being, in any 'technical' sense, homosexual? How should we regard these people?

The point I wish to make here is that serious problems of definition do exist which can seriously hamper our understanding of those we wish to help. In its determination to isolate 'homosexual' and 'heterosexual' into mutually exclusive categories of sexual behaviour, society has oversimplified the infinite range of human sexuality and substituted a system of classification and labelling which takes little account of human variety. By way of proof, consider the following four stories told by Felix, nineteen; Alec, forty-six; Tom, forty-seven; and Gerald, twenty-four.

I first met **Felix** in late 1974 at a GLF disco in London, where he played saxophone in a rock group called The No Name. At present Felix spends most of his spare time studying, which means 'listening to Vivaldi and Bach and maybe, if I'm in the mood, to Mozart'. He plans, in the not too distant future, to resume his music studies, and hopes eventually to have saved enough money to go to New York and enrol at Juilliard.

Though Felix's sensual experience has been with both sexes, he tends to make a firm distinction between emotional involvement, on the one hand, and 'sex for gratification, for the fun of it', on the other. 'I'm a sexual opportunist, I guess', he says, by way of explanation. Thus, although Felix has developed strong emotional feelings for both men and women, these have not generally led to sexual involvements. 'I just don't know what that would lead to, and I don't see how, just now, I'd hassle through it if the other person couldn't let go. Still, who knows? I keep changing, so I can't say for certain if I'll always feel this way.' Does Felix regard himself as either gay or straight? 'I'd say I'm roughly two-thirds straight, *today*,' he replies, 'though tomorrow it could well be the other way around. Let's just say I'm *polysexual*.'

Unlike Felix, **Alec** only fully recognized his homosexual component at the age of forty-two, nearly four years ago. It was then that he met Michel, a twenty-five-year-old schoolteacher from Paris who was, at the time, on holiday in London. 'I fell in love almost instantly', says Alec, 'and have never once questioned my feelings since the day we met.'

For the past three and a half years Alec and Michel have faithfully alternated in their monthly visits to London and Paris to see each other. They have made no plans to live together, as Alec is married and the father of five children ranging in age from six to twenty.

So far Alec, because of the nature of his business, has managed to explain his week-end absences to the satisfaction of his wife without, he hopes, arousing any suspicions. 'Though I don't know my luck will hold out for ever', he says, cautiously. And if his wife discovers? 'We'll cross that bridge when we come to it. This is all a "question-mark" in my mind. I would hope, if she were ever to discover, that she might try and understand that I love her and the children, but that I love Michel, too. This is the way I am . . .' 'Perhaps having two loves seems selfish to you', says Alec; 'I know it does to most people. But during these past four years, I've been as loving and, really, rather more so, than ever before, and to *everyone* involved, including, of course, the children. I'm happier now, so I feel I have much more love to give . . .'

'What I long for, says **Tom**, 'is a loving and mutually pleasurable relationship. This isn't easy for me, since my sexual preference is for children under the age of twelve . . . both sexes.

'People, you see, don't accept the sexuality of children. They teach children to be distrustful of an older person's attentions. . . . This makes it very difficult. Call me what you like— heterosexual, paedophile, or both . . . no, not homosexual. I'm not homosexual, though many have thought so. . . .

'I was married at eighteen. My wife and I lived together for, oh, some fifteen years, right up till she found out about me. Then she left me. . . .

'I was always this way, though I couldn't accept it till eight, nine years ago. . . . Paedophiles, you see, are still moral lepers, and worse, in the eyes of the public; and "child-raping monsters" in the eyes of the law.

'How many people realize that the average paedophile is as much opposed to child-molesting as the average man in the street? . . . Like I said, I look for a loving relationship. I love children, and I want to be tender with them.

'You know, if people could open their minds, they'd find a great deal that they don't know much about. And one thing is paedophilia.'

Gerald is now twenty-four years old and works in a wine shop in central London. Between the ages of twenty-one and twenty-two he served several months in jail for refusing to pay his rates. 'In jail I shared a cell with a bloke they all called Babes. "Babes", because he looked like a baby, a baby girl. He was eighteen, pretty, and had soft, blonde skin. A person like that has to be careful in jail. . . .

'I'm gay, but Babes wasn't. But gay or straight doesn't matter in jail if someone fancies you, providing he's a big enough lad. But I wouldn't do anything like that to Babes. I liked him. . . . No . . . more than that, I loved him. Every day was different with Babes around, even in jail. That's how he made me feel.

'But good things don't last in this world, do they? After a few months together, with no sex between us, mind, I began to hear rumours. You have to remember, a day in jail can be very boring. The lads think a lot about sex, and talk a lot about sex. Some of them began to talk about Babes and me, because I think they were jealous. I could tell by the way they looked at Babes. . . .

'One day, then, when no one was around, two louts claiming to hate gingers waited for us in the showers and took turns raping Babes, while a third geezer held me back, covering my mouth with his hand the whole time.

'I'll never forget that. It's not that this kind of thing didn't happen often enough, it does. But this time. . . .

'Of course, Babes knew about me from the first. It didn't matter, though. But after the rape, his attitude seemed to change. I don't know why. He didn't talk so much, and he ignored me a lot. A few weeks later he was outside . . . and I've never seen him since.'

Each of these four stories illustrates one of the principal difficulties involved in fixing sexual labels on to people: erotic feelings are not always rigidly focused on one or the other sex (Felix), nor any particular age group (Tom), though they may be repressed until comparatively late in life (Alec), and then surface in extreme circumstances under a guise of aggression which defends the individual from the threat which same-sex feelings of tenderness or desire might pose (the 'heterosexual' inmates in Gerald's story).

Concerning patterns of sexual behaviour, the voices heard in the preceding pages should warn us against assuming that all human beings fall neatly and co-operatively into two antithetical classes, 'heterosexual' and 'homosexual'. This is not so, as Dr Kinsey and his associates have pointed out:

> The heterosexuality or homosexuality of many individuals is not an all-or-none proposition. It is true that there are persons in the population whose histories are exclusively heterosexual, both in regard to their overt experience and in regard to their psychic reactions. And there are individuals in the population whose histories are exclusively homosexual, both in experience and in psychic reactions. But the record also shows that there is a considerable portion of the population whose members have combined, within their individual histories, both homosexual and heterosexual experience and/or psychic responses.

The division of the world into 'sheep and goats' is a great mistake, Kinsey concludes, for 'it is a fundamental of taxonomy that nature rarely deals with discrete categories; only the human mind invents categories and tries to force facts into separated pigeon-holes.'[2]

Only by realizing that the world is a continuum in each and every one of its aspects can counsellors understand the realities of sexual variation, as well as the difficulties and confusions of some within our sexual minorities. Social reactions to gays have obviously been based on the general belief that homosexuals are unique and, as such, need special consideration or 'treatment'. When it is recognized that homosexual response and/or activity is not fundamentally different from that had by a substantial portion of the total population (according to Kinsey, some thirty-two per cent),[3] then attitudes will begin to change. Such recognition could also be of great potential help to judges and social workers, officials in the Army, Navy, and Merchant Marine, administrators of penal and mental institutions, clergy, police, parents, and others who may be unaware of the incidence figures and who thus persist in calling for the condemnation, isolation, or institutionalization of nearly one-third of the nation's population.

Sex and Gender

In this chapter my principal concern is with questions of identity and definition. And because the gay person's very existence constitutes a challenge to the way society defines and categorizes human sexuality and its roles, such questions must also be of paramount concern to the counsellor. For the counsellor's role is to help the troubled gay define the nature of his or her conflict with society and, by so doing, to accelerate the process of self-identification. This, as we have seen, is a goal often thwarted by the careless use of sexual labels. Another major problem in dealing with issues arising out of social attitudes to sexual minorities is the general confusion surrounding the terms 'sex' and 'gender'.

Sex is not simply determined by biology, as most people would appear to believe; it is also *socially defined*. This fact is perhaps nowhere better illustrated than in the case of the transvestite, who, more than most in our society, understands the various ways in which each of us is conditioned from birth by the conventional dichotomies of 'man' and 'woman'. **Carl** is a transvestite, aged fifty, who lectures in physics at a college for further education:

> I was thirteen years old when I first began to take an interest in women's clothes. I can remember walking down Oxford Street looking at the windows, noticing the women's clothes—dresses, in particular, and shoes, lingerie. I adored fabrics, too: silk, satin, velvet, lace. I wanted to wear them close to me. . . .
> In the beginning, there wasn't an *overwhelming* desire to wear the clothes, though. But in my early teens I developed a strong identification with women and, alongside that, a need to be accepted as one. Not all of the time, but on occasions. From then on, I felt tense whenever wearing men's clothes.
> Still, it wasn't till I was seventeen years old that I actually dressed in women's clothes. One day, when I was all alone in the house, I decided to put on one of my sister's dresses. When the time actually came to do this, I was paralysed with fear thinking I'd be caught. But mixed in with those feelings was a sort of sexual glow. . . .

It's difficult to explain to someone who's never experienced the feeling. It was very arousing, although later in life it would lose this connotation, and then it became something more generalized. . . .

In the early days, after wearing women's clothes, I would feel convinced for a long time afterwards that everyone knew my secret. Because at this time I still believed that there was no one else in the world like me. My main concerns were loneliness, and this sense of being 'unique'. It wasn't until years later, in fact, that I actually heard the word 'transvestite' defined, and knew that there were others like me. . . .

I left home at the age of eighteen and took a job in London, where I knew I could cross-dress with less risk. Four years later, after completing my A-level work, I enrolled at a teacher training college, and today I'm a full-time lecturer in physics. . . .

All this time in London I would be dressing quite frequently as a woman, both in private and, less often, in public. When I was twenty-six, I married, and I still enjoy heterosexual relationships today.

What most people don't understand is that transvestites do *not* want sex-change operations. That's the transsexual. I know I'm male, but I also wish to preserve my female self, despite this outward 'proof' of my male-ness. But don't forget, I speak only for myself. No one can speak for *all* transvestites, any more than for *all* homosexuals, or *all* heterosexuals, or all whoever. . . .

We were saying before that one is always forced into apologizing for oneself. People expect you to do that when you're different. But I'm done with that now. There's nothing that I feel the need to apologize for. I am this way; I *enjoy being* this way; and I'm not hurting anyone. If other people don't like me, that's *their* problem.

You know, when the 'experts' speak of people like me as unhappy, they don't have a clue. . . . It does annoy me! They don't appreciate the risks we run in being ourselves. . . .

Certainly, I'm worried about people 'finding out'. And the reason is *other people* . . . other people and their reactions to me.

Let's face it: I can be arrested at any time and be publicly exposed. The only time you can safely cross-dress is at masquerades. . . .

What transvestites need, to begin with, is to be able to establish contacts with other transvestites. People also need to understand transvestism in terms of gender identity. It's more than simply wearing women's clothes; it's also a question of identification.

People who fail to distinguish between gender and sexual object choice are often inclined to regard the transvestite as a homosexual. As Carl's story reveals, this is often an incorrect assumption. In fact, according to a study involving 504 cross-dressers undertaken by a leading writer on the subject, Charles Virginia Prince, himself a transvestite, the majority of cross-dressers are heterosexual.[4] According to Prince, 'love of the feminine' is what characterizes the transvestite, and from this springs the desire to cross-dress. Yet not every cross-dresser is a transvestite, Prince insists: 'He may be a transsexual, a homosexual, a bank robber, or a person at a Hallowe'en party.' Here, as elsewhere, it's a taxonomic problem: 'Our society makes heterosexuality and homosexuality its chief distinction,' Prince argues, 'but you can cross-dress if you're either.'[5]

Transsexuals are often mistaken by the lay person as transvestites due to the interest of both these sexual minorities in cross-dressing. Generally speaking, though, the latter group derives emotional, psychological, and erotic gratification from dressing in the clothes of the opposite sex, while the former views clothing entirely as an outer expression of an inner identification. In other words, a transsexual is a person assigned by the anatomical structure of the body to one sex, but who feels to be, and wishes to function as, a member of the opposite sex.

Iona, who is twenty-nine was referred in 1974 to the gender identity clinic (London) for sex-change surgery:

> Biologically speaking, I'm a 'normal' male, that is I have the physical organs of a man. But inside I'm a woman. And I need to *live* as a woman. My problem is my body . . . it doesn't yet match the real me.
>
> It's no good asking me to give psychological reasons to explain why I am as I am, because I don't care. For several years I listened to people telling me how I over-identified with my mother, how my mother was 'too loving', over-protective, and all the other put-downs. Now I say, 'Maybe so, but I'm no longer interested. It doesn't matter. This is *me*. . . .'
>
> The difference between me and, say, a homosexual, is that the homosexual *knows* he's a man. He thinks to himself, I'm a man,

and I also want to have sex with other men. Transsexuals, on the other hand, are *not* homosexuals. I do *not* want to have sex with someone who doesn't see me as a woman. It's as simple as that.

A lot of people are uncomfortable with me. They wouldn't want to be seen in the street with me. This reflects more *their* insecurities. They're worried that people may 'get the wrong idea' about *them.*

Other people react a little differently. They feel uncomfortable because they're not 100 per cent certain which sex I am. People, you know, will behave differently depending on which sex you 'belong' to. With me, they don't know. I'm disorientating. . . .

I'm pre-surgery, so I think about being a woman twenty-four hours a day. What else is there? I only want to be accepted as the person I know myself to be. . . . Once I'm accepted as a woman, well, we'll see. . . .'

According to Iona, most of her problems are not internal, but rather are imposed by others—from the reactions others have to her desire to be a woman. Instead of regarding her feelings as real and valid, society tends to accept Iona's transsexualism as a manifestation of a psychological disorder. In other words, society refuses to accept her definitions (thus making it difficult for her to be totally self-accepting) and characterizes her situation as a symptom of mental illness. Rather than doing as Iona does and accepting her gender feelings as they are, the 'experts' speculate on causes, thus rendering her opinions less valid than their own.

Having made this point about definitions, let us return to the term 'homosexual', which we earlier attempted to define. In an ideal world, of course, no definition would be required; we would recognize, with Dr Kinsey, that there exists a continuum between homo- and hetero-sexuality, and that sexual behaviour reflects this continuity. This is not, however, an ideal world, and some workable definition must be found.

I am therefore using the terms 'homosexual' and 'gay', in a behavioural sense, to indicate any male or female with more homosexual than heterosexual experience in adult life; and, in a psychological sense, any male or female who is emotionally partial or erotically attracted to the same sex and who may or may not engage in overt relations with them. Thus, 'being homosexual' can refer to activity, preference, inclination, role, self-concept, status, or any combination of these; for example, a person who engages in homosexual activities but rejects the self-concept, or a married person who has the inclination but does not act on it.

How Are Sexual Preferences Acquired?

Before moving on to explore the ways in which gays recognize and learn to deal with their homosexual difference, we need first to consider the process by which human sexual preferences are determined. Contemporary science recognizes that all human sexual patterns are a product of learning and conditioning.[6] Human beings possess an inherent physiological capacity to respond to any sufficient stimulus, be it autoerotic, heterosexual, or homosexual. The tastes and preferences, goals and motives that determine any individual's pattern of sexual behaviour are *acquired* in the context of his or her unique experiences. It is, therefore, *experience* which determines the pattern of sexual responsiveness that becomes characteristic of a person.[7]

Prior to the development of experimental psychology it was generally assumed that human sexual behaviour depended upon innate, unlearned tendencies that were unrelated to an individual's environmental experiences. These instinctual influences were interpreted in terms of procreation, which was thought to be an inherent aim of the sexual drive. This is a view which, as we shall see in Chapter 5, is reflective of moral, and religious, rather than scientific, concepts. Homosexuality and other 'non-procreative' manifestations of the sexual drive were therefore dismissed as statistically rare 'perversions' having little relevance to prevailing views of sexuality. This position is no longer tenable, however, as the data of Kinsey and others have clarified the importance of homosexuality in the lives of substantial numbers of men and women in all cultures and throughout all of history.

It is the inherent physiological capacity of human beings to respond to *any* sufficient stimuli that provides us with the basic explanation as to why individuals acquire their sexual preferences. There is no need to hypothesize biological factors (genes, chromosomes, hormones), fixation theories, theories of childhood parental attachments, interpretations of psychopathic behaviour, or whatever, to explain the acquirement of homosexual preferences. Not only are such theories unsupported by scientific research and biased by religious and moral assumptions, but they fail to take account of recent data which persuasively indicate that (using Kinsey's formulation) the factors leading to homosexual behaviour are:[8]

1. the basic physiological capacity of every mammal to respond to any sufficient stimulus;
2. the accident which leads an individual into his or her first sexual experience with a person of the same sex;
3. the conditioning effects of such experience; and
4. the indirect but powerful conditioning which the opinions of other persons and the social codes may have on an individual's decision to accept or reject this type of sexual contact.

Though it is not possible to know precisely which experiences, or combination of experiences, may affect one's erotic orientation, childhood experiences have generally been emphasized. Advocates of cultural 'imprinting' claim that the age must be fixed at a period which coincides with the development of language, i.e. from eighteen to twenty-four months of age. Others, including the Freudians, claim that the Oedipal period of from four to six years of age sets the basic sexuality of a person, in addition to the all important facets of the personality. Behaviourists, for their part, argue that the ages of six and seven are more likely terminal points in the determination of a person's sexuality.

While there is no question of the crucial significance of these early years, the importance of later years has been largely underestimated. Individuals do, in fact, show a great deal of fluidity in their sexual preferences well into adult life, when the acquisition of new tastes remains a possibility. In my own personal counselling experience, I know of many people who did not 'come out' until they first had years of heterosexual experience, been married, and raised children. Then, during their forties and fifties, they developed conscious homosexual desires. Why this is so is a question explored at greater depth in Chapter 6.

On Discovering One's 'Difference'

Society goes to great lengths to ensure that its values and standards are learned by the child and adolescent. Thanks to the efforts of such efficient socializing agents as the family, school, religious institutions, the media, peer groups, etc., it is hardly any wonder that the majority of youngsters are drawn to the opposite sex. This is even more understandable when one remembers that homosexuality is never presented as a viable alternative lifestyle, but only as a *problem* within the community. It is this basic lack of acceptance which prevents gays from understanding the true nature of their sexual preferences in the same way as heterosexuals do. In fact, the discovery of homosexual difference is often accompanied by intense confusion and anxiety, as in the case of **Jack**:

> At about the age of eleven or twelve I began to feel attracted to some of the other boys in my class. I would want to be with them, and do things with them—kiss them, or see them naked.
> I had a crush on one slightly older boy. He joined our class at the end of the term, right before the school holidays. I remember that I couldn't wait for September to come so that I'd be able to see him again, and maybe to sit next to him.
> I was terrified by these feelings. I had never met or heard of anyone else who had felt like this. . . . I was really frightened, all the more because I felt so alone. There was no person I would dare tell. . . .
> And I felt guilty, too. I regarded my thoughts as 'mucky' and 'sinful'. I couldn't tell my parents, either. I knew that they would be upset and hurt; or angry, even.
> When these feelings later intensified, I would go to the library in the hope that somewhere in all those books I'd find someone like myself. I would read about boys who were lonely, unpopular, sensitive, misunderstood; about boys who hated sports and were ridiculed by their mates. But nowhere in all those books did I find anyone like *me*!
> It wasn't until several years later that I associated 'being different' with 'being homosexual'. And it was at least another four or five years before I dared allow myself to think that the word 'homosexual' might in any way apply to *me*.

With all the best intentions in the world, many a counsellor in the past has told someone like Jack that he's 'only going through a phase' and that, in the goodness of time, he will 'grow out of it'. Many youngsters accept this advice only to discover, much later, that their feelings have strengthened rather than abated. Such a discovery often leads to even greater anxiety, as well as a loss of faith in those whom one traditionally relies upon in times of need.

The following excerpts from interviews illustrate some of the

31

principal themes that appear time and again in stories dealing with the gay person's discovery of being different. To begin with, there is the sense of social isolation, of 'not belonging', as **Simon** and **Dora** describe:

> Before I even realized that I was gay, I felt different. It was a sense of not belonging, of being excluded by some understanding of classmates and friends that I was separate from the rest. I had no idea why this was. Later, I thought it had something to do with my shyness, a certain sensitivity, perhaps, and a generally non-aggressive manner (Simon).

> I felt alone, and different—as different as a circle in a world of squares. I didn't fit in *anywhere*, and I didn't believe anyone could be of help. There seemed to be a conspiracy of silence about the kind of feelings I had. I thought these feelings would go away if I ignored them—if I kept them secret in myself. But by doing this I found they soon became the most important part of me (Dora).

Another major theme that the counsellor will encounter is the feeling of 'being unique'. Both **Geraldine** and **Eleanor** experienced this.

> At about the age of thirteen I began to develop a crush on one of the other girls in my form. We'd sit next to each other, and meet after class. Quite often we would go the the Heath where we had 'our' bench. It was situated in a very secluded area. We would kiss, and even touch each other. At the time, though I enjoyed this, I felt it was wrong, even sinful. This was not only because it had to do with sex, but because I had never met another couple like us. We seemed totally unique, and that *had* to be wrong! (Geraldine).

> When I was growing up I always felt this vague feeling of discontent. It seemed to me that I had failed. My failure was in not being able to live up to some undefined but universally accepted ideal. In this I seemed unique—which is a very painful thing to be at that age. At times I felt so confused and frustrated by my feelings and emotions that I could scarcely endure it. I knew I was different from the other girls. About this there seemed no doubt in my mind, and certainly not in *theirs*. In that kind of situation, I can assure you, 'being different' means 'being worse' (Eleanor).

32

A further theme in stories dealing with the discovery of one's difference is self-denial as a means of earning the acceptance of one's peers. **Daphne** explains:

> All the girls were interested in boys. Of course! And being the good little joiner that I was, I entered into the spirit of things: I dated boys. I was about thirteen years old when I tried to take an interest in a dreadful boy called Joey, who knew I was interested in films. For him, films meant cuddling in the back row of the local cinema. I thought, well, I'll try; we'll see how it goes. And I did for several months, too, until I had established myself as 'all right' with the other girls. Unbeknownst to them, however, I was less 'all right' than ever. The reason is, I had at last defined my 'difference': it was that boys meant absolutely *nothing* to me!

And **Barry**:

> Other boys would never let me forget that I was different from them. They always called me 'cissy' because I wasn't 'hard'; I wore glasses; I played the piano; I was thin as a toothpick. All these things qualified me as a first-class cissy. But it wasn't too long before the word 'cissy' gave way to the word 'poof' and, in time, to even less pleasant terms. Because of these attitudes, and also because of my ignorance about sex, I denied my homosexuality till I was nearly thirty. . . .
>
> I tried dating girls during this time. I even had a long relationship with one girl. It was disastrous. I became very anxious and confused. I simply could not relate these difficulties with my fantasies about other boys. And it seems the more I tried to change myself in ways acceptable to others, the more unhappy I became.
>
> You can't run away from being different—no matter how hard you try.

Can Sexual Preferences be Redirected?

Conventional patterns of sexual maturity are painfully unsuitable to gays, as the above stories reveal. Because the awareness of being different precedes the knowledge of being homosexual, many gays grow up regarding themselves as 'failures'—an assessment based on their inability or refusal to conform to certain realities defined by convention. In order to strengthen a positive self-concept, counsellors should encourage such individuals to resist the rejecting attitudes of others by developing their own independent standards. What happens, though, if gays seek advice on changing their sexual orientation? How does the counsellor reply if a homosexual says: 'I can't go on the way I am. I want to be a heterosexual'? Is it, in fact, possible to change one's sexual orientation? The short answer to this question is 'no'. To suggest anything else by way of reply would be cruel and misguided. Although the counsellor will sympathize with those gays who encounter difficulties in withstanding social pressures, the fact of the matter is that such difficulties are *as nothing* when compared with those involved in attempting to 'convert' to heterosexuality. In short, it is simply not possible to expect that, by conforming to a heterosexual pattern, one can be made 'straight', any more than that, by conforming to a homosexual pattern, one can be made 'gay'.

There is a great deal of scientific evidence to support this claim. In fact, the majority of psychiatrists have experienced almost complete failure in their efforts to 'convert' gay patients to heterosexuality. Even in the extremely few and largely unconfirmed cases of 'success' that have been reported, we find no follow-up studies whatsoever on the sorts of adjustments achieved by the newly-made 'heterosexuals'. Indeed, an ever-growing number of psychologists argue quite persuasively that only very temporary change has been offered in these cases, and that such people were, to begin with, 'atypical' in so far as they demanded very radical changes in their lifestyle, in addition to possessing large amounts of time and money for the extensive psychotherapy or analysis required.

Self-acceptance, rather than submission to prejudice, is much the wisest course of 'treatment' for the counsellor to pursue. Troubled gays must be helped to resolve the guilt and conflict about their sexual preferences. In line with this advice, and by way of conclusion, consider the testimony of Dr George Weinberg, a psychotherapist who has written several outstanding essays on the issue of 'conversion':[9]

From what I have seen, the harm to the homosexual man or woman done by the person's trying to convert is multifold. Homosexuals should be warned. First of all, the venture is almost certain to fail, and you will lose time and money. But this is the least of it. In trying to convert, you will deepen your belief that you are one of nature's misfortunes. You will intensify your clinging to conventionality, enlarge your fear and guilt and regret. You will be voting in your own mind for the premise that people should all act and feel the same ways.

Summary

This chapter began with a statement concerning the importance to the counsellor of empathy in understanding and communicating with those who seek help. The capacity to participate in another person's feelings or ideas will greatly facilitate an understanding of what it means to be different-as-homosexual in our society.

The gay person's first awareness of being different is complicated both by society's failure to present homosexuality as a viable alternative lifestyle, and by a general tendency to label all individuals as either 'heterosexual' or 'homosexual'. But for many people erotic feelings are not rigidly focused on one or the other sex (**Felix**) nor on any particular age group (**Tom**). Erotic feelings may, in fact, be repressed until comparatively late in life (**Alec**), often surfacing in the context of extreme circumstances (see the case of (**Gerald**).

A major problem in dealing with social minorities is the confusion surrounding the terms 'sex' and 'gender'. One fact in need of emphasis is that in our culture sex is defined both biologically and socially (**Carl; Iona**). I therefore use the terms 'homosexual' and 'gay' in both a behavioural and a psychological sense to refer to activity, preference, inclination, role, self-concept, status, or any combination of these.

The unique experience of each person's life history determines the pattern of sexual responsiveness that becomes characteristic of that individual. However, indirect and powerful conditioning agents (the opinions of other persons and social codes regarding homosexual behaviour) often prevent an individual from recognizing or fully understanding his or her gay component. Thus, the discovery of homosexual difference is frequently accompanied by intense confusion and anxiety (**Jack**), causing those concerned to experience a sense of alienation from others in their environment (**Simon; Dora**), or to regard themselves as 'totally unique' (**Geraldine; Eleanor**). Although these reactions may lead to a temporary denial of one's gay difference (**Daphne; Barry**), an exclusive pattern of sexuality can never be permanently denied by 'conversion'. Though the counsellor will attempt to alleviate the social pressures that sometimes cause gays to think in terms of 'cure', self-acceptance rather than submission to prejudice is the only viable approach to these problems of identity.

3
Passing through Oppression

No man, for any considerable period, can wear one face to himself,
and another to the multitude, without finally getting bewildered as to
which may be the true.

Nathaniel Hawthorne, *The Scarlet Letter*

This chapter will attempt to identify those social pressures which
oppress gays and encourage a strategy of 'passing for straight', i.e. a
double lifestyle: heterosexual on the outside, homosexual on the
inside. But, first, let us consider the phenomenon of 'passing' as a
means of avoiding oppression.

The Passing Phenomenon
The homosexual is a member of a social minority. Unlike other
minority groups, however, gays can hide their distinguishing difference from the rest of the world. This crucial fact of the homosexual's
existence explains why gay people have been so long in demanding
their rights. In having to stand openly as a member of an oppressed
minority, one develops a sense of group identification, a sense of
sharing his or own 'differentness' with others of one's own kind. Not
so the homosexual, who is able to blend imperceptibly into the
heterosexual mass without ever having to face the experience of
standing openly with other gays as a member of a social minority. It
is for this reason, more than any other, that many gays are less likely
than other groups to understand their situation as social outsiders.[1]

Researchers are agreed that roughly three out of every four gays
'pass' as a means of avoiding social sanctions throughout most of
their lives.[2] This high ratio is all the more disturbing when one
considers that the figures include a disproportionately large number
of individuals who are prepared to identify with gay groups and
organizations.[3] To understand this seeming contradiction, it is

necessary to look more carefully at the phenomenon of passing and assess its significance in the experience of gays.

Passing is generally defined in the metaphor of theatre, that is, playing a role: pretending to be something that one is not. In the context of homosexuality, however, the emphasis should be placed on *concealment* rather than *pretence*. Hence, to 'pass' is to camouflage one's gayness by witholding information about oneself that might lead others to identify one as homosexual. Such a strategy of passing, motivated as it is by anticipation of the negative sanctions that would follow discovery, inevitably leads to increased confusion about one's sexual feelings, as well as a heightened sense of guilt and shame..

This passing strategy is not confined to the self-rejecting homosexual, either. Even those who have come to appreciate their gayness as an integral component of their self-identity will not always be completely free of the need to live a double life. As **James**, twenty, wrote to me:

Most of my friends know I'm gay. I've either told them, or they've worked it out for themselves. They're not naïve. . . .
I'm always aware of my gayness. It's difficult not to be always 'aware'. It's a straight world, and you are always being reminded that you're different. . . .
I'll be talking to people, not necessarily friends, but acquaintances, neighbours, the postman, the shopkeeper, and the conversation will turn to the subject of girls. I'm young, and they feel they can ask me these questions. They assume that, like themselves, and like everyone else in the world, I'm straight, and that I have straight interests.
I listen to them and smile, in a friendly way, yet all the while hoping they'll move on to other subjects. I don't want to say, 'Sorry, you don't understand; I'm gay', because most people aren't prepared to hear that. They don't *want* to hear it, either. Most people don't have the imagination to transcend this assumption of theirs that everyone that *they* know is going to be straight.
I know that this is not always such a big problem. And perhaps it is an educational experience for people to learn that someone they know is actually gay. But what about my feelings? It's difficult being 'that gay boy' all the time, having to deal with the negative or shocked reactions of people when you tell them that you're gay or, even, of having to deal with people who know but who now

see you *only* as a homosexual. I understand why people should think of me exclusively in terms of homosexuality. Perhaps I'm the only gay person they know (or *think* they know). But I get tired, sometimes, of having people look at me, however sympathetically, as a curiosity or an outsider. Worse yet, as someone to be pitied. And this is why, sometimes, I choose not to tell them I'm gay. I just keep quiet.

Being on stage, as gay, twenty-four hours a day is, as James implies, very demanding. It is difficult to be spontaneous in one's relations with people when one is seen always as a *type* rather than an *individual*. Yet such passing problems are minor compared with those confronting gays who *never* feel able to present themselves honestly to others, always being careful to manage their behaviour so as to maintain a pretence of heterosexuality.

Such concealment inevitably leads to alienation. The fear of exposure, of living a life that can be collapsed at any moment, forces one to be always 'on': to plot, to plan, to devise strategies of disguise and withdrawal. This anxiety follows closely on the heels of the decision to pass, as in the case of one seventeen-year-old girl, **Adele**, who was at last able to 'face up' to her gayness after months of worry, only to discover that

> . . . now, instead of having to worry about being a lesbian, I'm having to worry about anyone *finding out* that I'm a lesbian! I'm not certain I wasn't better off before. At least, before, I didn't feel such a hypocrite. Now I feel like an actress, always having to pretend I'm somebody I know I'm not. . . . I worry that people will see through me.
>
> Sometimes I think I'm not fooling anyone, least of all myself. I can never really tell whether people know or not. I'm always sort of looking after them to see if they have guessed.

Having to mask one's sexual orientation, like Adele, is not only conducive to anxiety; it can also create a permanent passing precedent. As author Robin Maugham writes in his autobiography, *Escape from the Shadows*, the decision to pass for straight— presenting 'a false façade to the world'—was the first step along the road to becoming 'two people'.[4] Such a schizophrenia of the human sensibility takes a heavy toll on the psychic state of the passer. Deceit of this kind quickly becomes a way of life, and the gay person emerges as one who is for ever alert to aspects of a social situation which others will treat as routine.

It is difficult to maintain one's self-respect under such circumstances, and the voluminous research of sociologists like Laud Humphreys provides persuasive evidence to suggest that self-hatred is much stronger among covert, passing homosexuals than it is among overt gays.[5] Thus, when **Gary**, a civil engineer in his late thirties, listened in affirmative silence to the 'queer joke' stories of his friends, it is hardly surprising that he should have come away convinced that

> I had degraded my character by offering tacit approval to the insulting stereotypes they drew. I listened to these stories of 'Larry Grayson gays' without saying a word. I even smiled, on occasion, which only appeared to confirm that I consented to everything they said.
> And yet, it was really *me* they were laughing at. Had I been braver, I would have said something. But I was afraid they would put two and two together and guess that I was gay, too. Then the mood would have changed in an instant, and I would have been the focus of attention. Only gays know what it feels like to be in that kind of situation. . . .
> I feel very ambivalent about effeminate gays. I'm not certain why. I hate the way they flout convention, mincing and fluttering about, drawing attention to themselves.
> Perhaps I don't mean that. I suppose it's no better or worse than the way straights behave, is it? I've been told that, really, I'm afraid of drawing attention to *myself*, to my homosexuality. Maybe so. But to be totally candid with you, I still avoid 'queens' at all costs; if you are seen with one of them, then that is it! Everybody knows about you!
> I don't like to hear myself say these things, but I can't help the way I feel. It takes time to change. It's easier to alter your behaviour than it is to change your psychology. . . .

One of the many negative effects of passing is the need of passers to take extreme measures in order to ingratiate themselves with unsuspecting heterosexual friends, e.g. by disassociating themselves from other gays or gay 'types'.[6] Thus, for Gary, 'Larry Grayson gays' were doubly disturbing: first, because they presented an unacceptable image of homosexuality to others (and, therefore, to himself); and second, because their very existence enhanced the possibility of his own 'exposure' as gay ('they would put two and two together and guess that I was gay, too').

It is understandable that those who have internalized society's sex/role assumptions should make such strenuous efforts to prove, both to themselves and to others, that, despite appearances to the contrary, they are every bit as 'normal' as everyone else. Yet such a strategy of survival often produces intense feelings of anxiety and self-hatred. For this reason, passing for straight is the most efficient means available of destroying group cohesion among homosexuals; there is no better way than this to stir up mutual animosity and create a community of persons who think so little of each other and who offer one another so little comfort and love.

Passing as a Product of Oppression

The passing strategies outlined above may seem somewhat extreme. The majority of gays will not be so concerned with hiding or disguising their homosexuality. However, the issue is not the numbers of people who behave in such ways but, rather, the extent to which such alternatives to self-acceptance reflect the pressures that force some gays to regard them as inevitable. If, as Laud Humphreys maintains, the 'self-destructive ego is a product of oppression', then only the loosing of bonds will heal it.[7] It is my thesis that passing is largely motivated by an assumption of failure, a conviction that one has failed to measure up to society's concept of 'man' and 'woman'. As Dennis Altman has pointed out,[8] our society is one that defines masculinity and femininity very much in heterosexual terms, so that the social stereotype (and, often, self-image) of the gay is that of someone who rejects his or her masculinity or femininity. Those who are unwilling to accept their socially defined roles are appropriately stigmatized. Proving one's 'manhood', or being a 'lady', are thus closely tied up with the rejection of homosexual characteristics. In women, repression is often internalized; in men, it is often externalized in aggressive behaviour.

What is so fundamentally wrong and cruel about this ideology of sexual repression is that, in encouraging the adoption of rigid postures as a means of rejecting tender, warm, or loving feelings towards others of the same sex, society further inhibits many gays from exploring either the meaning or the value of same-sex closeness. Society does not wish homosexuals to form loving relationships: hence the difficulty for some of ever doing so. It's as simple as that. (This is a point further explored in Chapter 7.)

The mechanics of this socially induced repression are clearly described in three autobiographies by homosexuals. In the early chapters of *To Fall Like Lucifer*, the former MP Ian Harvey recalls that 'particular friendships', even those 'strong enough to be called love', were quite common in his student days. Yet a combination of secrecy and contempt always surrounded gay love, which was, he says, 'regarded as effeminate, and effeminacy in our eyes was degrading'.[9]

The experience of T. C. Worsley, the drama critic, further illustrates how stereotyped definitions of masculinity/femininity are transmitted and internalized. While a student at Marlborough, Worsley's yearning for acceptance led to a passion for games which, in turn, satisfied a need for reassurances about his virility. But friends of a more conventional frame of mind demanded additional proof, which took the form of the cricket captain's cousin—an attractive and 'experienced' girl who suffered silently through several physically uneventful sessions with Worsley before at last informing him:[10]

> 'You're a homosexual! . . .'
> 'Am I?' (Worsley replied, with genuine surprise).
> For how was I to tell? The word, after all, implied if anything, 'cissiness'. Cissy I certainly wasn't. Wasn't I, on the contrary, if not a tough, at least a very masculine, athlete?

But the most outstanding example of society's success in programming sex/role expectations is the case of William Aaron. Beauty for him was in the eye of the heterosexual, and it is there that he found himself to be ugly. 'Disgusted' by what he regarded as his homosexual 'retreat from normalcy', Aaron yearned to be 'reconditioned', 'a lover of women and therefore a complete man' (i.e. one who has 'penetrated a woman' sexually). As Aaron explains it:[11]

> I'd love to be able honestly to downgrade the importance of this 'achievement', to pose as someone so rational and 'together' that I could separate potency from masculinity; make a humane distinction between manhood and the ability to perform sexually with a woman. But that would be a lie.

The experience of William Aaron, like those of Ian Harvey and T. C. Worsley, helps us to understand just how painfully unsuitable to gays are heterosexual patterns of sexual maturity. Sadly, too, they illustrate the extent to which internalization of these attitudes and values makes the phenomenon of passing a key fact of the gay experience. Self-acceptance can be a reality only when gays are enabled to evolve a means of proudly embracing their sexual identity. Part of this adjustment involves an understanding of the means by which society stigmatizes homosexuality, and this we shall consider next. (The impact of AIDS on gay self-acceptance will be considered in Chapter 8; so, too, will the forms of discrimination being employed against those carrying the AIDS virus or who are ill with the disease.)

Weapons of Oppression: The Law

No one who has ever counselled homosexuals can be in much doubt about the continuing reality of gay oppression under the law. For those who are not totally familiar with the subject, however, a brief introduction follows.[12]

Gay people in Britain encounter oppression of two basic kinds: persecution and discrimination. Persecution refers to the illegality of homosexual activity, and discrimination to its social and psychological consequences. So long as our society continues to legislate morality, it is fairly obvious that large numbers of people will consistently and consciously break the law. Not all these people will pay for their 'crimes', of course; in fact, it is quite safe to assume that only a small fraction will ever be apprehended. But those who do run foul of the law may well find their lives dramatically altered as a result; so, too, the lives of their friends and loved ones. Those who are not apprehended may be more fortunate in so far as they escape the wrath of the law; however, the awareness of one's lawlessness is bound to have damaging psychical consequences in the long run.

The Sexual Offences Act was passed by Parliament in 1967, ten years after the published Report of the Wolfenden Committee.[13] Regarded by many at the time as a piece of enlightened legislation, it has since been shown that in certain crucial respects the Act upholds and reinforces many of the traditional biases against male homosexuals. Indeed, according to Lord Devlin, one of its architects, 'the Act of 1967 was an act of toleration. It was not an act of approval . . .

43

In 1967, and probably still today, homosexuality is regarded as undesirable and not to be encouraged.'[14] Although the Act legalized sexual activity between consenting males over the age of twenty-one, time has proved that certain provisions of the Bill are more harmful than beneficent in their effects:

· 1. Members of the Armed Forces and Merchant Navy may not participate in homosexual activity, regardless of the circumstances in which such activity takes place and even if those involved are both over twenty-one and make love in private (when the Armed Forces Bill recently came up for review, the Commons Select Committee refused to allow oral evidence on the subject from the Campaign for Homosexual Equality, the National Council for Civil Liberties, and the Conservative Group for Homosexual Equality; thus, lesbians and gay men in the services can still be—and *are* being—arrested for what the Bill calls 'disgraceful conduct amounting to indecency');[15]

2. homosexual acts between consenting adults in the Channel Islands and the Isle of Man remain, in law, criminal offences (in 1981 the European Court of Human Rights ruled in the *Dudgeon* case that the United Kingdom had failed to justify the maintenance of legislation in Northern Ireland which, in effect, criminalized private consenting homosexual relations between two men; the government was thus compelled to introduce legislation—the Homosexual Offences (Northern Ireland) Order 1982—which brought Northern Irish law into line with the rest of the UK);

3. homosexual males are not accorded the same latitude as heterosexual males in so far as the right to privacy is concerned, e.g. homosexual acts are illegal if performed on premises where more than two persons are present, even if they are all over the age of twenty-one, consenting, and in absolute privacy;

4. no provision is allowed for amendments to take account of changes made in other legislation, e.g. at present the age of consent for male heterosexuals is sixteen, but twenty-one for male homosexuals;[16]

5. homosexual males are not accorded the same parity of treatment under the law as heterosexual males in respect to penalties, e.g. two years can be given for indecent assault on a woman, but ten years for indecent assault on a man;

6. no fair and just balance between the concepts of freedom and protection is achieved, e.g. in regard to cases of soliciting: police evidence is sufficient *in itself* (the complainant not being called upon

to give evidence) to substantiate a charge made by one man against another; it is an offence for a man (or woman) to solicit another man for 'an immoral purpose', but not for a man to solicit a woman for an identical purpose;

7. the law assumes that male homosexuality is more anti-social than heterosexuality (and, therefore, inherently more criminal), e.g. by the use of such negatively toned words and phrases as '*lewd* homosexual practices' [emphasis added].

One final point: the 1967 Act, in line with all past legislation dealing with sexual morality, does not prohibit homosexual behaviour between women. In fact, when a private Member introduced a clause into a 1921 Commons Bill, it was rejected by the House of Lords on Government advice which argued that such a measure, in addition to encouraging blackmail, would involve unwarrantable interference with the freedom of the individual.[17]

As far as prosecutions for homosexual 'offences' are concerned, most of these fall into one of two categories: breaches of the age of consent and sexual activity in a public place. Most 'age of consent' cases involve adult males charged with offences against one or more than one boy between the ages of eight and fifteen. A boy under sixteen is treated by the law as being incapable of consenting to sex. Consent is therefore not considered a defence in the case of an older person who may be charged with 'indecent assault', a crime punishable with a maximum of ten years' imprisonment. Although the Director of Public Prosecutions (DPP) does not always press charges, the decision on whether or not to do so can take a long time—a period of great uncertainty for the accused. (Between 1984 and 1987 thirty-five men, on average, were each year sent to prison for having consensual sex with other men aged between sixteen and twenty-one, even though such 'offences' do not exist for heterosexuals. The average sentence was twenty-two months, with a minimum of three months and a maximum of five years. It is also a criminal offence if both of the partners involved in 'homosexual acts' are below the age of twenty-one, though the DPP would need to give its permission to prosecute.) If the accused has offered money as an inducement, or is a teacher, a social worker, or a member of one of the caring professions generally, then imprisonment is more or less automatic.[18]

The above account of existing legislation and prosecutions for homosexual 'offences', though brief, should be sufficient to alert readers to the fact that, in situations involving the law's attitudes to homosexuality, it will not always be an easy matter to determine the point at which counselling leaves off and social services begin. The point is borne out in the case of **Reg**, twenty-seven, who is at present living and working in North London. Reg is 'fortunate' in so far as his involvement with a sixteen-year-old boy never came to the attention of the law. But when he first came to see me, nearly two years ago, he felt certain that arrest was imminent. As he recalls:

I fully expected to be hauled into the police station, put on trial, and then be sent to jail for corrupting the morals of a minor.

I'll start at the beginning, when I first met Tony. Actually, I had seen him dozens of times before we ever spoke. We lived on the same road, just a few houses apart. Tony had moved in with his family about three months before. . . .

It was Tony by the way who spoke first. He was always a bit flirtatious, I should say. Oh, I had already noticed him, of course. He could tell that I was . . . curious. I guess it showed in my eyes. It was during our very first conversation that he mentioned the fact that his parents were spending most weekends in Norwich with his gran, who was poorly. 'Why don't you keep me company? We've a colour telly', he says. . . .

Well, to keep a long story short, I dropped round to see him that weekend, and on several other occasions. I needn't tell you again all that happened. Let's just say he wasn't in the least bit shy. Mind you, I wasn't unwilling; but it wasn't *me* who corrupted him. At sixteen he was well and truly corrupted, believe me, for all that innocent look of his. . . .

People talk about predatory old men in dirty macs! It was *he* who seduced *me*! And as for being a dirty *old* man, I was barely twenty-five at the time. . . .

I'll skip to the point. Tony's parents discovered that the two of us had been seeing one another, and they threw a fit. Obviously Tony made it appear as if I had hypnotized him or something because they *really* were outraged. . . .

There was no doubt in my mind they were going to the police. In fact, I couldn't be certain they hadn't already done so when I came to see you. The father was *furious*!

But then you spoke to them, and I suppose that changed his mind. . . .

In fact, Tony's father had little inclination to discuss matters rationally when I first spoke to him over the phone. Tony's mother proved far more sympathetic to Reg's situation, as well as to her son's. It was she who arranged for a meeting of the two families, urging her husband 'not to take things so personally'. This advice was much to the point. Many fathers view their sons, at least in part, as proof of their own masculine accomplishments. For this reason their self-image is threatened should the son exhibit homosexual tendencies, or express feminine traits, or prefer artistic pursuits to games and sports. Tony's father was therefore perfectly prepared to believe, in the face of much evidence to the contrary, that his son had been seduced by Reg.

Some semblance of the truth did emerge, however, when the two families met to thrash the matter over, and Tony's father finally decided it would be best to 'keep this whole affair to ourselves'. It was not so much the 'truth' which persuaded him to take this course of action but, rather, the argument of Tony's mother that to file a complaint with the police would do their son far more harm than good. In this opinion the Wolfenden Committee appears to be in complete agreement: 'The fact of being seduced', it says in its Report, 'often does less harm to the victim than the publicity which attends the criminal proceedings against the offender.[19]

As for Reg's parents, though shaken by the manner in which they learned of their son's homosexuality, their love and concern for Reg has in no way changed. As **Alice**, Reg's mother, says:

We had a long talk, and I'd say we understand each other a little better now. Mind, things won't ever be the same way as before. They can't be, really.
I'm having to look at my world differently. I've changed some of my ideas. The future looks a bit different. Reg is our only child, and I know I won't be a grandparent now. . . .
I can't say I'm in any way pleased Reg is homosexual. I'm sorry, but I can't. . . . My generation is one which looked at things very differently than what they do today. Like I said to Harold, I know it's old-fashioned, but it's the way I am. . . .
I'm trying to do the best I can. I can't do better than that. . . .
You see, this is all new to us, Harold and me. We've never had to think about . . . this, or anything like this, before. . . .
Still, Reg is our son, and we love him. . . . He's not changed, has

47

he, just because we know? If anyone has changed, I suppose you can say it's us.

The reaction of parents to their children's homosexuality will be further considered in Chapter 6. For now, it is sufficient to say that the suffering caused by the five-year disparity in the age of consent is by no means limited to those taking part in homosexual activity. The families of those involved also suffer in consequence of a law which, as Bob Sturgess has argued:[20]

is a bad law . . . because it invites—and suffers—widespread violation by otherwise law-abiding citizens; bad because the ministering professions are also prone to disregard it in the name of common humanity; and bad, finally, because it is not in accord either with current knowledge or with this country's best traditions of toleration and enlightened reform.

Homosexual activity can also be prosecuted under the Sexual Offences Act of 1956, s. 32, which states: 'It is an offence for a man persistently to solicit or importune in a public place for immoral purposes.' Though originally intended to deal with men procuring for female prostitutes, it has, in practice, been directed almost exclusively against gay men in situations having nothing to do with prostitution, but which, rather, involve unobjectionable pick-ups and casual encounters.[21]

At the time of writing, this law is still being enforced, the maximum sentence being two years' imprisonment and/or a fine (in Scotland there is no statutory maximum sentence, though the usual sentence for a first offender, as in England and Wales, is a fine plus the payment of police prosecution costs). It is also worth noting that, since the advent of AIDS, cases of arrest for 'gross indecency' have dramatically increased.[22]

Unhappily, the police, despite the fact that they are no longer under any obligation to detect homosexual activity between consenting adults, continue on occasion to treat gays as if the very fact of their sexual orientation was an indication of anti-social tendencies. Indeed, cases known to the Albany Trust and the Sexual Law Reform Society indicate that patterns of arrest in public places, as well as interrogation procedures concerning aspects of a man's private life which are no longer criminal, give cause for continuing concern.[23]

Although the police insist that they no longer use *agent provocateur* tactics, the overwhelming evidence of many homosexuals contradicts this claim and, I am convinced, demands the most serious consideration by the counsellor. Let us listen to the voice of **Jeff**, whose story reveals many of the circumstances which frequently lead to the arrest of a gay person in a public lavatory.

I'm twenty-nine and I'm currently unemployed. Six months ago I was arrested for soliciting in a public gents. I pleaded guilty. The judge gave me a £25 fine.

At the station they told me that my employer would be informed, so I quit. I quit my job the next day. I didn't want to be fired first. I won't deny that I've cottaged from time to time. But on the afternoon of my arrest, I wasn't looking for anything but a quick pee.

Why did I plead guilty, then? Ask anyone who's been in the same spot, and they'll give you the same answer: because the police tell you it will be easier for you if you do. They act like they're concerned, like they're giving you this advice in your own interest.

And you want to believe it, you know, because, let's face it, you're scared, you're in a panic. So you go along with their story. You plead guilty. Later on, you appear in court. You pay your fine. It's over. A minimum of fuss. And you don't want fuss, because that's bad for you, for your family, friends, job. It was bad for *me*, and I pleaded guilty!

People don't believe you, either. They think, well, you know, the police, they don't lie. They're the police! You have to put your trust somewhere, don't you? People don't want to believe cops aren't perfect. So you must have done what they say you did.

The day I was arrested, I had gone into a toilet at 5.30 in the afternoon. Maybe a little later. It was crowded at that hour. The urinals were all taken up, so I started to leave. Then this bloke zipped up and left, and I went over to this urinal next to a skin-head type in faded denims.

I wasn't looking for 'action', but you'd have to have been blind not to have seen this bloke next to me playing with his penis, and looking right down at it, with a sort of frown on his face. I looked over at him, not obvious, though. Just a glance to the left with my eyes, if you see what I mean.

Funnily enough, I was beginning to feel a bit nervous. I guess I suspected something. I couldn't urinate, either. I never can if I'm feeling nervous like that. I looked up, then, at his face. Just curious, because I thought to myself, is this bloke 'rent', or what? It was at that moment, as I looked at the bloke's face, that this other bloke who'd been standing at the wash-basin combing his hair, he came over and put his hand on my shoulder. And with that the fellow next to me quickly zips himself up and looks at his mate, then at me.

They were cops. I couldn't believe it, because they told me I was under arrest. Then they took me back to the station house.

The police are anxious that the public should understand that they do not enter toilets looking for homosexuals unless a complaint is lodged.[24] Let us assume that this is true. Who, then, makes the complaints? In the course of a sociological study involving close observation of hundreds of homosexual encounters in public rest-rooms, Laud Humphreys came to the conclusion[25]

> that an unwilling participant may withdraw at any time from a (cottage) encounter without creating a scene or losing his purity or his composure. Because of cautions built into the strategies of these encounters, no man need fear of being molested in such facilities; he must first demonstrate by showing an erection that he wants to get in on the action.

Humphreys is not alone in this conclusion. It is the carefully considered opinion of a research team on law enforcement at the University of California's Faculty of Law that[26]

> the majority of homosexual solicitations are made only if the other individual appears responsive and are ordinarily accomplished by quiet conversation and the use of gestures and signals having significance only to other homosexuals. Such unobtrusive solicitations do not involve an element of public outrage. The rare indiscriminate solicitations of the general public do not justify the commitment of police resources to suppress such behaviour.

One final provision of the law affecting gays to be considered here is the common law charge of conspiracy to corrupt public morals. This law is of immediate concern to the counsellor, for interpretations of the 1967 Sexual Offences Act aim to inhibit all those who recognize and are attempting to alleviate the social isolation and loneliness of gay people through the provision of social facilities and meeting places.

It was in June of 1972 that the House of Lords upheld convictions for conspiracy to corrupt public morals brought against the directors and company of an 'underground' newspaper, *International Times* (*IT*). The prosecution arose because *IT* published contact advertisements for gays who wished to meet with other gays. Despite the fact that the prosecution never suggested the homosexual meetings or activities envisaged by the ads were in any way unlawful, the court ruled that there is a 'material difference' between 'exempting certain conduct from criminal penalties' and 'making it lawful in the full sense'.[27] In other words, the Sexual Offences Act of 1967 was read as saying that if people chose to corrupt themselves (i.e. if homosexuals chose to meet and engage in sexual activity) they were entitled to do so, and the law would not interfere. On the other hand, no licence had been given to others (e.g. counsellors?) to encourage such a practice of 'corruption'. (The law seems to have wearied of prosecuting newspapers and magazines for publishing contact advertisements, and there are now a number of publications which regularly include such ads, directed at both homosexuals and heterosexuals.)

It seems, as a lawyer writing in the *Guardian* pointed out, that we are, in regard to homosexual behaviour, in a no-law area where 'the law now appears to be what the Director of Public Prosecutions wakes up in the morning and says it is'.[28] As a consequence, police are given wide powers of discretion in carrying out their duty to preserve the peace and protect the 'public good'. Thus, police can and do infringe upon the civil rights of gays who are not conducting themselves like heterosexuals. Consider this story, reprinted from *New Society*:[29]

> In September 1968, the Manchester magistrates fined a club owner for having allowed men to dance together. Evidence was given by the police who had visited the place in plain clothes that it was 'a haunt of homosexuals'. Presumably the homosexuals themselves were not outraged by single-sex dancing. Nevertheless, the owner pleaded guilty to having permitted dancing of a nature likely to cause a breach of the peace.

Twenty years later, one continues to hear of such blatant cases of discrimination. It has even been argued (and there is substantial evidence to support the claim) that, due to the anti-gay climate

51

created by the AIDS crisis, such assaults on the civil liberties of
homosexuals are actually on the increase (see Chapter 8).

Finally, it should be pointed out that new legislation may well be
passed which would radically change the domestic laws on obscenity
and further restrict the publication or sale of much pro-gay literature. Gay's the Word bookshop, in particular, has been victimized
by the arbitrary interpretations of 'obscenity' used by HM Customs
and Excise, which seized numerous books imported to the shop from
the USA. 'Perhaps', as the shop's manager, Paul Hegarty, has
speculated, 'homosexual material is considered to be obscene simply
because it's homosexual.'

Weapons of Oppression: Employment

It is not only the law that oppresses homosexuals and encourages
passing. Discrimination comes in a great variety of shades, as
Eileen, thirty, explains:

> Rejection is expressed in many ways. The law in this country has
> never discriminated against women *as lesbians*, yet I don't feel any
> less oppressed than gay men.
>
> The hushed conversations people have about 'one of them'; the
> newspaper stories about lesbian scandals that are blown out of all
> proportion; the jokes about 'dykes' and 'bull dykes'; the sexist
> assumption that 'all we need' to be 'real' women is a 'good man'
> (and you-know-what-else!); the icy stares that greet you when you
> arrive at dinner parties with a girlfriend rather than the expected
> boyfriend; the social functions you never get invited to because
> you 'simply don't fit in'.
>
> I could go on endlessly, relating my experiences and those of my
> friends. I won't, though, because you're always thought 'para-
> noid' when you say anything. One is always thought paranoid by
> people who have no idea what it's like to be someone else.

Nowhere is discrimination more pronounced than in the area of jobs
and employment. The counsellor will doubtless encounter many
cases where, in being open about themselves at work, homosexuals
have jeopardized their prospects for promotion, or even lost their
jobs (though other reasons are generally given in such cases). There
is still no legal protection for homosexual workers. Furthermore,
industrial tribunals tend overwhelmingly to support the employer in

sacking lesbian and gay workers. We have recently seen a disconcertingly large number of cases in which gay men have been sacked from their jobs simply due to the fears of workmates that they might, because of their sexual orientation, have AIDS. In all too many instances an industrial tribunal has backed the sacking.[30] The risk run by self-respecting gays is, of course, peculiar to their status in society; hence, doing one's job well is not always sufficient in itself to prevent the gay person from being sacked. Professions particularly at risk are (in addition to the military) those in government, the church, education, the social services, and caring professions; elsewhere efforts are frequently made to keep 'known homosexuals' out of 'sensitive' posts.

It is sometimes thought that gay women, because of their more favourable legal status, encounter less discrimination than men in this area of employment. This is not so, and counsellors will eventually find themselves confronted with women from all spheres of work who seek help with broken careers. For **Nancy**, a twenty-eight-year-old former nurse, the problem was one of 'not knowing for sure whether anyone knew, or whether, really, it would make a difference if they did':

> There are a lot of gay nurses. It's an open secret. But don't mention the subject to *other* nurses. They take the attitude that it gives the profession a 'bad name'. It's the wrong image to present to the world outside. . . .
>
> I remember once confiding in an older nurse while in training. She was straight. I felt so lonely then. I told her about myself because I was looking for understanding. I was very young. Her immediate reaction was to assure me repeatedly that I shouldn't breathe a word to anyone else. She left me feeling that mine had been an unwelcome confidence. After that, we scarcely talked when we passed in the wards, except to nod, or say 'hello'.
>
> I felt frightened by this reaction. 'Discovery' suddenly loomed as an awful possibility in my life. I would have to keep up my guard, pretend to be straight. This is how I interpreted her reaction. . . .
>
> In many ways, it's fortunate that I didn't come out until recently. I don't believe I could have lasted those five years in hospital otherwise. Even so, it was difficult sticking it for that long. . . .
>
> Being a nurse . . . I don't know . . . it's not easy separating the profession from the rest of your life. You have to be open about

yourself, otherwise you always find yourself in difficult situations, always pretending. . . . It's the small talk, for example, with all the girls enthusing about 'the kidney case' in such-and-such a ward, or 'Dr Mallory's latest patient', or whatever. . . .

It's having to *pretend* all the time! Using the body language women are expected to use in conducting business with male colleagues and patients! I had become my own worst enemy. Pretending to be something that I wasn't, because that's what other people wanted.

It wasn't till I started talking to other *gay people* that I began to realize what was happening to me, and what I could *be*. . . .

Nancy's story helps to explain why so many homosexuals fear coming out, preferring instead to hide or disguise those facts about themselves which might lead others to the right conclusions about their homosexual orientation.

Dennis Altman does not exaggerate, then, when he claims that[31]

. . . if I am simply *known* as a homosexual, I will encounter discrimination even at times when no one seriously believes my sex life is directly involved. This is most obvious in the field of employment, and there are homophile leaders who believe that *job discrimination* is the greatest single reason why homosexuals fear disclosure.

Outside certain areas of work, of which entertainment and some personal services are the major examples, one's career can only be adversely affected if one is known as—or suspected of being—a homosexual. . . .

In my (own) case I realized some years ago that I was precluded from entering conventional politics, because I was not prepared sufficiently to hide my homosexuality. There are, of course, a number of politicians who are in fact 'closeted' homosexuals, but I would not be prepared to live the quite tortured life of secrecy such men must suffer.

Organizations which work for homosexuals—both self-help and referral agencies—report numerous instances in which individuals, both men and women, have lost their jobs or have been asked to vacate their lodgings because it was either known or suspected that they were homosexual. And such allegations are almost always made *without* any sexual misconduct being alleged. As for those gay people who take recourse in the law, they soon discover that a homosexual charge which is made in court—no matter how trivial it may be—is usually followed by the most disastrous professional (not to mention personal) consequences. This is a point I have made elsewhere in this chapter, but it is an important one which cannot be emphasized enough.

Weapons of Oppression: Housing

In both the public and the private sectors, most of the housing regulations are designed to meet the needs of heterosexual married couples and their children. The social security system clearly ignores the existence of gay relationships under the existing DHSS housing regulations, while access to mortgages, especially in the private sector, also reflects this discriminatory policy, all the more so with the advent of AIDS (see Chapter 8). Perhaps lesbians are the hardest hit since, in common with all women, they have a lower standard of living than men. As a result of their weaker economic position, they are less likely to have access to mortgages and much more likely to be forced to choose between expensive rented accommodation and sub-standard council housing. Lesbians without dependants, along with many single heterosexual people, find themselves restricted to this form of housing. The housing problems are varied, and the consequences of discrimination often traumatic, as in the case of **Gilda**, who was forced out of her council house on the death of her lover, Rose:

Rose and I were among the lucky ones. We had a council house. Or, I should say, Rose had the house. The tenancy was in her name. We lived together there for eight years, and before that Rose was there for two. We were really nicely settled, and we got on pretty well with the neighbours, too, who didn't seem to think anything about our living together. They just liked us . . .
Then last year Rose, who'd had a lot of trouble with her heart, had a coronary, and she died within twenty-four hours of the attack. I was shattered, really in shock for days, and in a terrible state of depression for weeks. It seemed so sudden.
But I won't go into that, except to say that before I could get myself adjusted to things, to sort my future out, I had notice from the local authority saying I had to leave the house which had been

55

my home, Rose's home and mine, for the last eight years. I went to the legal aid centre and they were very sympathetic and understanding, but in the end they said, 'sorry', the way things now stand a lesbian relationship didn't qualify as a heterosexual one would in securing tenancy. If we had been a married couple, I'd have had inheritance rights.

So I was out. It wasn't just having to leave, to find another place. Not that *that* was easy, I can tell you.

It was leaving behind those memories, everything that reminded me of my years with Rose.

Most liberal opinion in Britain is appalled by the discrimination and persecution of gay people which I have outlined; and, no doubt, it would support the efforts of gay groups such as the Campaign for Homosexual Equality (CHE), the Gay Rights Office of the National Council for Civil Liberties, the Northern Ireland Gay Rights Association and the Scottish Homosexual Rights Group in their drive to reform the laws affecting homosexuals. Unfortunately, though, such toleration is not incompatible with a suspicious and even hostile attitude towards homosexuality—particularly when this psychosexual orientation is perceived as posing a threat to such institutions as (heterosexual) marriage and the nuclear family.

Tolerance must be replaced by both understanding and, most of all, by acceptance of homosexuality as a valid lifestyle. Until such time as attitudes are substantively changed, however, gay people will continue to regard passing as an attractive alternative to being open and self-accepting. And such a decision, as we have seen, can only be accompanied by the most unhappy consequences.

Summary

This chapter has been concerned with the phenomenon of 'passing' and the nature of that oppression which sustains it.

Passing means concealing information about oneself which might bring others to conclude that one is homosexual. This strategy of survival in a hostile environment inhibits spontaneity (**James**), and often leads to intense feelings of anxiety (**Adele**) and a sense of alienation (**Gary**).

Passing is the product of oppression, and we have examined here some present legislation which discriminates against the homosexual. As far as prosecutions for homosexual offences are concerned, most of these fall into one of two categories: breaches of the age of consent (**Reg; Alice**), and sexual activity within a public place (**Jeff**).

Discrimination comes in many shades, and it is not only the law that oppresses gays and inhibits the search for self-identity. For example, gay women, though they are not discriminated against as lesbians under present legislation, nevertheless feel the impact of anti-gay attitudes (**Eileen**), and are particularly vulnerable in view of the unwelcoming posture taken by certain professions, such as nursing (**Nancy**). Discrimination is also reflected in a social security system which clearly ignores the existance of gay relationships under existing DHSS housing regulations (**Gilda**). It is only when such rejecting attitudes as these are substantively changed that gays will more fully accept themselves and reject passing as an alternative to being open.

4

The Halo of Marriage

To be or not to be: that is the question.
Shakespeare, *Hamlet*, III.i.56

Hamlet's question of whether 'to be or not to be' is one with special resonance for homosexuals. Gay people, as we observed in the previous chapter, are confronted with a wide range of possibilities in dealing with the stigma attached to their sexual orientation. Almost as soon as gays have discovered their difference, the question arises as to whether or not they will reveal this fact to others. Many choose to pass for straight. Another form of adjustment, and one which is frequently overlooked in the literature dealing with the subject, is heterosexual marriage.

In this chapter, I shall consider the situation of married gays and the reasons why homosexuals enter into heterosexual marriage. Some modes of adjusting to the conflicts which develop in married life will also be considered. But first of all a warning regarding the statistical generalizations often made concerning the prevalence of marriage among homosexuals. Such figures must be viewed (as should so much else that has been written on the subject of homosexuality) with a fair degree of scepticism. The reason for this is that, generally speaking, only self-accepting and publicly identified homosexuals are interviewed by researchers, whereas the majority of married gays are likely to remain reticent about their homosexual component. This fact is not often taken into account, thus casting doubt on the accuracy of the present data.

The experience of many gay counsellors is that the number of gays who are, or who have been, married is higher than is generally supposed. Perhaps the following tentative findings based on my own counselling experience combined with the most recent and reliable statistical evidence[1] will be of some help to readers in gauging the numbers of married homosexuals, the ages at which gays are married, the duration of marriages, and the numbers of gay parents:*

1. approximately one-fifth of all gays are married at some point or other in their lives;
2. approximately four-fifths of this number are married by the age of about twenty-nine, and the remaining one-fifth at a later age;
3. approximately three-fifths of all marriages among gays last for up to three years, and approximately two-fifths last for a period of more than three years;
4. approximately two-fifths of all married gays have had one or more children in the course of their marriages.

Why Gays Marry

Why should some homosexuals choose to enter into such a seemingly conflicting situation as heterosexual marriage? The reasons are various, but four explanations tend to be given with greater frequency than others:

1. insufficient awareness of one's homosexuality at the time of marriage;
2. a conscious desire to escape in some degree from the knowledge of one's homosexuality;
3. rational choice;
4. social pressures.

Let us consider each of these in turn.

The story of **Judith** clearly illustrates the 'delayed recognition' factor in the gay person's decision to marry:

I didn't fully believe myself to be lesbian until some while after

---

*Although it would be difficult to verify this conclusion, it is my feeling that since the advent of Gay Liberation in 1969 fewer homosexuals choose to enter into heterosexual marriages. My basis for this assertion is, in addition to my own counselling experience, an interpolation of past and present research into the incidence of marriage among homosexuals, e.g. Kinsey, *Sexual Behaviour in the Human Male* and *Sexual Behavior in the Human Female* (1948 and 1952); Weinberg and Williams, *Male Homosexuals* (1974); and Saghir and Robins, *Male and Female Homosexuality* (1974). However, it is possible that the advent of AIDS, in so far as it has caused some to reconsider coming out as gay, may see a further increase in the number of homosexuals who enter into heterosexual marriage.

my marriage. I expect the evidence was plain enough for *anyone else* to see, but not me.

My first romantic crush was on a woman in her late thirties. I was about eleven or twelve. Very vaguely, too, I recall having had several dreams in which I was sexually involved with other girls at school. That's when I was about thirteen or fourteen.

But I never applied labels to myself. I mean, I never said, 'Aha! I'm lesbian!' *That* possibility never entered into my head. I wasn't aware homosexuality even existed.

In any case, I rather liked boys. More as companions, I think . . . as equals. Frankly, I felt superior to most boys I knew, though I enjoyed the company of the more intellectual ones.

I'm afraid I was never much good at taking a subordinate or *submissive* role. . . .

Still, I dated. And there were one or two boys I was rather serious about. One boy, I discovered, was gay. He was nice—very sweet, intelligent, gentle, considerate. . . . We're still friends.

When I was twenty, I married Carl. Eleven months later I was pregnant. In the middle of my pregnancy Carl began to spend more and more time with his friends, or his hobbies. He had a number of outside interests. He was, and is, very interested in politics. So there's always been quite a bit to keep him away from home.

After Tim was born, I felt fairly content. Perhaps I should be ashamed of saying this, but I regarded being a mother as a challenge. I've always enjoyed taking on challenges. . . .

I certainly enjoyed those first few months of being a mother. But then, about four months after Tim was born, I was pregnant again. This second pregnancy was unexpected. I had been careless about taking the pill, and was beginning to feel very nervous about just everything. I was now seeing less of Carl, and although we never had serious arguments, it seemed as though a formality had developed between us. . . .

After Mandy as born, I virtually refused to have sex. I don't think this greatly worried Carl. His lack of concern might have bothered me (on some level) if I hadn't been so pleased by his casual acceptance of the situation.

About a year later I met Mary, a girl I knew at my college some years before. She was sitting in the park, where I usually went in the afternoons with the children. . . . I saw her several days a week after that. Within a few months we were in love. . . .

When I met Mary, everything changed. I began to see myself more clearly. Three years after marriage I suddenly understood: 'I'm gay!' I still like men, but it's basically women I care for. . . . As I say, I don't know why it took me so long to understand, and I don't care. . . .

I'm still married to Carl and, on the surface, at least, things appear much as before I met Mary. But *I'm* changed. I'm happier. I feel more complete.

Carl is away a great deal, but this is temporary. He begins a new job in the spring. I can't say yet what will happen—tomorrow or next year. One thing I can say, though: I'm at last beginning to enjoy life.

Although Judith was unaware of her gay component at the time of her marriage, it is probably true to say that most gays who decide to marry are fully aware of their homosexuality. Some of these decide on marriage as a means of escape: a 'solution' to the 'problem' of being gay. Unfortunately, such an adjustment is sometimes encouraged by counsellors in the belief that homosexuality is a kind of situational phenomenon that will disappear once the opportunities to have regular heterosexual relationships present themselves. Consider, for example, the case of **Toby**.

When I was seventeen I sought the advice of my doctor. I was having these sexual fantasies about other boys. I thought there might be something biologically wrong with me. . . .

My doctor's face turned crimson when I told him. He asked me if I had told my parents. I said that I hadn't. 'Well, don't,' he said, 'because many boys go through this sort of thing and it doesn't mean anything.' No use worrying my parents, he said.

He seemed more concerned about my parents than me. Yet I did feel a *bit* better for having seen him. I hadn't realized that other boys felt this way, too.

The trouble is, my fantasies continued. A few months later I felt so depressed I went to a teacher. He became very solemn when I told him. He asked me how long I had felt this way. When I told him he seemed . . . well, I don't know, disturbed.

'Don't you have *any* feelings for girls?' he asked. But before I could answer, he was telling me how sensitive I was. He thought I was worried about taking advantage of girls, and that this concern had driven me to boys.

I didn't understand this. He seemed very encouraging, though, and told me I should think of marriage—having a family, children, responsibilities. He said that if I began going out more often with girls, I would soon find them less frightening.

I hadn't said anything about being *afraid* of girls. I *wasn't* afraid of girls. . . .

For the next year or so I forced myself to fantasize about girls whenever I masturbated. . . . At nineteen, almost on the spur of the moment, I asked this girl I had known for years to marry me, and she said 'yes', she would.

I truly believed that getting into the routine of marriage—having sex on a regular basis—would tone down my homosexual fantasies, make them less intense, less threatening.

It didn't work out that way at all. My fantasies were no less intense. Marriage was going to 'cure' me, but it didn't. After about a year, Millie and I almost began to hate each other.

Prior to his marriage, Toby had no sexual experience of any kind. This fact left him particularly susceptible to the advice of counsellors whom he believed to be experienced in this area. Other gays who marry are aware of their homosexuality as a permanent feature of their total make-up. Such individuals, under no illusions about the power of marriage to redirect their erotic preferences into heterosexual channels, still conclude that happiness is possible only by marrying and living out a conventional (heterosexual) home life. **Arthur**, thirty-five, is a case in point.

I've always preferred sex with men. I never tried to deny that to myself. But by the age of twenty-nine I had given up believing in gay relationships. Basically, I was *afraid* to believe. . . .

I accepted, uncritically, everything people said about homosexuals. That made it easy for me to see only the bitchiness, the broken affairs, the transiency. . . . And this I didn't want for myself. I wanted something *permanent*. . . .

Right up to the time of marrying, I viewed my homosexuality as a total negative. If that's the way you see yourself, then everything in the gay scene is going to reinforce that conviction, including gay partnerships.

I had this fantasy of a snug and secure family life. All my friends, the people I grew up with, they were married, and . . . yes, I envied them. I imagined family life as the ideal. You know, you watch the box, you listen to the radio, you read the papers, you talk with your friends, and it's always the family that's assumed to be everyone's goal in life . . . the home, family, getting married. . . .

For Margaret, my wife, marriage meant 'true love'. For me, it meant security, being accepted as 'normal', being like everybody else.

A fourth reason why some gays decide to marry relates to social pressures. Being known about or being publicly identified as homosexual may have undesirable consequences for those concerned with maintaining a socially acceptable façade. According to Erving Goffman, sex is more significant even than social class, profession, or personal qualities in determining a person's inner, as well as public, identity.[2] For **Edward**, a civil servant, being married was 'a decided advantage' because '. . . marriage imparted a respectable image':

I'm not saying you must be married to 'get ahead'. But people do wonder when you're single after a certain age. And you must be above suspicion at all times. People are quick to jump to conclusions. . . .

Certainly to be labelled 'homosexual' could lead to a variety of professional avenues being closed off. It can make a difference to one's career prosepects . . . generally speaking, people don't require a great deal of evidence in order for this assumption (of homosexuality) to be made. . . .

The insistent demands of one's relatives and friends who feel something is *wrong* with you, or in your life, if you've no marriage prospects—this constitutes a subtle form of blackmail. . . .

It's assumed you're somehow irresponsible if you're homosexual. Men who are married, family men firmly ensconced in a conformist home life, are thought more 'solid'; marriage confers a halo of respectability upon them.

The demands of relatives and friends can be even more insistent in the case of women. As **Cheryl** says:

There are very strong cultural drives on women to be wives and mothers. Throughout childhood and adolescence I can remember hundreds of occasions at home when I was reminded of my future as some man's wife, or the mother of his children.

At school, teachers never failed to emphasize the different roles and goals for men and women. The underlying assumption was that all women, except for the very unfortunate few, grew up, *matured*, and took their place alongside their men. Perhaps I was more conscious of this process of indoctrination because I always felt a man's lot was a more fulfilling one, potentially. . . .

It's difficult to get free of the conformist cycle most of us are caught up in. I admire those women who do break out, but in those days I wasn't strong enough. You feel so desperately lonely and isolated when all your friends are dating boys and getting married. . . .

I loved my parents and never wished to hurt them. It was from them that I learned what was expected of me as a daughter and a woman. I remember my mother describing 'poor Beryl', my cousin, as 'mischievous' and 'loose-moraled'. 'My poor sister,' she would say, 'the disgrace!' Mum would then compare me to Beryl, saying how happy she was that I never shamed her. I put the two messages together, and when I did they read: 'We love you, Cheryl, so long as you don't do anything *different* to disgrace us.'

This is why, after becoming aware of my sexual feelings for other women, I understood that if ever I was to become a lesbian, I'd be unloved—as much an outcast at home as in the world outside.

My parents, and especially Mum, were so worried I'd develop into a 'lonely old spinster'. How that term 'spinster' haunted me! Sitting by the fire, a little old lady with white hair, shoulders wrapped in a shawl. The thought of having no one to look after me—no husband, children, grandchildren to keep me company. This frightened me. The day I was married, Mum says, was the happiest of her life. She's pleased I married Stewart, though, frankly, I think, in *my case*, it could have been 'most *anyone*. . . .

I know that Mum always sensed, deep inside, that I was different, but could never guess *how* I was different. She was very relieved, then, when I decided to marry. . . .

The Heterosexual Spouse

The above stories present the counsellor with a variety of motivation to account for the gay person's decision to marry: delayed recognition of one's true sexual orientation; conscious flight from the knowledge of one's homosexuality; rational choice; fear of loneliness; social and economic considerations; family pressures. But what are the reasons for the heterosexual partner's agreeing to marry a homosexual? The answer to this question is that, in most cases, the heterosexual spouse is not aware of his or her partner's homosexuality. This situation arises either because the gay person (e.g. **Judith**) is not conscious of being homosexual at the time of the marriage, or because the gay person chooses to keep this fact a secret (e.g. **Toby**; **Arthur**). However, if counsellors have the opportunity of meeting the spouses of gay people, they will also find that occasionally 'an undefinable difference' is what the heterosexual spouse regards as the gay partner's most attractive asset. This was so in the case of **Flo**, the young wife of Bruno:

> I respected Bruno, and still do, for his gentleness and consideration. . . .
> Bruno didn't tell me about being homosexual until quite recently. It must be the only thing he's kept from me. . . .
> In a way I always knew. Oh, not that he was gay. I only thought he was different, but in a very special sort of way.
> I suppose gay men don't try so hard to prove their virility. Most straight guys I've known make a big show at being manly. They have this hard exterior. I find it very difficult to relate to someone like that. You can't *talk* to them. . . .
> Bruno always shared his feelings with me. This is something else that made him seem so different. Most men feel it's cissy to show their feelings.
> . . . Unlike a lot of men, who are generally too proud to admit they may be lonely, or in need of affection, Bruno was always open and direct, never cold or distant.

There are also cases in which the heterosexual spouse takes the decision to marry in the full knowledge that the partner is homosexual. Some, like Meg, Vincent's wife, are 'too much in love to let anything stand in the way'; others act in the belief that the partner's sexual orientation 'will change after being married for a time'; still others, who are relatively ignorant about homosexuality, are unable to accept that this fact will 'in any way make a difference to the way we feel about each other'.

Causes of Conflict

However optimistic the partners may be about the future of their marriage, conflicts often do develop over waning sexual attention and the formation of outside relationships. As **Vincent**, Meg's husband, explains:

> I love Meg, in my own way. Not passionately. I respect her, though. My emotional involvement could never match her own for me. . . .
> Sexually, I've been . . . how does that expression go, 'I've been faithful to thee, Cynara, in my fashion'. . . .
> Meg tried to be understanding. She always meant well. But often her concern made me feel like an invalid. . . .
> There was quite a bit of sexual contact for the first six months or so. I enjoyed it. Of course, it didn't have the same meaning for me as I know it did for Meg. Still, I enjoyed it. Those who say that gay men are all frightened of women, or their bodies . . . they don't know what they're talking about.
> After about six months to a year, there was much less sex between us. I simply felt less inclined to express my feelings for Meg, sexually. Meg took this as an ominous sign. She thought she was losing me. She began to talk about having failed me. . . . The relationship grew very tense.
> It was then that Meg began to carp away about my being gay, about my gay friends. I told her, more out of anger than anything else, that I was having an affair with Larry. She said she couldn't accept that. . . .
> We've been separated for over a year now. We see each other from time to time, and Meg has hopes that eventually we'll be together again. I don't share that hope.
> I should never have married. I can see that now. . . .

Another source of conflict, one frequently reported by gay women, is dissatisfaction with the restrictive roles of married life. As **Harriet**, thirty-two, explains:

> Being a housekeeper, wife, nursemaid, and cook didn't suit me. I tried, but I never felt I succeeded. I felt trapped, a prisoner of chintz and nappies, with a lifetime of dusting, cooking, cleaning, and washing ahead of me. . . .
> When Jerry was born, my feelings became incredibly mixed. I was happy and miserable all at once. And after a year I was largely miserable again, because there seemed no escape. I felt I couldn't cope. I didn't *wish* to cope. I wanted 'out'.

Yet for three years I carried on as before. I tried to be a good mother, a good housekeeper, a good wife. It seems I had no time to be myself. All my energies were exhausted in helping others, and keeping things tidy for them.

Finally, when Jerry was about three years old, I met Isobel. This was at the same time that I started evening classes. I wanted to get away from the house, really.

Andy wasn't too happy about my classes because it meant his having to stay at home with Jerry. He felt rather put out, and told me I was shirking my responsibilities.

Isobel and I hit it off straight away. She was in much the same situation as I. So we had something in common to begin with . . . there's no 'happy ending', though. Isobel and I are still friends, not lovers. There's not much likelihood of the relationship developing on another level.

Andy was always resentful of Isobel, though. That *did* upset me, and one evening I just lashed out at him and with all my pent-up feelings and frustrations. I told him what I owed to Isobel, that she had brought me out and helped me to see myself as I am. . . .

Andy nearly hit the roof. He threatened to take Jerry away, saying I wasn't any good for him. Which wasn't true. I love Jerry. It's just that everything was getting on top of me. . . .

Andy soon moved out of the bedroom and slept on the couch. After a few weeks he calmed down. And then, quite suddenly, he moved out. Without a word. There was a note on the kitchen table one morning. It said: 'Dad [Andy's father] will have collected us by the time you read this. Will be in touch.' And now, of course, it's in the courts.

Gay Mothers: A Court Case

It was Andy, rather than Harriet, who was given the custody of Jerry. This is not at all unusual. In the majority of cases where the mother is known to be lesbian, the father is given custody of the child. The law does not, in itself, make any reference to lesbian mothers. Discrimination is the result of anti-lesbian views among judges and legal workers who assume that a lesbian is an unfit mother. Most lesbian custody cases concentrate upon the mother's lifestyle and how this might 'damage' the child, rather than upon the quality of childcare offered. By contrast, very little time is spent investigating the social and sexual lifestyle of the heterosexual father or his parenting abilities. 'It is assumed', as the GLC Women's Committee has pointed out, 'that a heterosexual household is naturally superior and preferable.'[3] A classic instance of such thinking can be seen in a court case reported in the *Guardian*, in which a mother's application for custody of her seven-year-old daughter was denied after the father, who had since remarried, protested that his former wife was living with another woman 'in a lesbian relationship'.[4] Although the judge agreed that the child had been well looked after, and a psychiatrist, called in as a character witness, recommended that the mother be given the custody of the child (which was also the child's wish), the view from the Bench was that the mother was lacking in 'femininity', i.e. that she possessed a strong personality and refused to 'sacrifice her lesbian proclivities' for the sake of the child.

The judge concluded that homosexuality was unnatural. The child, he felt, would be the recipient of 'unhealthy attitudes' if left with the mother, and would also be left vulnerable to the taunts of friends. Although the father was said to be 'less intelligent' than his former wife, the judge was satisfied that he possessed 'hard-working habits'. His new wife, who had made a favourable impression on the judge, had helped the court to conclude that the child would have a happier and healthier life if the father was given custody, care, and control.

This particular case was never taken to the Court of Appeal because the mother's barrister persuaded her that such a course of action was hopeless. It would not be possible to persuade the Appeal Court that the judge's decision ought to be reversed, the barrister informed her. In view of current custody laws, one might regard this as realistic advice. Courts decide what is in the child's best interests, and the child's 'best interests' are reckoned on the basis of conventional middle-class standards. Hence, though the courts 'would probably not feel', as Anna Coote has pointed out, 'that a child should be protected from the corrupt atmosphere of a stately home with a full contingent of servants or freed from the repressive influence of a strict religious upbringing',[5] it would (as we have seen) protect a child from a mother who was thought to be lacking in 'femininity'.

Fortunately, there are a minority of cases in which the mother receives custody, though even here there may be problems, as the case of **Vicky** testifies.

During the two years that hearings were going on, the hardest time was when it seemed certain I was going to lose my kids on the sole grounds of being lesbian. I felt totally powerless and angry. I couldn't come to terms with the idea of no longer living with them.

After two long court hearings and the threat of my children being put into care, the judge grudgingly allowed me care and control with joint custody, but only after my husband had agreed to let me have them under very specific conditions. A supervision order was put on me until the children were eighteen—a disgusting insult, I think. But even that, and some really *very* harsh words of warning from the judge, didn't matter at the time. I had been given permission to live with and care for my kids. I was just so happy . . .

It's been four years since I left my husband, two years since the court hearings. I'm now thirty-six, my children are nearly twelve and ten, and I'm still angry at the ordeal I was forced to go through—the most humiliating experience of my life.

A Gay Father

Gay fathers also suffer from conventional ideas about what constitutes a 'good parent'. **Lawrence** is the twenty-nine-year-old father of an eight-year-old daughter by a marriage which recently ended in divorce. He speaks here of some of the answers he gave to his daughter's questions concerning his relationship with a male lover:

You don't hear many gay fathers tell their stories, do you? Until I joined a group of gay fathers, about a year ago, I had no contact with others in my situation. I had no idea about how they managed to deal with the questions of their children. . . .

The questions can be tricky. But, really, if you're honest with your kid, they're not difficult to answer. Let me give just one example. A few weeks ago Kit, my daughter, was dropped off at the flat by her mother. Jon, my lover, was in the kitchen, in his pyjamas, putting together a late breakfast.

We had been expecting Kit, but Jon was a bit anxious. He had never met Kit before, though he had heard me talk about her a great deal. . . .

After Kit had tucked away an egg, an orange drink, and three slices of toast, she looked over at Jon for a long, long minute.

Then, turning towards me, she asked: 'Who do you love the most in the world, Mum or Jon?'

I said that I loved them both in different ways. I loved her mother with one kind of love which I wasn't able to give to Jon or anybody else; and that I loved Jon with another kind of love which belonged to him and him alone.

'And other men? Do you love other men besides Jon?' she asked.

I thought about that for a moment, and then said, yes, I did.

'Why?' she asked. 'Because', I said, 'loving people is something I've learned to do very well, something I hope I'm very good at.'

Kit thought about that for a few seconds, and then said, 'All right; so long as there's enough left over for me.'

A lot of people think that the child suffers from the knowledge of a parent's homosexuality. These people don't give children much credit . . . I didn't have to go into any lengthy expositions about gays, or homosexuality, or any of the rest of it.

I'm certain, however, that Kit *understands* at a feeling level, and that's good enough, for the present. I was honest with her. She knows who I am, and she loves me. That means more than the silly things some people might say about gays.

Resolving Marital Conflicts

Although many homosexuals choose to separate from their hetero-sexual partners as a way of resolving the conflicts and strains of marriage, there are several other modes of adjustment with which the counsellor should be familiar. The first of these is a platonic arrangement, as described by **Sam**:

We stress the non-sexual side of our relationship. Don't laugh when I say it, but we're 'good friends'. You might say Plato's been our guide.

Look at it this way: we've been married eighteen years. Joy was nineteen and I was twenty when we married. So we've spent nearly half our lives together. You don't separate easily after so long together. I doubt if I could be as happy with anyone else.

Joy and I have careers. We enjoy our work, *love it*! That means a great deal to us. We're people who love to work. We also have many outside interests . . . hobbies, and so on. . . .

I've had many affairs with men, almost all of them short-lived.

That's the sort of person I am. The last affair I had was almost a
year ago. Joy? I don't know. We never talk about our affairs, our
sexual affairs. . . . Why should we? As long as they don't cause
problems. . . .

Another form of adjustment is the 'open marriage'—one in which
both partners tolerate the existence of extra-marital sexual relationships. As **Lydia**, a writer, aged fifty, explains:

The most successful marriages are those in which each of the
partners respects the other's needs and wishes. . . .

Angus and I have what they call, nowadays, an 'open marriage'.
Neither of us prevents the other from growing in our own special
way. . . .

We have three children, all grown up, living away from home;
two are married. They know I'm bisexual. They accept it. That's
the way we brought them up: to be tolerant, accepting kids. . . .

It's odd. I have the deep love of my children, and yet my
children, in the past, have often been obstacles to the love of other
women. Lesbians will stereotype me as 'heterosexual mother/
wife'. If you are bisexual, or a married gay, you're something of a
sexual pariah. Perhaps it's changing now. But I remember when
it was very difficult for the bisexual to relate to the gay scene. It
was the biggest 'problem' of all. . . .

Why did I get married? I loved Angus. I never had a woman lover
before marrying. I don't know if being more experienced, sexually, would have made a difference. Angus and I were in love, and
we wanted to affirm our relationship in some way. Angus saw
marriage as a mature statement of our commitment to each other,
the supporting bond of our relationship. I went along with that. I
still do.

Some of my friends say it's 'politically incorrect', marriage, that
you shouldn't seek validation from society for your relationship. I
can't agree, though. I don't see anything wrong in using social
institutions to shore you up, if that's what you need. If institutions can be of help in making you happier and stronger, then use
them.

Of course, marriage *has* been corrupted, but I don't know that *in
itself* it is corrupt. There's a potential there for supporting, as well
as controlling. It's not the *only* arrangement for people in love.
It's only one of many.

71

You can, of course, make yourself a victim of marriage if you choose to. I think, though, that I'm one of its beneficiaries. Then again, Angus and I are perhaps a bit special. We have an open marriage; marriage is what *we* want it to be.

Of all the means of resolving a marital conflict so far considered, the 'open marriage' would appear to be the most 'successful'. It is also the most rare, depending as it does on the sexual versatility of the one partner and the broadmindedness of the other. Less happy variations of this and the platonic arrangement are more usual, and it is these that the counsellor will most frequently encounter. The anti-gay bias of our culture induces gays to marry, but then prevents their mutual acceptance of each other in marriage. This is a situation that must be viewed in the light of our religious views of homosexual behaviour, which is one of the concerns of my next chapter.

Summary

In this chapter I have considered the situation of married gays. There are four basic reasons for gays choosing to enter into such a seemingly conflicting situation as heterosexual marriage: first, insufficient awareness of one's gayness at the time of marriage (**Judith**); second, a conscious desire to escape from the knowledge of one's gayness (**Toby**); third, rational choice (**Arthur**); fourth, social and familial pressures (**Edward; Cheryl**).

In most cases, the heterosexual spouse is not aware of his or her partner's homosexuality (**Flo**), either because the gay person is not fully conscious of being homosexual at the time of marriage, or because the gay person chooses to keep his or her homosexuality a secret. There are also cases, however, in which the heterosexual spouse takes the decision to marry in the full knowledge that the partner is homosexual. The motives here are (1) love; (2) the hope of a change taking place in the sexual orientation of the gay partner; and (3) the belief that the factor of homosexuality is insignificant to the success of the marriage.

Conflicts often develop in such marriages due to waning sexual attraction; the development of outside relationships (**Vincent**); and dissatisfaction with the restrictive roles of married life (**Harriet**). When couples with children decide to split up, the gay parent is, in law, at a distinct disadvantage, since the custody laws operate according to conventional middle-class standards (**A Court Case, Vicky** and **Lawrence**).

Not all homosexuals choose separation or divorce as their means of resolving marital conflicts, however. At least two other forms of adjustment are fairly commonplace: a platonic arrangement in which the non-sexual side of the relationship is developed (**Sam**), and an open marriage in which both partners tolerate the existence of extra-marital sexual relationships (**Lydia**). In general, though, less happy variations of these two adjustments are pursued.

5

Gay Sex, Straight Religion

JESUS CHRIST
WANTED: For Sedition, Criminal Anarchy, Crimes against Nature,
Vagrancy and Conspiracy to Overthrow all Established Governments
by Revolutionary Love.

Dresses poorly. Said to be a Carpenter by trade. Ill-nourished. Has
visionary ideas of establishing a free and loving society. Associates
with common working people, national and racial minorities, the
unemployed, and prostitutes. Is often to be found in the company of
twelve other highly suspicious men, one of whom, John by name, he
calls his Beloved. Alias: 'Prince of Peace', 'Son of Humanity', 'Servant
of the People'. Bearded. Dark-skinned. Marks on hands and feet as the
result of injuries inflicted by an angry mob led by bankers, generals,
church officials, educators and other respectable citizens and legal
authorities.

from the Summer 1975 *Calendar* of The People's Church:
Community of the Love of Christ (New York City)

Sex versus Faith: Five Cases

Opposition to homosexuality is closely bound up with the nature of
our Judaeo-Christian heritage. Counsellors will therefore need to
know what advice is appropriate for gays whose religious beliefs
appear to be in conflict with their sexual orientation. Such advice
depends, in part, upon counsellors' familiarity with those passages of
Scripture and their interpretation which have traditionally been used
to legitimize the oppression of gays. These passages, along with
present church attitudes on homosexuality, will be considered below. To begin with, let us listen to five voices, each of which
illustrates one or more aspects of possible conflict between homosexuality and faith. The first belongs to **Deirdre**, sixteen, who writes:

> I am only sixteen years of age, but I am as certain as I can be that I
> am a lesbian. I am not happy about this because I know that in the
> eyes of God I am a sinner. It says so in the Bible. I have read the
> Bible through and through and everywhere (homosexuality) is

74

condemned. You can check this if you like, as I know exactly where it is, it is 1 Corinthians 6.9. There are other places in the Bible, not only Corinthians, and if you would like to know where then I will tell you in my next letter. The list is long. . . .

What I want to know from you is, does this mean that I will go to hell, or will it make a difference if I marry, like other girls?

Please give me the answers to these questions, because there is no one else to whom I dare to turn for help. I am asking you even though I think I know the answer. . . .

I am so worried, I cannot tell you. Inside I feel a nothing. Sometimes I want to hide myself when I have bad thoughts but I know how silly that is, to think that you can run away; you can't.

Please, write. You are the first person I have ever told anything, and though you are someone I have never met, already I feel I know you.

Love,
Deirdre

If Deirdre had been troubled by any other moral issue, she might well have taken it to some responsible member of her church. But because of the expected traditional attitudes of the Church towards homosexuality, she felt unable to share her anxieties and doubts with a fellow Christian. Why is this the usual course of action when the issue involved is homosexuality? After all, it stands to reason that if those to whom one generally turns in time of distress are thought likely to be sympathetic, gays like Deirdre would not hesitate to share with them their doubts and worries. If, on the other hand, there exists only a condemnatory attitude, then gays may well isolate themselves, perhaps for ever, from those whose very ministry it is to be of help.

The fear of having one's confidence greeted by icy disapproval has forced many gays to question the very foundations of their faith. A counselling group which I once facilitated consisted of twelve gays, including myself. Of this number, ten had been raised in the Christian faith, and two in the Jewish. Yet not one person in twelve could honestly say that his or her religion had offered any significant support during those periods when faith and sexual orientation seemed most in conflict. Some of us had sought help and been rebuffed. Others were fearful of seeking help owing to the 'bad experience' of friends, or because the church's attitude on homosexuality was already all too clear to us.

Lorraine, one of the twelve members of this counselling group, spoke for several others when she said:

I left the Church because I wasn't accepted as a lesbian. It took me a long time to understand this, but, once I did, there was no alternative except to leave. It was that simple. . . .

I would say that the real crisis came when I met Margo. We attended the same church. Our religious convictions were very much the same. We love each other very much, and when we first discovered these feelings, we wanted to share them with others in the church.

Any hopes we may have had that friends in the church would accept us were soon dashed. We're both very sociable people. We like to entertain. Before we moved in together, we were invited into people's homes fairly frequently, for dinner, drinks, parties. . . .

Once we set up house together, everything changed. Not dramatically, but in subtle ways. We weren't invited out so often, and only rarely would we *both* receive an invitation to someone's home. . . .

I spoke to the vicar about this. He listened, and when I was finished he thanked me for sharing with him my 'problem' (as he chose to call it) and then, very firmly, and at considerable length, informed me that, given the generally unsophisticated views, which *other* people held on this 'sensitive subject', it wasn't altogether surprising that people should behave as I described.

This was followed by a brief sermon, during the course of which I was informed that being a lesbian wasn't exactly a sin, but that homosexual acts were wrong in the sense that they made 'unnatural' use of sexual organs—sexual organs whose proper use was restricted to heterosexual marriage.

Well, I'm sorry to say that this exchange marked a turning-point in my relationship with the Church. For years I had worn blinkers. I wouldn't allow myself to see the hypocrisy of some of my fellow Christians. I was afraid to face up to facts. I knew what might happen if I *did* face up to facts. . . .

The Church seems split on this issue of homosexuality. . . . It refuses to take a stand. It does nothing substantial for fear of alienating its members. . . .

In refusing to lead the way, it's lost my respect. . . .

Not everyone who joins a counselling group or who contacts a gay organization seeks help with an immediate problem. There are many gays like Lorraine who, as she says,

> . . . would simply like to meet other gays as a way of renewing that sense of *belonging* to others, or to a community. This is something I feel I've lost since leaving the Church. In coming together with other gays who are also trying to raise their level of consciousness, I'm hoping to recover that sense of sharing goals and commitments. . . . By exchanging feelings and experiences, I feel that I've come much, much closer to understanding myself and others. It's been very stimulating. I've been made aware of possibilities in my life that I never knew existed.

Lorraine's disillusionment with the Church springs from a sense of being rejected by her fellow Christians. This feeling was once shared by **Paul**, thirty-two. Although in recent years he has managed to reconcile his homosexuality with the teachings of his church, he was once deeply troubled by feelings of guilt. As he explains:

> At first I found it impossible to be both a 'practising' homosexual and a 'practising' Christian. At age twenty I was confirmed as a member of my Church. At that time I promised I would not again receive Communion if I had sexual relations with another man. I kept that promise for over three years. For the next two years I had occasional sexual experiences and always felt guilty about it. Then I met Malcolm, and for the next six years I had sex exclusively with him. I lost all feelings of guilt and at the same time became more open to others and more involved in the Church. Slowly I forgot that there was ever a contradiction between my sexual preferences and the teachings of the Church. Of course my Church is not as rigid on this matter as some other branches of the Church are. There is, for example, an organization of gays who are working for a better understanding with the Churches, and they seem, slowly, to be working out a reconciliation of sorts. I do believe that it is possible for a homosexual to be a sincere and faithful Christian. Just as fathers or mothers care for each of their children, so I believe that God cares for each person. This holds even if a person is not exactly like the majority (like a member of the family that is not exactly like all the other children).

Moreover, God calls all his children to reconciliation, and he exhorts each of us to use what abilities we have both for our own good and the good of others. Regardless of what we are, I believe that God will use us to the extent that we will allow him to do so. . . .

The Churches are slowly coming to this point of view, and there will probably be more drastic changes in my lifetime. This is what I pray for. . . .

The sense of guilt which Paul experienced is one which most gays will readily understand. In some cases, such as that of **Olga**, twenty-six, feelings of guilt are exacerbated by a morally scrupulous nature weaned on the sexually oppressive attitudes of people around her:

I was born in Sheffield, but my memories of the place are bleak. Until recently these were my only memories: Sheffield, the home I was born in, the church and schools I attended for more than ten years. . . .

My home was like a church. Evenings, Dad read chapters from the Bible. I remember having nightmares. Dad read half a book each night, and then expounded on several passages. He had a great reverence for family life, my father, and he dwelt a great deal on 'crimes' that marred the sanctity of the family unit. I particularly remember the passages dealing with sexual impurity. Several times I became ill after readings from Leviticus or Deuteronomy. . . .

All this must have greatly inhibited me in ways that, even now, I don't fully understand. . . .

After school I went to secretarial college, and then to university. My father thought university a bad idea for a woman. His grumblings became so insistent that, after a year, I decided to leave. I took a job as an editorial assistant in a publishing house. I quite enjoyed that. . . .

When I was twenty-four, my father died. He had been ill for two years, and his dying was long and painful. Within eight months of my father's death, my mother died. Her heart stopped beating one night. . . . I remember how lonely I felt, how lost and stranded.

There was this boy, Geoff, whom I had known since we were

children. He was a great favourite with my parents. He was
studying for the ministry. My parents always hoped I'd marry
him. He was always asking me to marry him. When my parents
died, I said yes.

It was crazy. You see, I hadn't yet convinced myself that I am
lesbian. No, that's not right. It would be more true to say that I
was too terrified to even think of such a thing. And that meant not
thinking about my sexual identity at all. . . .

Two weeks before the wedding was to take place, I called it off.
Something happened which I'm ashamed even now to talk about.
. . . I knew this girl, a friend, and she seemed to know me better
than I did. She told me that I was marrying Geoff to fill a gap left
by my parent's death. And then she said: 'I expect you're a latent
homosexual.'

It was awful! She told me straight out, in the most unfeeling way
imaginable. . . .

I put the house on the market, sold everything, quit my job. I said
goodbye to Geoff, then packed my bags and left for London. Just
like that! Everyone thought I had gone made. Perhaps I had.
Perhaps, too, I had finally come to my senses. My original motive
was to put as much distance as possible between myself and my
friend. Or, if you like, between myself and the truth. Yet one of
the first things I did on arriving in London was to confide in the
vicar of the church near the flat I had rented. He wanted to be
helpful, I could tell. He said he had little experience in this area
but recommended a gay women's organization. He thought they
could probably help me. I followed it up. I went there and
attended these weekly discussion groups. At first I was too
nervous and shy to speak. The other women were so open in
discussing the most intimate matters. But I was far too inhibited,
so I stopped attending after two meetings.

Two months went by and I decided to go back again—more out
of loneliness than anything else. Whatever motive, I'm pleased
now that I did return.

I managed to talk about myself in a way I had never done before,
particularly about my fears, and sex. It was good for me to talk
about these feelings, to share them . . . and very exciting, very
creative. . . .

No one laughed when I told them how my mother had long ago
said that sex between a man and a woman was sinful if the motive

was pleasure. . . . I never saw my parents show any physical affection for one another, *never*. . . .

I told them about a teacher at school who warned us against masturbation. I'm certain the teacher saw me blush. She said that masturbation 'saddened God' because the body was a 'sacred vessel' that should never be polluted by 'self-lust'.

She was also the first person to mention love between women. 'Such women are lesbians', I can remember her saying—it was said with a sort of hissing sound attached to the word 'lesbians'. These women, she said, were an 'abomination', and were condemned in the Scriptures. . . .

All the girls seemed horrified that lesbians might be walking the streets of Sheffield. Afterwards, oh, for *months* and *months* afterwards, if girls happened to be standing close to one another, or if any two girls were special friends—you know, seen together a great deal—there would always be someone close to hand who would shout 'lesbian'.

During those last two years at school, I remember that 'lesbian' was the most rude and hurtful word you could possibly use against another girl.

It's funny, though. When this teacher used the word 'lesbian'— the way she said it—I seemed at once, at that very moment, to understand *everything*. And, just as quickly, something deep inside—something unconscious, I guess—seemed determined that I should *forget* everything.

Growing up lesbian in a heterosexual environment can be very alienating. Only in exceptional cases do parents or teachers pause to consider the possibility that a child or student might be homosexual. Thus, some gays, like Olga, will listen in silence as others speak belittlingly of an aspect of their personality which is absolutely crucial to their sense of self.

Stan, a twenty-six-year-old post-graduate student, is Jewish. His memories of being excluded are no less intense than those of Olga.

The problem faced by Jewish gays are different only in emphasis from those of Christians. . . .

One thing a Jew is always conscious of is his Jewishness. It's the product of 2000 years of persecution. Oppressed peoples have long memories. Jewish institutions help to preserve and perpetuate those memories. The best example of this is the family. Jews are fiercely proud and protective of the family unit.

You can trace this Jewish pride in the family way back to ancient times. In the Jewish struggle for survival, barrenness was a curse. It was vital to the survival of the small Jewish tribes that they increase and multiply. Homosexuality was therefore shunned as subversive to the procreative function of sex and a threat to family life. . . . These attitudes continue, though twentieth-century society is very different. . . .

Religion was an integral part of family life in our home. I never realized until I was an adult that you could actually separate the two. From the moment I was born, I found myself being initiated into a ghetto mentality: circumcision, religious training, Bar Mitzvah and manhood!

And then, of course, dating 'nice Jewish girls' and preparing for marriage and a family of my own. . . .

My mother was as much the matriarch as any of those caricatures we're all so familiar with. In the novels of Philip Roth, for example, or in the jokes of Jewish comedians. Mother ruled the roost. She made absolutely certain that family ties were maintained, religion reverenced, etc., etc., etc.

Mother also acted as a sort of non-unionized marriage broker. 'Shirley, she's a nice girl', she'd say to me. 'What's the matter, you don't like nice girls?' And if it wasn't Shirley, it was Sara, or Naomi, or Miriam. . . .

It's still difficult for young Jews to break out of this mould. The problems are enormous. Like other gays, I grew up believing my gay difference was unique. Everything reinforced this conviction, particularly the stress on marriage, and the religious beliefs deeply embedded in my Jewish heritage that I was conditioned into since I was a small boy. . . .

Despite the story of David and Jonathan, I come from a religious background which suggests I don't really exist. If you don't believe this, you have only to look in a recent edition of *The Encyclopedia Judaica*. What you find there is truly astonishing; for example, the author of the entry on 'homosexuality' speaks of a 'virtual absence' of gays or of the 'rare incidence' of gays among Jews! Now this just isn't true! Yet even Maimonides followed the Talmud in holding that Jews are 'not suspect to practise homosexuality'.

81

So you can see how far back this myth goes. Talmudic law makes homosexual relations a capital offence (just as in Leviticus) and is based on the general warning not to indulge in the 'abhorrent practices' of the Egyptians and the Canaanites. . . . Believe me, the situation is scarcely better today. The Progressives are only *slightly* more sympathetic than the Orthodox wing. . . .

It wasn't until I prised myself loose from the heterosexual embrace of my family and synagogue that I was able to *even begin* to come to terms with the reality of being gay. It was then that I realized, as never before, how very much of a disappointment I was going to be both to my parents and to my religion.

Our culture is one in which most individuals derive some clues as to who they are from the faith into which they were born. This being the case, any religion which is intolerant of homosexuality may therefore be encouraging gays like Deirdre, Lorraine, Olga, Paul, and Stan to develop a self-image characterized by terms such as 'sinner', 'a source of scandal', 'dishonourable', 'unnatural', 'abomination', 'abhorrent'.

Homosexuality and Scripture

Such terms as these reflect the opposition to homosexuality that is closely bound up with the nature of our Judaeo-Christian heritage. Hence, many of today's Christians (and Jews) are victims of a condemnatory view of homosexuality that is deeply rooted in the Old Testament and perpetuated by the New,[1] Unfortunately, the use of Scriptures to condemn homosexuality—a tendency which exhibits many of the worst possible features of uncritical biblical exegesis—is still practised as a means of oppressing gay people.[2] This being the case, the counsellor will need to be familiar with the principal biblical texts employed to censure gays. There are six: three from Pentateuch and three from the Pauline epistles.

The Sodom and Gomorrah story (Gen. 19.1–28) is often viewed as the *locus classicus* of divine wrath against homosexual behaviour. It was the Code of Justinian which first alluded to 'the most reprehensible vices and . . . *crimes contrary to nature* . . . [which] incur the just anger of God, and bring about *the destruction of cities* along with their inhabitants' [emphasis added].[3] This reference to Sodom and Gomorrah is of crucial significance for Western law codes dealing with homosexuality. The Justinian Code was the model used by legal students at Bologna when Roman law was revived in Europe in the eleventh century and is, therefore, the progenitor of a legal tradition dating back some 900 years.

Notwithstanding this fact, the story of Sodom and Gomorrah remains much less a product of history than of folklore and legend. This is the same story, let us not forget, wherein women are transferred into salt; men are struck blind by angels; and two cities of Palestine are destroyed by apparent volcanic eruptions in an area of the world where volcanoes have never been recorded.

It is also true that when Old Testament writers such as Isaiah, Jeremiah, Ezekiel, Amos, and Zephaniah speak of Sodom, as they frequently do, they make no reference whatsoever to homosexuality. Thus, the prophet Ezekiel, speaking more as a socialist than as a fundamentalist, interprets the sin of Sodom and Gomorrah not as homosexuality but, rather, as luxury, idleness, and lack of concern for the poor. Indeed, it was only at the beginning of the Christian era, about 2000 years after the events were supposed to have taken place, that the Sodom story became, as Lewis Williams points out, 'the vehicle for anti-homosexual propaganda in the hands of Jewish philosophers and historians who were in revolt against Hellenic manners'.[4]

If the Sodom and Gomorrah story is a fanciful medley of fact and fiction, the Levitican code is depressingly clear. It is here that we read: 'Thou shalt not lie with mankind as with womankind; it is an abomination' (Lev. 18.22); 'If a man also lie with mankind as he lieth with woman, both of them have committed an abomination; they shall surely be put to death, their blood shall be upon them' (Lev. 20.13).

Such prohibitions as these will doubtless prove disturbing to many gays. It might be helpful to remember, then, that these are but two injuctions falling within a very complex series of prohibitions which, were one to use the same process of random selection as in the case of homosexuality, could lead to theologies of food (Lev. 11.10–12; 17.10; 19.26), clothing (19.19), and hairdressing (19.27) that would cause havoc with many of our present cultural patterns.

Yet some will still insist that the injunctions cited against homosexuality are clear and incontestable. Let us assume, for the sake of argument, that this is true. In that case, other prohibitions found in Leviticus are no less clear and incontestable, e.g., that which requires adulterers to be put to death (20.10). Of course, we reject the latter injunction, which refers to *heterosexual* relationships, but accept the former, which refers to *homosexual* relationships. What is it that enables some to say that certain laws of God are obsolete while others should remain operative? The answer, it seems to me, is that each religious group claims its own version of the truth, and that each of us, in turn, decides between contending viewpoints by a process of personal judgement. When it suits our purposes we change, modify, and reinterpret the law. Thus, we may decide that adultery is not to be punished by death, but that homosexuality should still be regarded as an abomination.

Still others will argue that the advent of Christianity has imperceptibly brought about a rejection of many Old Testament commandments. Let us turn to the New Testament, then, and consider briefly the Pauline epistles. There are two passages of special relevance:

> For this cause God gave them up unto vile affections: for even their women did change the natural use into that which is against nature: and likewise also the men, leaving the natural use of the women, burned in their lust one towards another; men with men working that which is unseemly, and receiving in themselves that recompense of their error which was meet (Rom. 1.26–7).

> Know ye not that the unrighteous shall not inherit the kingdom of God? Be not deceived; neither fornicators, nor idolaters, nor adulterers, nor effeminate, nor abusers of themselves with mankind . . . shall inherit the kingdom of God (1 Cor. 6.9–10).

Perhaps the most important point to be made about Paul's two statements on homosexuality[5] and his comments on other sexual ethics is that they constitute a direct reflection of his Jewish background and must be seen in that context. Being a product of his time, Paul associated homosexuality with the tendency to idolatry and heresy. In neither of the above passages does he attempt to deal with the morality of homosexuality as a human condition but, rather, as a deviation from the religious practice which made of Judaism the monolith that had withstood the infiltration of Canaanite, Babylonian, Greek, and Roman influences. Thus, in *Homosexuality and the Western Christian Tradition*, Derrick Sherwin Bailey has argued that Romans 1.26–7 and 1 Corinthians 6.9–10 must be interpreted as 'the Christian reaction to the dissolute sexual behaviour of the Hellenistic world, which was regarded as the inevitable concomitant of idolatry'.[6]

For Paul, then, *all* sexuality was suspect.[7] His condemnation of homosexuality, as Rattray Taylor has pointed out,[8] was simply one aspect of the general condemnation of all sexual activity which was not directly necessary to the races. Hence, in Romans 1.18 we read that 'the wrath of God is revealed from heaven against *all* ungodliness and unrighteousness of men' [emphasis added]. Indeed, it sometimes appears that for Paul the most Christian society imaginable was one in which all men remained bachelors, just as he did, and completely abstained from sexual relations. 'It is good for a man', Paul remarks in 1 Corinthians 7.1, 'not to touch a woman.' But if the 'unmarried . . . cannot contain themselves, then, says the apostle, 'let them marry; for it is better to marry than to burn' (1 Cor. 7.8–9). Though even here, within marriage, one must add, severe restrictions were imposed on sexual relations, the husband and wife being admonished to give themselves over to 'fasting and prayer' (1 Cor. 7.5).

These teachings of the Bible, when combined with the moral theology of St Augustine, constitute the main weights of Christian doctrinal tradition against homosexuality. This tradition, in its interpretation of the fundamental purpose of the sexual drive as procreation, and in its classification of sexual acts as 'natural' and 'unnatural', has militated against the full acceptance of the homosexual. Gays are still regarded by many in the churches as a threat to family life—a belief which has often led to outright condemnation of homosexual acts and relationships. Still others within the churches, while more amenable to a greater toleration of homosexuality, are anxious lest any re-examination of the issue should lead to questions concerning all other canons of sexual morals. It is this worrying possibility of an extension of the subject into a much broader area of Christian sexual ethics which may well pose the principal obstacle to full acceptance by the churches of several million homosexuals.

The Gospel of Love

While recognizing that counsellors must abide by their own religious convictions, it is possible to offer helpful advice to gays who are troubled by scriptural prohibitions without compromising one's own moral principles or imposing exclusively Judaeo-Christian ethics on others. For example, counsellors might stress the fact that the authors of the Scriptures interpreted their faith in terms of the world in which they lived. Many modern churchmen, on the other hand, are convinced that contemporary morality should not be based on ancient rules as interpreted by medieval scholars but, rather, on the basis of all the insights and discoveries made available to us over the past 2000 years. It might also be helpful to remind gays that the overwhelming majority of religions outside the Judaeo-Christian tradition are largely unconcerned with matters of sexual morality; hence, such proscriptions against homosexuality as do exist reflect philosophical convictions that are entirely subjective.[9]

But most important of all, the counsellor might remind gays of the gospel of love in action. Christians could look to the ministry of Christ, where one finds no direct references to the subject of homosexuality, Jesus preferring to restrict his very occasional pronouncements on sexual matters to guidelines and standards for use in human relationships. Indeed, the moral teachings of Christ regarding sexual expression are just as adaptable to homosexuals as they are to heterosexuals. After all, it was Jesus who reminded us that 'God so loved the world, that He gave His only begotten Son, that whosoever believeth in Him should not perish, but have everlasting life.' He did not qualify this by adding 'but with the exception of homosexuals'.

When we stop to consider the ways in which this gospel of love is communicated in our contemporary world, we find that the churches reflect a very broad spectrum of theological views on homosexuality. To begin with, the Jewish faith holds that homosexuality frustrates the procreative purpose of sex; it does 'damage to family life'; and it constitutes 'an unnatural perversion, debasing the dignity of man'. Jewish teaching firmly rejects notions of homosexuality as an illness or as something which is morally neutral, although this latter view has gained some support among contemporary moralists. Generally speaking, Jews appear to regard the more liberal attitudes found in certain modern Christian circles as possibly due to the exaggerated importance Christians have traditionally accorded the term 'love'. But Jewish law, according to one influential writer on the subject, holds that 'no hedonistic ethic, even if called "love", can justify the morality of homosexuality any more than it can legitimize adultery, incest, or polygamy, however genuinely such acts may be performed out of love and mutual consent.'[10]

The most monolithic position on homosexuality is taken by the Roman Catholic Church. In considering the morality of this sexual orientation, the Catholic Church makes a distinction between responsibility for the homosexual 'condition'; the objective morality of the homosexual act; and the subjective responsibility of individual gays for particular acts.[11] According to Father John Kane, author of *What is Homosexuality?*, there is no doubt that homosexual acts are 'objectively sinful' in all cases. However, the 'subjective guilt' of the individual is less easily determined since this depends on each gay person's 'total personality structure'.[12] However, the official position, as stated in 1985, refers to homosexuality as a 'moral disorder', and insists that sexual acts which are not intended for procreation are always wrong. 'Homosexuality', Pope John Paul II proclaimed, 'cannot be tolerated in a Christian society.'[13] Guidelines issued to the bishops by the Sacred Congregation for the Doctrine of the Faith (the former Holy Office) in October 1986 with the full consent of the pontiff argue that homosexuality can never be approved because it is 'contrary to the creative wisdom of God'.[14] In Britain, Cardinal Hume endorses these views, asserting that homosexuality is 'an impediment to one's fulfilment and happiness', and claiming that 'the Roman Catholic Church cannot be expected to lend support to any measures which tacitly accept sexual activity outside marriage'.[15]

Father John F. Harvey, whose writings on homosexuality have received wide circulation within the Catholic Church, has advised counsellors to direct homosexuals to undertake a course of psychotherapy which would 'change the direction of their instincts'. Those individuals who feel they are too old for such therapy, or those who are otherwise unable to pursue such a course of treatment, should be advised to follow 'an ascetical plan of life if they desire to be fully human and Christian'. An element of proven worth within such a programme, says Harvey, is 'the actual performance of apostolic and charitable work . . . [rather] than the achievement of satisfactory sexual relationships'.[16]

Furthermore, a document entitled *Declaration on Certain Questions Concerning Sexual Ethics* issued by the Sacred Congregation for the Doctrine of the Faith firmly opposes any relaxation of the Roman Catholic Church's traditional rejection of homosexuality. Drafted by an international group of moral theologians with the approval and confirmation of Pope Paul VI, who ordered its publication, this document advises the faithful that 'homosexual acts are intrinsically disordered and can in no case be approved of'. It further adds that 'in sacred Scripture [such acts] are condemned as a serious depravity and even presented as the sad consequence of rejecting God.'[17]

The Protestant Churches offer a much broader range of opinion. As far as the Anglican Church is concerned, the Archbishop of Canterbury stated in the debate on homosexual relationships at the General Synod of 1981 that the Church is 'not united on this subject'. Three principal points of view, he said, prevail in the Church. The first is that homosexuality 'is, simply, a sin'. Those who support this make much of the Sodom story. The second is that homosexuality is 'a sickness and may be catching'. Those who still think in this way, the Archbishop argues, 'must have the obligation of exercising compassion'. The third—and this is the view to which the Archbishop says he inclines—is that homosexuality is neither a sin nor a sickness, but a 'handicap', that is, 'a state with which people have to cope, with limitations and hardships, in which the fulfilment of heterosexual love and marriage are denied'. The 'handicapped', it is further argued, should be treated 'with deep respect and an awareness that often through their handicap they can obtain a degree of self-giving and compassion which is denied to those not similarly afflicted'. In short, there is no acceptance of the validity of gay love. As the Archbishop puts it: 'I do not believe that it is possible for anyone to be loyal to the Christian tradition and to see homosexual and heterosexual relations as having equal validity.'[18]

This line of argument was affirmed at the November 1987 meeting of the General Synod. Although it rejected the Revd Tony Higton's motion that 'homosexual acts' should be regarded as 'sinful in all circumstances' (and that clergy should adhere to this as a condition of being in office), the Synod did accept the Bishop of Chester's motion that 'homosexual genital acts' fall short of the ideal of sex 'within a permanent married relationship'.[19]

Hope for the Future

Although religious groups are far from anxious to reconsider the subject of homosexuality, many individuals within the Churches are now urging a reassessment of traditional attitudes. Some of these critics are themselves gay, and they argue that condemnation of homosexuality inhibits personal and religious development. Others tend to see the issue in the light of sexual ethics, while still others regard it as, quite simply, a question of justice.

Such critics as these are determined that the subject of homosexuality should find a permanent place on the Christian agenda. They have already met with some success. Both the Unitarians and the Social Responsibility Council of the Society of Friends have now published studies on homosexuality. The former group has posed the question of whether society or the Churches are justified in expecting gays to abstain permanently from any physical expression of love and affection for their own sex. The Quaker study raises the same question, and offers an 'inside' account of homosexuality as a basis for future discussion.

In December 1979, the Church of England published its long-awaited report on 'Homosexual Relationships', stating (rather grudgingly, it must be admitted) that 'in the light of evidence we have received we do not . . . deny that there are circumstances in which individuals may justifiably choose to enter into a homosexual relationship'. More encouraging was the publication in November 1980 of the British Council of Churches' influential 'God's Yes to Sexuality', which concluded that 'in the light of the abiding central message of the Bible . . . we find it impossible to reckon homosexual orientation as a vice or a disorder of nature'.

More recently Dr John Habgood, Archbishop of York, stated that 'as a Christian' he would 'always value stable relationships; when these are homosexual, many church people do not now condemn it', though he himself regards homosexuality as 'a misfortune' and he acknowledges that the Church of England still speaks 'with a divided voice on homosexuals in stable relationships'.[20] The Bishop of Stepney, the Right Revd James Thompson, has urged that there be 'a better understanding of the problems of homosexuals' in the 1980s,[21] while the Revd Malcolm Johnson—speaking at the November 1987 General Synod of the Church of England—proposed (unsuccessfully) a motion that would give acceptance to all committed relationships, regardless of sexual orientation: 'The essential of the Biblical message', the motion argued, was that 'human love is a reflection of divine love and should be characterised by the permanency and commitment of relationships.'[22]

These pleas for a more sympathetic approach to the subject of homosexuality have been taken up by various organizations which seek to assist the Church in its understanding and support of gays. In addition, various ecumenical communities such as the Lesbian and Gay Christian Movement and the Metropolitan Community Church have been established. These groups are open to all, but with a special interest in, and concern for, Christian gays.

A group of Catholic homosexuals have formed a group called QUEST, which aims to reconcile the Church's moral theology with an acceptance of homosexuality. In line with this objective, Father Fabian Cowper OSB, writing in *Christian Renewal*, has given his support to a claim made by a number of distinguished continental theologians that 'natural law' has been based on outdated conceptions of nature, and that moral theology should concern itself not simply with acts, but also with the spirit and values which motivate gays in their lifestyles and relationships. This point is reiterated by Father Neil Grey, who adds that 'the sin which seems to annoy Jesus more than any other is that of judging and condemning other people'. Commenting on the lack of compassion and outright hostility shown by many to those with AIDS, he says: 'If it is true that Christ suffers with his people through membership of his body, the Church, then the face of God is most appropriately shown in an icon of Christ covered with the distinctive purple blotches of Kaposi's Sarcoma.'[23]

According to Lewis Williams, a contributor to a collection of essays on ethics, theology, and homosexuality, one of the Churches' top priorities must be the development of 'a theology of engagement aimed at undoing the effects of two thousand years of religious anti-homosexualism'.[24] The Revd Thomas Maurer, writing in the same volume, agrees with this, and argues for a theology that will spring from 'one's experience, and out of one's own visceral being'.[25]

But if the Churches are to evolve such a theology they must begin with the premise that no sexual orientation is superior to any other. Such an assumption of equality should extend to the realm of moral responsibility, too—an acknowledgement of the fact that homosexuals are no less responsible for their sexual lives than are heterosexuals. After all, true religion recognizes that sexual maturity and self-realization are essential parts of the gospel of wholeness preached by Judaism and Christianity alike. Such tensions as arise derive from the historical attitudes towards homosexuality and the modern interpretation of sexual fulfilment as a Christian way of life. Those Churches which contribute to the oppresion of gays by regarding homosexuality as a sin need to be persuaded that such an attitude produces many of the very evils which they so vociferously condemn. This is a point which is forcefully made in a pamphlet entitled *Towards a Quaker View of Sex*:[26]

> Sexual activity is essentially neither good nor evil; it is a normal biological activity which, like most other human activities, can be indulged in destructively or creatively. [But] if we take impulses and experiences that are potentially wholesome and in large measure unavoidable and characterize them as sinful, we create a great volume of unnecessary guilt and an explosive tension within the personality. . . . A distorted Christianity must then bear some of the sexual disorder of society.

In short, self-realization is never possible when one accepts a philosophy that encourages conformity to a set of rules which run directly counter to one's true nature. It must be recognized that sexual morality requires both conviction and decision. A morality which is neither believed nor felt is no morality at all. It is for this reason that 'sexual virtue', as Wainwright Churchill observes, 'begins with the joyful acceptance of one's own sexuality and the sexuality of other people'[27]

Summary

This chapter has dealt with those issues particularly troublesome to individuals who feel their faith is in conflict with their homosexuality: **Deirdre** was deeply disturbed by the scriptural injunctions against various sexual practices; **Lorraine** expressed feelings of disillusionment with fellow Christians who failed to accept homosexuals on an equal footing with heterosexuals; **Paul** was once inhibited from developing satisfactory relationships with other men because of intense feelings of religious guilt; **Olga** internalized the sexually repressive attitudes of her parents and teachers and, in time, came to regard herself as an outcast and a sinner; **Stan** discussed the problems of Jewish gays in relation to a religious tradition which regards homosexual acts as 'abhorrent practices'.

Many gays have been oppressed by a condemnatory view of homosexuality which is deeply rooted in the Old Testament and perpetuated in the New. It is therefore important to remember that the Ancients interpreted their faith in terms of tradition of sexual virtue which was preoccupied with procreation. As far as Paul is concerned, his aversion was for sexuality generally, and not simply *homo*sexuality. When we look to the ministry of Christ, we find nothing to support such an attitude, Jesus preferring to restrict his very occasional pronouncements on sexual matters to guidelines and standards for use in social relationships.

In turning our attention to the present day, we find that the Churches reflect a broad spectrum of views on homosexuality. The Roman Catholic Church regards homosexual acts as always sinful, though it reserves judgement on the guilt of individual gays. A broader range of opinion prevails in the Protestant Church, while modern Jewish teaching tends to fall somewhere between the Catholics and the Protestants.

Although the Churches are still far from eager to reassess the subject of homosexuality, an ever-growing number of individuals in the Churches are now prepared to speak out on behalf of change and reconciliation. The question of homosexuality has already found a tentative place in the Christian agenda, and the Unitarians, Quakers, Anglicans, and others have published studies or set up working parties to explore the subject in the light of our new understanding of human sexuality.

6

Families and Friends

The death of Satan was a tragedy
For the imagination. . . .
  How cold the vacancy
When the phantoms are gone
  and the shaken realist
First sees reality.

Wallace Stevens,
'Esthetique du Mal', VIII, in *The Collected Poems*

Coming Out

'Coming out' is the most significant step in the gay person's progress towards self-acceptance. Like all important changes occurring in the life cycle of the human being, this phenomenon is accompanied by after-effects that are both pleasurable and painful. We shall consider some of these below. But, first, an attempt at definition. 'Coming out' is a term that may be unfamiliar to many readers. Even gays will often differ in their understanding, each stressing that particular aspect of the coming-out process which has proved most important to him or her. Here, then, are several definitions provided by individuals who have already been introduced to the reader in the preceding chapters:

Coming out is the realization that you're gay; it's when you begin thinking of yourself as homosexual for the first time. In a way it's like a foreign language you've been studying. You have always got to think in your own language before speaking. Then, one day, you find yourself *thinking* in this other language and, suddenly, it's no longer 'foreign' in the way it once was (**Claude**).

It's more than just telling yourself that you're gay; it's sharing this fact with other people, as you might share anything else about yourself that's important (**Lorraine**).

Coming out is the reverse of passing, which is a way of hiding

93

yourself from others. Coming out means being as open as you are able with your friends . . . (**Nancy**).

It is having sex for the first time with someone else of your own sex (**Simon**).

Coming out implies a great deal in addition to a first sexual encounter. It's part of the whole process of self-recognition— identifying yourself as homosexual, bisexual, or whatever. And 'coming out' also demonstrates in the most positive way a willing- ness to involve yourself in the wider community of gay people— to be *a part of* that community (**Lydia**).

Coming out is coming of age. It's like Bar Mitzvah for the Jew, or Confirmation for the Catholic, or a boy's first pair of long trousers (**Stan**).

I would say it is a state of mind, a process of recognition. Coming out is understanding that you are part of a stigmatized minority; but it also entails a willingness to cope with the knowledge of being an outsider. I would say it is, basically, feeling positive about yourself as a gay person (**Cheryl**).

Gay people *discover* that they're homosexual. This is not the usual way of learning about your sexuality, which is a taken-for-granted thing in the life of heterosexuals. Once you can *accept* that you are different; once you can *accept* that there are people in this world who will think of you as 'queer' and a 'poof' (in others words, someone feared or hated), then you've done it! You have come out! (**Lawrence**).

In short, coming out means 'being open'. Passing, as we have seen, is a response to the stigma of homosexuality; it indicates a desire to escape negative sanctions. Coming out, on the other hand, is a courageous act of defiance, a refusal to be intimidated by the rejecting attitudes of others. But coming out is *not* the concluding chapter in a happy romance, or the proverbial sunset into which the hero rides in the final frames of a Western. Having come out, gays must still deal with all the people in their lives who will now know, but perhaps not fully accept or understand, that they are homosexual.

Coming Out at Home

Rejection by one's family is a particularly painful, and very distinct, possibility for the gay who has come out. (Recent research shows that eleven per cent of all gays are asked to leave home after coming out to their parents.) The counsellor should bear in mind that only rarely, or if specifically told, are parents aware of their child's homosexuality. As **Alice**, Reg's mother explains:

> I always knew Reg was a bit different as a youngster; he was more sensitive than my two older boys. . . . Reg was a bit of a free spirit, really very independent, even as a small boy. . . . It wasn't until he took me aside one day and actually told me about himself that the penny dropped. It was only then that I was able to say, 'Oh, so that's what this or that was all about!'

A further explanation of why parents may not guess that their child may be homosexual is supplied by **Rita**, Lawrence's mother.

> You teach your children the same way as everybody else. You don't stop to question whether this is the heterosexual way or not. I mean, it didn't occur to me that I had any choice in what Larry would grow up to be. . . .
> I can't truly say that I knew anything about homosexuals. Only what I picked up in the papers. I never *thought* about it, really. We never discussed it. I suppose if I thought about it at all, it was, you know, something that happened to *other* people's children. And then I might think, you know, I wonder what *they*, the parents, did wrong.

When parents do discover that a child is homosexual, their reaction is often one of anger, disappointment, and revulsion, as in the case of **Kay**, forty-five, the mother of Ken:

> I felt horrified, and was literally sick for days. I don't know why he's become homosexual. As his mother, I blame myself. . . .
> My husband knows, and he's *terribly* against it. He feels as I do, that it's not natural. Casey, my husband, doesn't understand how people can be like that. His attitude towards Ken is just polite now. . . .
> When I don't think about all this, it's all right. But it so upsets Ken to think that he's disturbing me. And he is terribly disturbed. But as I said to him, we each have our own lives to lead. I cannot be expected to involve myself in his life, and I don't wish to. . . .
> I find the sexual aspect distasteful. When I think of homosexuality I think of the sex aspect. It's unnatural. And to think that my

son is involved in something so unnatural is very worrying for me, and for my husband. . . .

But we are also disappointed because we were so looking forward to grandchildren. We do feel deprived, as there are no other children. We were so looking forward to being one big family. . . .

Ken wants me to accept his friends, but I can't. I'm sorry, but I simply *can not*. . . . When I first saw him, his . . . friend, I was taken aback. . . . a seedy type, long hair, no job. He said he was a student, but I don't know. . . .

It is in relation to the family that the stigma of homosexuality weighs heaviest. The fact that gays feel unable to be open and honest with their parents is a source of great unhappiness and frustration. How odd it is, then, that in all the literature dealing with homosexuality there is scarcely any reference to the difficulties of such relationships. Even when one turns to the mass of psychiatric source material available (where parents invariably play crucial roles in the formation of a homosexual commitment), the difficulties of the gay child in dealing with parents (and vice versa) are never discussed. Yet this estrangement from the family is but one more illustration of the many ways in which *social* attitudes create the 'problem' of homosexuality. Indeed, it is in this area of parent-child relationships that the homosexual's passing lifestyle of concealment and disguise is learned and perfected. Consider the experiences of **Sandra** and **Colin**. Sandra says:

My parents think of themselves as ordinary people who, as my father is given to saying, like to 'keep 'emselves to 'emselves'.

I was seventeen when I told them about being gay. I had just broken up with this girl at college. My mum sensed something was wrong, and when she asked me about it, I burst into tears and told her.

Her first words were: 'What are you *saying* to me?' She repeated that twice. Then she told my father. He came into the room and slapped me across the face. . . .

I was sent to our GP and he advised therapy. One month after telling my parents, I had my first appointment with a psychotherapist. I continued to see him on a weekly basis for the next two and a half years. . . .

I would talk a great deal about my childhood. My therapist was interested in *how* I came to be a lesbian, even though, on the surface, his attitude was that, you know, if you didn't do it in public and scare the horses, it was all right.

In reality, though, he was for ever warning me not to become emotionally involved with other girls until I was 'ready'. He never encouraged me when I mentioned any of the relationships I had formed. . . . He could be so stern in his silence. . . .

As for my parents, they kept hoping I'd be 'cured'. They also warned me against ever telling anyone about being gay. They were very concerned about what our relatives and neighbours would think . . . I'm certain that isn't because they stopped loving me in any way. It's only that they never had to think about this before—having a lesbian as a daughter.

I think they thought, at first, I had devised some cruel means of hurting them. In fact, my guess is that if you had asked them whether or not they had ever met a lesbian in their lives, they would have replied, in all honesty, that No, they hadn't.

Many parents find it extremely difficult to deal with their child's homosexuality. 'Where did I go wrong?' is perhaps the most frequently heard lament of a parent upon discovering a child's gayness. There is, in other words, a tendency for parents to think, first and foremost, of themselves. 'What are you *saying* to me?' was Sandra's mother's initial reply, followed, later, by a concern lest the rest of the family and neighbours should learn of Sandra's gayness. Given this usual pattern of response, **Colin**'s parents would appear to be a happy exception:

After I'd finished with this fellow I was deeply involved with, I wanted to tell someone who I felt cared about me. I needed a bit of sympathy. Who better than Mum and Dad?

I decided to go home for the week-end. But for two days I felt, and acted, miserable. I couldn't bring myself to say anything. There never seemed a 'right' moment when I could say, 'Well, I'm upset because I've broken up with the love of my life'. . . . I couldn't bring myself to tell the truth. Instead, I pretended I was upset because I wasn't happy with my new job. . . . Two weeks later, though, I was feeling worse than ever. So I phoned on the Thursday night and, well, I broke down on the phone. Mum said, 'What's the matter, Colin? Both your father and I know you have some problem; what is it?'

97

I told Mum that I couldn't tell her yet, that it was something I would have to sort out by myself. 'But we want to help you so much,' she kept saying, 'and we feel awful because we don't know how.' There was a long pause, and then she said: 'Can I ask you questions?' And without waiting for a reply, she said: 'Is it your flat?' I said that it was, but only partly. Mum was very persistent. 'And the rest?' she asked. 'Is it your feelings for someone?'

She *knew*! Because, you see, she had noticed that while I talked a great deal about my friends in London, there was one friend that I spoke about a great deal more than the others. Mum thought, as she later told me, that she guessed this was probably the first time I'd cared a lot for a boy and that perhaps I couldn't understand my own feelings. She said, too, that on more than one occasion she had given me a lead which I hadn't taken up. Over the Easter holidays, for example, she invited me to bring a 'friend' round for dinner, when, really, she had in mind this one *particular* friend of mine. But she phrased her invitation in such a way that it could have meant *anyone*. I didn't know what she had in mind, of course, so I said, 'No, there isn't anyone I'd like to bring round.' Mum said she felt so clumsy and helpless because she knew I'd have loved to have brought him home but, well, just couldn't.

Colin feels that, though his own mother and father may be exceptional in their ready acceptance of his homosexuality, that most gays will none the less underestimate the ability of parents to cope with the knowledge of their gayness. 'There is no doubt in my mind', says Colin, 'that I am much closer to my parents now than I was before. It's true, my dad had more difficulty in understanding, but he's come round. Perhaps not *completely*, because it's a big thing for a father to get over. But, still, we can talk to each other now whereas before we both found it a bit of a strain.'

It is perhaps even more of a strain for the parents of gays who come from a different culture than ours to accept a child's homosexuality. **Ananda** is Hindu, an Indian of twenty-three who has lived in East Africa for most of his life, who came to London several years ago with his older brother, sister-in-law, and three younger sisters. His parents have returned to India, but eventually plan to settle in England. Last year Ananda joined a counsel group consisting of seven other gay people, all of whom, with the exception of himself, were born in Britain. After explaining to the group how concerned

he was that his parents would discover his homosexuality, Ananda
recalls that

no one in the group understood. Maybe one person. I explained
that parents have done so much for you, have sacrificed so much,
have had such hopes and dreams. . . .

They would be so unhappy to learn that a son is homosexual. This
would be a very great shame to them.

How can I tell them, my parents? One boy said, 'Grow up,
Ananda, you're a big boy now, why should you let your parents
stand in the way of your happiness? Why should you let your
parents prevent you from being your true self?'

How can I answer that? This is someone from a different world,
a different culture, asking me this question. In my country, the
family . . . it's different, it has a meaning, a different meaning.
. . . The son marries. Then, perhaps, he goes to the home of the
wife to live, as my brother did. You see? Everyone is very close
together. . . .

My brother tells me, 'In two years in England, see how Western
you've become!' Maybe. If he means, how homosexual I've
become, yes. But no, he doesn't know about me. . . .

It's against my religion. Homosexuality is immoral in my religion.
. . .It means sleeping with many men, but caring for none. That's
what they say. . . .

Someone said to me 'Ananda, go to this pub, it's a gay pub, there
will be other homosexuals. You'll make friends.' 'I don't drink', I
said. 'It is against my religion.' Why should I go? What will I do?
Stand around and do what?

I want one person. My love will be for that one person always.
Why should I need anyone else if I love one person? It doesn't
make sense to me. . . .

I still live with my brother and his family, and my sisters. We
have a big house. It's nice, and I have my own room. They don't
ask me, 'Where have you been, Ananda?', and questions like
that. But I am close to my sister-in-law, and she says to the baby,
'When is your uncle going to introduce you to your aunt?' She
means, when does Ananda get married and bring his wife home?
And I say, laughing, 'Ananda will never get married.' My brother
and sister-in-law always laugh at that because they are thinking to
themselves, you wait, he'll meet the right one soon and then see

how different it will be. I won't, but what can I do? I'm not brave. . . .

Once, a year ago, in class at college, we were talking about the law, about blackmail, and someone mentioned homosexuals. I shivered, as if I were sitting on ice, and I shouted out, 'They should kill them all! Exterminate them!' I'm so ashamed now, but I felt I must protect myself, keep the others from looking at me. They thought, after that, laughing when they said it, Ananda, he hates homosexuals. And then I felt safe. . . .

How can I tell my family? Only last week, watching television, we saw a comedian who acted like a woman, who dressed up as a woman, and my brother shook his head, saying, 'Sad people, sad people'. I left the room, thinking, he will never understand; how can I ever tell him? And what will I do when my parents arrive? They will arrive in, maybe, two years. I will not be a little boy then. . . .

How to Tell Your Parents

There is no single answer to the question of 'how to tell your parents'. The manner in which a child reveals that he or she is homosexual will depend on all the personalities involved, as well as on the existing relationship between the parents and the child. What follows, then, are only suggestions, all of which are offered by gay people who have already revealed themselves as homosexual to their parents:

It all depends on how you feel about being gay. If you're miserable about it, your parents are likely to feel the same way once you've told them. If you feel good about it, then that is also likely to affect their reactions. I told my parents at the worst possible time: when I was really depressed about things— everything, from school to pimples, to feeling lonely, to being gay. And, of course, they were horrified. Not about my skin, or my loneliness, or my bad grades, but only about being gay. Nothing else seemed to matter (**Gavin**, eighteen).

I can tell you what *not* to do. Don't tell your parents if you feel they are unlikely to understand. Don't do as I did: I folded up completely when I saw the look of shock in their faces. I'll never forget that look as long as I live. It's like a scar, now, that's never going to go away. I know that. Better that you phone and tell them, if you must, than to be unprepared for a reaction like that. I'm still feeling very guilty because I know I am hurting them by being myself. They won't tell me this in so many words. They won't come out in the open with their feelings. They are *so English*! Maybe if they did come out with their feelings, I could tell them how much I'm hurting inside when they act this way. There is no understanding on their part; their minds are closed. Never tell your parents if you think they are likely to react this way. Try and prepare them first (**Mandy**, twenty-one).

You must choose the time very carefully. Don't blurt it out during an argument, because then your homosexuality becomes a weapon to wound them with, and not what it should be: something important you wish to share with them (**Brigid**, twenty).

What you must do is to decide whether or not to tell both of your parents or just one of them. It depends on what your relationship is like with your mum and dad. I told my mum first because she never flaps, and I felt she would understand. She did understand, but she said I was right to tell her first because father, she said, 'needs a little preparation for this'. A week later the two of them came into my bedroom one night and my father kissed me on the forehead and cheek and said 'Katy, we love you now as much as ever, and we are very proud of you for confiding in us as you did' (**Katy**, nineteen).

With my parents, I decided it was best to tell them gradually. I knew they would be wanting to visit me at my flat, and I didn't want to have to lie and pretend all the time about who Ruth was, or why I wasn't dating men, or about anything else that would mean having to deny that I am a lesbian. I began by explaining to them that I needed to go in with another girl to purchase the flat because of the high costs involved. Then one evening I told them a few things about Ruth, and on another evening I told them *quite a bit* about Ruth, so that they would know that this was not just 'another friend'. And by the time I actually told them I was gay, I think they had already guessed! (**Yolonda**, thirty-one).

If I was a counsellor, I would tell all gays who came to see me that they should expect the worst when they tell their parents. I would say, 'be prepared'. That is the main thing. The news is going to surprise your parents, perhaps upset them. They will not take it calmly. I told my parents last year, but I had thought about telling them a long time before. I weighed the reasons very carefully in my mind before deciding to say anything. In the end, I felt it would be best to tell them. As I expected, they lashed out at me. It was as if I was gay because of something *they* did, and I was reminding them of that by telling them. Mum said, 'You are doing this to hurt me', but my father, he wouldn't accept it. He kept saying, 'No son of mine is a poof' . . . (**Dan**, twenty-seven).

I don't think that anyone should force the issue with parents or, you know, be defiant. I would not try and force my parents to accept my girlfriends because, well, I don't think you can force someone to change simply because you would like them to. It takes time. When I told my mother and dad, I tried explaining to them that I was still the same daughter as before, and that maybe they could try looking at it that way (**Melanie**, nineteen).

After telling my parents I made certain that I kept the lines of communication open. I had the advantage, maybe, of reading dozens of books and articles before finally deciding to tell my parents. I also had the experience of other gay friends to work on. So I think I understood that parents have their own defences, and that my parents would have to change their ways of understanding me, and that this was not going to be easy for them. I was far more concerned about *them*, actually, than I was about myself. I felt proud of being gay, but I knew they would be unlikely to feel the same way. It was a case of my helping *them* to grow up, rather than the other way around (**Eve**, twenty-two).

What to Say and Do as a Parent

Once the parents learn of their child's homosexuality, what can they do to help their son or daughter? This is the question I put to **Ann**, Colin's mother, who replied:

It would help immensely to think of homosexuality as a kind of loving, and not concentrate exclusively on the sexual aspect of things. This was the most difficult thing of all for Mel, Colin's father. At first, he couldn't come to terms with the sex that was going on. It took a while for him to begin thinking about the sort of *relationships* that Colin might be developing. . . .

I strongly suspected that Colin was homosexual long before he ever told me. This understanding was very disturbing to me at first. A parent wants what is best for the child. As a homosexual, there are problems. You must always deal with other people's negative attitudes, even if not directed at you personally. As a consequence, life can be very difficult.

The best that parents can do for their children is to help them develop the personal resources necessary to resist the disappointments and the rejections that they will meet in life. It doesn't matter if the child is heterosexual or homosexual, you would still do the same thing. . . .

If you love your child, you love that child *as it is*. And if there is something about that child that you don't like or that you can't understand, then my advice would be to talk about it as openly as you feel able to. But *don't* put a lid on your feelings. Don't tuck your feelings away somewhere.

Some Further Advice to Parents

1.   Listen to your sons or daughters as they are coming out to you. Try and discover how *they* are feeling. Most important, establish in your mind what being gay means to your children. You may well be surprised by the answer you receive.

2.   Be honest in your reactions to your child's 'revelation'. If you think you may say something that you will later regret, say so. It isn't necessary to say you accept a son or daughter's homosexuality if you don't. You can say that you find it very difficult to understand; that it will be a struggle for you; that you need time to come to terms with this. *Don't hold on to your feelings*. If your child is in the least bit sensitive and intuitive, then beware lest you lose his or her trust and confidence by hiding the way you feel. *Share your feelings*—these can be a crucially important aspect of your bond together.

3.   It is also important to meet your child's friends. You needn't feel obliged to *like* them. The important thing to remember is that your attitude should not be influenced by the fact that a friend happens to be homosexual. After all, so too is your child. Be as accepting as you are able, and you might learn a great deal about your child's homosexuality. You will also learn a great deal about yourself.

4.   It might also be helpful to read some books on the subject of homosexuality. Be careful. So much of what has been written reflects a strong homophobic bias which is not always immediately obvious. You might, to begin with, take a look at the Critical Bibliography.

5.   Never consider the matter of your child's homosexuality closed. If you are accepting, then your child may well feel the need on many occasions to talk to you about being gay. That is what coming out is all about.

6.   If there are others in the family who you feel should know, tell them. But only tell them when the time is right. Don't rush in to tell others simply because you will feel better if others can share something that may be very heavy for you to carry alone.

7.   Don't relate every little annoyance you may have with your child to the fact that he or she is homosexual. Remember, gays are no less complicated than heterosexuals, and all actions will have a multiplicity of causes.

8.   Finally, and most important, let your child know that your love remains as firm as always. Remember, it took a great deal of courage, trust, and love on your child's part to tell *you*.

Coming Out at Work

The home is not the only problematic area for homosexuals who choose to be open about themselves. Discrimination in employment also means it is difficult for gays to be open at their place of work. This leads to the constant pressure of concealment and exclusion from common workplace topics—for example, home and family life or problems with personal relationships. It also means that gays are isolated from an important potential support network. Heterosexual workmates, doubtless without realizing, refer constantly to their heterosexuality (spouses, dates, weddings, anniversaries, offspring, domestic problems), and help create a climate which effectively silences and excludes homosexuals.

Many employers equate sexual orientation with job performance. Thus, the homosexual—and particularly those who exhibit traits which the general public identifies as gay—will be at a disadvantage in finding and retaining employment or in being considered for promotion. With the advent of AIDS, the employment situation is even more precarious. Recently, an industrial tribunal sitting in Bedford ruled that it is acceptable to sack gay men from their jobs simply because their workmates are afraid of catching AIDS—and this despite a much publicized and widely distributed booklet issued in late 1986 by the Department of Employment informing employers that infection with HIV should not be a reason for job discrimination. It is for reasons such as these that many gays choose to erect a heterosexual façade between themselves and their employers and workmates. When one considers that most of us spend perhaps a quarter of our working lives at our place of employment, such a passing strategy can be seen as constituting a potentially serious strain on the psychical well-being of gays.

Until the early 1980s, when the figures for AIDS cases in Britain began to climb and the media took a keen interest in publicizing the subject, the situation in this general area of jobs and employment was more advantageous to gays than at any other time in the recent past. Many more gays felt freer to come out to friends at work, and were doing so with very positive results. With AIDS, the situation is considerably less encouraging, with many gays now showing reluctance to make their homosexuality known for fear of being shunned or sacked.

But even if AIDS had not intervened to cast a cloud over the brightening employment prospects for homosexuals, we must be wary of underestimating the hazards of being open-as-gay in one's job. To illustrate this point, consider the case of John Saunders, a gay maintenance man sacked from a Scottish campsite in 1980, *not* for committing any offence but because his employers were informed that he was gay. When Saunders took his employers to an industrial tribunal, he lost because it was ruled that it is quite legitimate to sack someone on the basis of a commonly held prejudice. The Employment Appeal Tribunal later upheld the industrial tribunal's ruling, arguing that, though it might not be 'scientifically sound' to think so, 'a considerable proportion of employers would take the view that the employment of homosexuals should be restricted, particularly when required to work in proximity and in contact with children'.[1]

Although women and members of ethnic minority groups are offered some protection under the law, lesbians and gay men seem less entitled to the benefits of equal opportunities. Confirmation of this can be found in a statement of Home Office minister David

105

Waddington, who has said: 'I cannot imagine anything which is more likely to damage the Equal Opportunities Commission than for it to become identified in the public mind with such crankish notions as that it should be wrong to discriminate against people on grounds of homosexuality.'[2] It is not surprising, then, that in 1986 alone the group known as LAGER (Lesbian and Gay Employment Rights) dealt with well over a hundred cases of homosexuals losing their jobs because of their sexual orientation, and most of these, LAGER concluded, because of panic over AIDS.[3]

The most significant issue of principle to emerge from these cases is that the 'general public' has 'strong views' against homosexuality, and that the hostile views of other workers, customers or, in the case of teachers, parents, can justifiably be acted upon by an employer who wishes to remove a lesbian or gay male worker.

In the case of *Wiseman v. Salford City Council* (1981), similar issues were raised in relation to a teacher in a college of further education. The Manchester industrial tribunal ruled that a lecturer had been fairly dismissed following a conviction for gross indecency. Although the college Principal accepted that there was no evidence to suggest that the teacher's homosexuality had at any time in the past affected his teaching duties, he argued that there was a 'risk element' in continuing his employment due to the teacher's close contact with the young. The majority of the industrial tribunal hearing the case considered that the college had been unprejudiced, although one dissenting member argued that 'in treating a homosexual male more harshly because of his homosexuality, the governors showed themselves to be less than "unprejudiced" and "open minded" as the Employment Tribunal requires them to be'.[4]

The cases discussed above reveal at least two basic assumptions prejudicial to gays: first, that homosexuals are, in themselves, a threat to children; and, second, that 'known' homosexuals are an even greater threat. (Such assumptions, the reader will recall, ignore the fact that gays are no more likely than heterosexuals to be paedophiles, and that a paedophile will not necessarily subject children to unwanted or violent advances. Further to this, a 1986 GLC Women's Committee report found that 'ninety-five per cent of child abuse is the responsibility of heterosexual men and the victims are young girls'.)[5] It is the conclusion of a 1975 report by the National Council for Civil Liberties (NCCL)[6] that, though there has been some progress made since the days when homosexuality was, in itself, sufficient justification for dismissal, there still exists 'a considerable degree of prejudice' in the area of employment, especially when homosexuals come into contact with children.[7] It is my belief that, more than a decade after the publication of the NCCL report, this conclusion still holds valid.

The case of **Shirley** highlights some of the problems confronting the gay teacher, and also illustrates some of the confusions of many educationalists when confronted with what they regard as a homosexual 'problem'.

In February 1975 I decided to resign my teaching post at an all-girls grammar school, and I will attempt in this letter to explain the circumstances surrounding my decision.

I will begin by stating the obvious. We know that in all our schools there are lesbians on the staff who remain above suspicion by carefully hiding their homosexuality from others. They do this because they are unwilling to challenge the bigoted assumption which holds that a teacher who is known as lesbian undermines her authority in the classroom. I do not accept this assumption. Of course, there doubtless exist students who have been conditioned to distrust or dislike homosexuals, just as there are students who have been conditioned to dislike blacks, Indians, the elderly, people with working-class, middle-class, or upper-class accents. The question we must ask ourselves is whether we should bow to such prejudices, or reject them.

Many students grow up believing that none of the people they know are homosexual. The gay image is supplied by television comedians or the uninformed and often malicious gossip of the street. Homosexuals thus come to be regarded as sick, worthless, ridiculous, criminal. Students who are gay, but who do not fully understand homosexuality, will therefore resist the truth about themselves. As a result they may feel guilty and ashamed about their feelings long after their heterosexual friends have learned to deal with their sexuality.

A teacher who is openly gay could therefore play a very positive role in the school. In eight years of teaching, the one thing I regret more than anything else is that I remained too much in the closet. You see, I too feared for my position. . . . Of course there are many ways that we reveal the nature of our sexual orientation. Many teachers will speak informally to students of their personal lives, of their spouses, or about their children. Engagements and weddings are often discussed in and out of the classroom. The students talk about these things, and no one ever seems unduly distressed. But could I, as a lesbian, assume the same degree of tolerance if I chose to be as forthcoming about my domestic arrangements with a female lover?

I now know that the answer to this question is 'no'. Some months ago I was discussing the Sex Discrimination Bill in my Current Affairs class. It was a lively and interesting discussion, and when the bell rang for lunch, most of the students remained behind to continue the discussion. We began talking informally about the wider implications of the Bill. One girl wondered whether lesbians would be affected. Another girl laughed at this, and said that the girl who raised this question must be lesbian herself, 'or something even worse'. A few laughed uneasily, and a flurry of comment followed.

I remained largely silent throughout. But then one girl remarked that lesbians were 'disgusting creatures'. When asked if she had ever met any, she said no, she hadn't, and explained that 'lesbians never show their faces'. No one dared to disagree with her, for they knew she would level the same charge at them: *Lesbian!*'

It was then that I spoke out. I spoke out not because I was angry with this girl; I was not. I spoke out in order to explain what it means to live with the need to hide, to disguise, and to deny oneself. I came out to my students and told them that I was gay, but not for myself. I came out to increase their awareness, especially those in the group who might themselves be gay.

The reaction of the girls was interesting. They were not shocked or upset. They were *interested*. They were interested because my admission had made them think about certain unquestioned, *negative* assumptions about lesbians. You see, they knew and liked me as a teacher, and as a person. They were surprised, therefore, that someone they knew, liked, and respected was lesbian. They had learned something about themselves, about me, and about life. And I believe that most of them will never feel the same about lesbians again.

Several days later the Head called me to her office and asked for an explanation of my behaviour. It seems that the students had been discussing this particular class at lunch, and one of the other teachers overheard. This teacher then informed the Head.

My explanation proved unsatisfactory. I was told that I had been 'indiscreet' and that I had allowed my 'private life' and 'sexual tastes' to interfere with the professional exercise of my duties. I was also asked to give an undertaking that under no circumstances would I ever again mention or 'allude to the fact' that I am homosexual. I could not, in conscience, give such an undertaking.

I was not asked to resign, nor do I believe the Head could have forced my resignation. However, when my Current Affairs class was assigned to another teacher (ostensibly so that I would have 'more time for preparation and marking'), I felt that I no longer wished to teach in this particular school. And so I resigned. I felt then, as I do now, that there is no place for me, as a self-respecting gay woman, in an educational establishment which has made it transparently clear that it regards lesbians as a threat to pupils *in a way which heterosexual women are not*.

There are many more such cases. The general public will never hear about these. I hope that my experience will help in some small way to make the truth more available to those who are in a position to help in changing the sort of attitudes which led to my resignation.

To conclude this chapter, here is an excerpt from an address delivered in November 1973 by **Dr Howard J. Brown**, at a conference held by the Gay Academic Union of Hunter College, New York.[8] Dr Brown, who died in early 1975, was a former Health Services Administrator and Chairman of the Board of Health of the City of New York. He was, at the time of his death, a Professor of Preventive Medicine at New York University. Dr Brown speaks here of his reasons for coming out, as well as the consequences of doing so:

Seven weeks ago I got up one morning and, as usual, shut my closet door. Twenty-four hours later I had no closet door to shut; in fact the closet door had been ripped away from around me, and thanks to *The New York Times* I was the best-known homosexual in the East. . . .

I did it for political purposes. . . . I had a heart attack about eight months before I really decided to announce, and for about two days, as a physician, I knew it was possible and perhaps even probable that I might die. And I thought a great deal about the fact that you can't wait endlessly to do things. And certainly if I was going to leave some legacy to the gay cause I had to act as soon as I could. So it was really during that period that I decided it might be useful if a physician announced his homosexuality. . . .

Now I should mention that I also had some safety, though I don't think this was a central factor in my announcing. I had tenure. . . . [But] the thing that was more important to me, that gave me a greater sense of security, was that I knew the student evaluations of me were very good. . . .

I then decided that I'd ask the Public Health Association of New York City (that's an organization of public health people of which I was a member) whether they would appoint a committee to fight discrimination against homosexuals in public health. So I spoke to the president, and went to the board of directors, and I told them that I thought they should pass an anti-discrimination resolution, and listed a number of other things they could do. And then I said, 'Really, we should appoint a chairman of the committee who's a homosexual, and I'd like to be chairman.'

Well, there was a long pause, and there were a few conservatives in the room that suggested a committee and a study, but the majority came right out and said, 'No, we'll pass the resolution, and you can be chairman of the committee'. . . .

As many of you may know, the announcement appeared on the front page of *The New York Times* and was followed by some other stories in the *Times*. I appeared on every television network in the city; and across the country I'm still getting clippings from little towns—from front pages of little town newspapers. . . .

The stories that were written were kind stories. . . . Across the country the headlines weren't, you know, 'Doctor Caught as Homosexual' and 'Doctor Announces He's Pervert', but they were 'Homosexual Doctor Praised for His Candour' or 'Colleagues Praise Homosexual Doctor'. . . .

Meanwhile, back at the university, everyone had to face the fact that they had a gay professor in their midst. And the reaction from the university has been uniformly positive.

I started out saying that I announced my homosexuality for political reasons, and that was clearly the reason. I would now do it for personal reasons, because I have found that I can associate much more honestly and clearly with the straight faculty mem-

110

bers. I had not realized how many things about myself I really hid, and how many times during the day I was still programmed to be a shadow of the way I am. . . .

Summary

This chapter has been concerned with the consequences of coming out, a process variously defined as 'thinking of yourself as homosexual for the first time' (**Claude**); 'sharing' your gayness with others (**Lorraine**); 'being as open as you are able' (**Nancy**); 'having sex for the first time with someone of your own sex' (**Simon**); 'part of the whole process of self-recognition' (**Lydia**); 'coming of age' (**Stan**); 'feeling positive about yourself (**Cheryl**); 'accept(ing) that you are different' (**Lawrence**).

Once gays have come out, they must deal with all the people in their lives who will now know, perhaps for the first time, that they are homosexual. Rejecting attitudes are not uncommon. These are most painful when they come from within the home. Most parents, unless specifically told, are unaware of their child's homosexuality (**Alice**; **Rita**), and when they do discover, their reaction is one of 'anger, disappointment, and revulsion' (**Kay**), or concern about what the neighbours will think (**Sandra**). It is much less common for a parent to be accepting and helpful (**Colin**), and it may be particularly difficult for the parents of gays who come from a different culture than ours to accept a child's homosexuality (**Ananda**).

There is no single answer to the question of 'how to tell your parents', although the following suggestions have been offered: be positive about your gayness before you tell (**Gavin**); don't tell parents if they are unlikely to understand (**Mandy**); don't say anything during the course of an argument (**Brigid**); decide whether or not you are going to tell both parents or just one (**Katy**); break the news gradually (**Yolonda**); prepare yourself for the worst (**Dan**); don't force the issue (**Melanie**); understand that your parents have their own defences (**Eve**).

On discovering a son or daughter's homosexuality, a parent should endeavour to help the child develop the personal resources necessary to resist the disappointments and rejections that life may provide (**Ann**). Some further advice to parents would be: understand the importance of feelings—your child's and your own; meet your child's friends; read some books on the subject of homosexuality;

never consider the matter of your child's homosexuality closed; don't rush to tell other members of the family; don't relate every little annoyance to the fact of your child's homosexuality; let your child know that your love remains as firm as ever.

Another problematic area, in addition to the home, is one's place of employment. Many employers equate sexual orientation with job performance, thus making it difficult for gays to come out at work. Discrimination is also severe in the field of education. **Shirley**'s story highlights some of the problems confronting the self-respecting gay teacher, while the case of **Dr Howard Brown** reveals that the consequences of coming out to colleagues may be extremely beneficial to oneself and others.

7

Coming Together

'So here we are. Who am I? Why am I what I am? At the beginning of this book I told you how I feel about people trying to find reasons for me. I am what I am, and I fully embrace that. I am human—much to the amazement of some people.'

from *Being Different: The Autobiography of Jane Fry*, ed. Robert Bogdan

In coming out and proclaiming their true inner identity, gay people are rejecting society's definitions of them as abnormal, sick, sinners, and criminal. The guilt and shame that formerly accompanied the passing strategy of pretence and disguise is now replaced by a greater sense of pride in self. Instead of perceiving homosexuality as a failure in development, gays begin to realize the full measure of their success in resisting the overwhelming pressures of society to deny their true selves and be heterosexuals. It is thus that homosexuality ceases to be a source of guilt and shame and becomes, instead, part of a creative process of self-actualization.

Once gays have set themselves free from the tyranny of their conventional social roles, they are immediately confronted with the problems of readjustment. Part of the creative process of homosexuality consists of evolving a new basis for existing and potential relationships. Another way of putting this is to say that homosexuals, in taking the decision to come out, have chosen to relate to other people on the basis of honesty in regard to their sexual orientation. This may lead to rejection by some, as we have seen, but it also allows for the fulfilment of one's needs and desires in ways which have hitherto been hampered by the determination to pass for straight.

The 'Gay Scene'

Heterosexuals can meet other heterosexuals at any moment of the day or night. A friend, a lover, or a prospective spouse can be found at one's place of employment, at a relative's flat, at a party, in a bus queue, at college or university, in church, and so on. This is the 'ordinary' way of meeting someone. Unfortunately, though, homosexuals cannot expect to meet other homosexuals through the usual channels of social activity. This fact, which springs from society's continuing disapproval of any overt expression of homosexual behaviour, accounts for the popularity of the 'gay scene', i.e. all those public places and activities which provide homosexuals with many of their social, sexual, and psychological needs. Although the gay scene constitutes a very small corner of a much larger gay community, it none the less remains one of the few areas on the heterosexual map where gays can be certain that the people they meet and like will not be confused or angered by friendly overtures, be they social or sexual.

Critics of the gay scene (and there are many) often forget that a basic emotional need of human beings is a sense of belonging to something or someone. It is extremely difficult to live without community. The need for identity, for the comfort and affirmation of being with others of one's own kind, is particularly intense in the case of homosexuals. Indeed, as any member of a minority group, be it political, religious, racial, social or sexual, will testify, there are few things more satisfying than the positive reinforcement which comes from being with one's own when so many of one's day-to-day activities are shared with those who hold different views, interests, and goals. Hence, most gays, at some point or other in their lives and to a greater or lesser extent, will involve themselves in the gay scene.

The traditional gay scene consists principally of pub, club, and disco. The key fact of this world is the need for many of those who inhabit it to lead a double life. For if homosexuality were acceptable to straight society, there would hardly be the need for a scene totally apart from the mainstream. If identification with other gays in this milieu too often accentuates the negative and eliminates the positive, thereby causing intense distress for individual gays, then the counsellor will need to understand why this is so. As a partial means of answering this question, let us take a look at the gay pub, undoubtedly the central and most popular institution within the scene.

The Horse's Tail is located in an area of London best known for its bedsitters and transient population of tourists and students. The public bar of the pub (the private bar remains the almost exclusive preserve of the local inhabitants) is entered through a longish mirrored, 'modern thirties' hallway, complete with palm trees and oak panelling. The room, largely dominated by the colours blue and green, is fairly large, yet maintains a relaxing intimacy. The décor is similar to the entrance-way, with small upholstered chairs clustered around eight smallish, oval-shaped tables. At one end of the room is situated, somewhat incongruously, a 'one-arm bandit' and, at the other end, a juke box which plays everything from pop to Puccini. Drinks are noticeably higher in price than in non-gay pubs, but this is a form of exploitation which most gays have lived with for so long that it now seems an unquestioned fact of gay life.

Ernie, licensee of The Horse's Tail, is gay. He is a large and jovial man of fifty-three, and he talks here about the changing nature of the scene in which he has lived and worked for all of his adult life:

In the past, the gay pub was virtually the only place we could congregate, *as gays*, without revealing our 'terrible secret' to the outside world. The reason we came to the gay pub was to be ourselves. You felt a release when you walked through that door. And it was good to meet people you *knew* would be gay. Outside the pub, you could never be certain that someone who turned you on was gay or straight. You might say that visiting a gay pub avoided a lot of black eyes.

Of course, not all gays knew where the pubs were located. We couldn't advertise. If you were a shy sort of person it might be years and years, *if ever*, before you learned of a place like this. I first discovered gay pubs through a pick-up. He asked me if I had gone to such-and-such a place, and I said no, and he gave me the address. . . .

You'll find a lot of customers here who don't much like the 'scene', but don't know where else to go. There are people who say to me, 'It's so tense; I don't feel I fit in; no one talks to me.' They come here all the same in the hope that tonight will be their lucky night. . . .

No one likes to be rejected. Your self-esteem is at stake. Gay people are hassled so often that they want to be supercautious before showing interest in anyone. Look at it this way. In a place like this, your physical appearance counts for a great deal. If you're straight and you go to a dance, you go up to the girl who turns you on. It works the same way here. You go up to the person who attracts you and you start a conversation. A lot of people are afraid of being pub wallflowers, though, and this accounts for some of the tension.

One of the great myths about the gay scene is that the *only* thing that brings people to the pub is sex. This isn't true. Sex is one thing, certainly. But for many gays the pub is a place to meet friends, to chat with new people, relax, have a quick drink on the way home from work or the theatre. In other words, it's a place to be sociable with people who have similar interests. . . .

The gay club differs from the gay pub in several respects; the former requires membership, tends to be more intimate in terms of atmosphere and size and, like all clubs, is generally inhabited by a regular, if changing, core of members. **Guy** is a gay club owner, about fifty years of age. Here he talks about his club, and about certain aspects of the scene which militate against the development of personal relationships.

Our club is very small, and that gives it a feeling of intimacy, which is what I wanted. We have two bars, though, and also a juke-box, and a small dancing area. . . . The word I'd use to describe the decor is 'utilitarian'. It's comfortable. You'll notice, too, the stained glass windows, and on them are the club's initials. One thing about this place: the people are friendly. If they're not, they won't come back a second time. The staff are pleasant, and that really creates the atmosphere. I think you've probably discovered that for yourself. You can see how friendly they are. They chat to customers, but only when they have a free moment. . . . We're very busy here from about nine in the evening till closing time. And, of course, week-ends are absolute murder!

The subscription is nominal. We only charge £1 a year. And we try to keep the prices as low as possible without actually going broke. We also try to make newcomers feel at home. A little conversation, if it's a new face, helps the person to feel more at ease. . . .

You may find the place a bit conservative, and perhaps it is. You have to remember, though, that in the old days (and my memory in the business goes back some thirty years) clubs were registered institutions. We had a committee! Everything was *impeccably* run. It was like a council meeting, really: minutes and motions, and all the rest of it. We didn't have too much interference from the police for that reason. Things were run in a very orderly way, so the police didn't interfere. Problems? One, in particular: the vagaries of the licensing laws. One is terribly vulnerable, even though you have a club licence. The police can close down clubs more or less at will. You mentioned the Manchester club case a little while ago. Well, that's not at all unusual . . . police can enter the club in plain clothes, and if they see men dancing they may decide it's a breach of the peace. The police are entitled to use their own discretion in preserving the peace.

If you're homosexual, you can never keep yourself clean enough. That's the lesson I've learned from being in this business all these years. No matter how jolly it is in here, there's always a great deal of uncertainty, as well. And that's bad for getting to know people.

The formation of relationships on the scene can also present problems for gay women, as **Ursula**, thirty-three, explains:

Any woman who has ever stood uncomfortably on a dance floor waiting to be noticed will understand one of the principal drawbacks of the gay club as a meeting place. . . .

The prevailing atmosphere is one of sexual urgency. I don't want to put the scene down. I know that for many women there is no other place to go. And clubs have the advantage of being accessible. They are there when you need them.

On the other side of the coin, the world of the club is as hidebound by etiquette as the world outside. The lines that are drawn between one woman and the next are rigidly prescribed. Even making a first move can be an incredibly complicated process. You must always ask yourself, who is the woman standing next to her—are they together? What will she expect of me? Am I her type? What do I say after I have said hello?

For a gay woman, there are two big options: 'butch' and 'femme'. When I first arrived on the scene, the pressures to identify with one or the other were irresistible. I know that roles are not so sharply defined today, but the desire to be accepted is still very great. Let's face it, a gender-defined situation is comforting, especially for women who aren't yet confident enough to relate to other women in their own independent ways.

Since the pub/club/disco is often the point of entry into the gay scene, the young lesbian who is still uncertain of her identity and susceptible to new images of herself may find it safe to take refuge behind the comforting stereotypes of 'butch' and 'femme'. In time, though, many gay women come to feel trapped by the constricting roles they have learned. 'Thus,' say Sidney Abbott and Barbara Love, authors of *Sappho was a Right-On Woman*, 'the lesbian has two identity crises: the first is over being heterosexual or homosexual; the second, over the old but still existent choice of butch or femme'.[1]

Sexual Contacts

The gay scene, it should be stressed, does not have equal significance for males and females. The sexual marketplace character of many pubs and clubs holds less appeal for the latter than it does for the former. It is important for the counsellor to understand that the different learning and conditioning processes of men and women have resulted in certain psychosexual differences between the two sexes. Given the fact that women in our culture are conditioned to play different roles than men, sexual contacts tend to carry different meanings. For the majority of women, Ford and Beach have pointed out, 'sexual satisfaction demands more than simple genital stimulation; it usually rests upon a complex type of interrelationship with [one's] partner. . . . This simply emphasizes the fact that for the human female, physical climax in and of itself is less sufficient than it is for the male.'[2]

The social implications of these differences between the sexes are considerable. 'Among all people, everywhere in the world,' says Kinsey, 'it is understood that the male is more likely than the female to desire sexual relations with a *variety of partners*'[3] [emphasis added]. The propensity of the male (hetero- or homo-sexual) to find sexual stimulation in a greater number of situations, relationships, and things means that he is far more likely than the female to find himself in socially provocative situations. It would, for example, be very rare for a woman to cruise the streets or public toilets in search of a partner for sex; not so a man. There are lesbian clubs, as we have seen, but these are few, in relation both to the number of gay men's clubs and to the total lesbian population. In addition, gay men are far more likely than gay women to begin a potentially sexual relationship with an immediate sexual encounter.

It is also important to remember in this connection that in no two people is the intensity of the sexual instinct the same. Hence, the physical satisfaction of sexual needs may be left unsatisfied by a single partner. This is particularly true in the case of many men who, though they may enjoy the emotional satisfaction and companionship of one other person within a primary relationship, will still seek out others in an attempt to deal with their own surplus sexual needs.

'Cottaging' is, as we have seen, perhaps the most readily available means of obtaining quick and anonymous sex. If the research done by Professor Humphreys in the United States is any guide to the British situation, then it appears that a substantial percentage of the men (fifty-four per cent) involved in cottaging are married. Finding their sexual needs unfulfilled by their wives, these men find in cottaging a convenient means of obtaining sexual satisfaction without in any way endangering their primary relationships.[4]

Generally speaking, cottages are particularly well suited to men whose immediate interest is focused upon genital contacts. Of course, pubs and clubs are also available, but such places have certain crucial disadvantages: they necessitate an expense of time and money; they are very competitive in nature; they do not allow for complete anonymity. Of course, there are also gay men who, long after they have rejected feelings of guilt and shame, will continue to cottage, simply because they have learned, through conditioning and habit, to enjoy it. For such people, cottaging has two important advantages: first, it can provide sexually satisfying and emotionally non-involving encounters; second, the risks involved, though potentially disastrous to one's domestic life and professional career, may heighten the sense of sexual excitement.

From the vantage point of the 'ordinary person', it is easy to condemn cottaging. Yet such condemnation, as David Blamires reminds us, is 'more in the idea than in the reality of the act committed'.[5] Many gays who have been turned away from the mainstream of social life may find in cottaging something which cannot be found elsewhere: a temporary escape from loneliness and isolation. Such social isolation, we must never forget, is a direct consequence of the fact that homosexuals, as a minority group within society, are subject to sanctions which encourage a fragmentation of sex from the rest of their everyday lives. Such a process of fragmentation not only militates against personal happiness, but can also be damaging to one's social well-being.

If, as some critics have argued, gays are more concerned with their sexuality than heterosexuals, the reason is simply that society has chosen to regard the sexual feelings of homosexuals as a 'problem'. Fearing the penalties which might result from openness, the gay person may seek sex by furtive means. Some will make sexual contacts in cottages as a way of ensuring their anonymity. After all, if the identity of one's sexual partner is unknown, then there is no possibility of developing the relationship any further than the initial sexual encounter. In time, however, such individuals, having successfully internalized society's prohibitions against same-sex intimacy, may find it virtually impossible to respond sexually to others in a safer or more relaxed atmosphere. It is thus that the promiscuity so vociferously condemned by heterosexuals (who blithely ignore their own, leaving it to the media to reveal all the sensational details) is no more than a direct by-product of those very prohibitions imposed by society against gay relationships.

Creative Alternatives

A constructive examination of the traditional gay scene is today being undertaken by homosexuals themselves. The awakening of gay consciousness that followed the Stonewall Riot of June 1969* has given a new impetus to the development of a true gay community. The essential qualities of this community are an assertion of one's gay difference and a sense of solidarity with other gays. This gay affirmation has led to a retreat from many of the more oppressive aspects of the pseudo-community of the gay scene. **Glen**, thirty, speaks for many gays when he says that, for him, 'the scene was generally a last resort rather than a free choice':

> It isn't difficult to get hooked on the scene. It depends on what the alternatives are, and until recently there weren't any. So, no matter how much I disliked the scene, I would feel compelled to

*The Stonewall Inn was an after-hours gay bar on Christopher Street in New York's Greenwich Village. On the night of 27 June 1969, the police raided the pub over an alleged infringement of the state liquor laws. Local gays had grown accustomed to police harassment, and could be relied upon to put up no resistance. But on this occasion they reacted in anger, so that the police were forced to barricade themselves inside the bar. The next evening, crowds of gay sympathizers gathered in the vicinity of the Stonewall and protested against the vice squad action. Within a month of the riot, the GLF was organized and with it came the birth of the Gay Liberation Movement.

use it. If I wanted to meet other gays, where else could I go to meet them? Only the pubs and clubs.

In the past it was necessary to defend the scene, if only to yourself. You had to preserve your self-respect. If you attacked the scene, you felt a hypocrite, because you knew that you'd be back there. You needed the scene, even though the scene didn't need you.

The scene was generally a last resort rather than a free choice. This is why I never felt relaxed there . . . I was leading a sort of programmed gay life, doing things and behaving in the ways expected of me as a gay. It was on the scene, in fact, that I learned how to be gay; how to be a stereotyped gay, that is. . . .

In the short run, the gay scene can be useful. It can be an important part of a gay person's coming out. Walking into a gay pub for the first time is a way of saying 'I'm gay', not just to yourself, but to others like yourself. It's like an initiation rite. . . .

But in the long run, the scene holds you back. It's a ghetto and like all ghettos it narrows your vision of yourself and the rest of the world. . . . What matters most in the gay scene is being accepted—not for the person you are, but for the person you appear to be on any particular evening. It's the *appearance* that counts, and the role you happen to be playing. And if you're short on looks, youth, a good body, or the right gear, you're in trouble! This is also true of life on the commercial straight scene, but that doesn't mean gays should be the same way. . . .

I think my principal objection to the scene is that it's so difficult to get to know people. The competitive atmosphere of the pubs and clubs isn't right because it develops a spirit of rivalry, which is bad. In my own case, I remember always trying to protect myself against being rejected. I would pretend to be tough and indifferent. I'd stand there at the bar, a drink in my hand, looking around at everyone with a slightly disinterested look on my face. Like everyone else, it seems, I was determined to set up my own role from the moment I stepped into the pub.

That's the sort of role-playing the scene encourages. . . . I would say that the scene is a big obstacle to starting up a relationship, because when you're in the pub or club, you're presenting only a small part of yourself to other people. I know this for a fact, because I've had years of experience in doing exactly that. . . .

If the gay scene that Glen describes is to change, its inhabitants must first alter their perception of themselves. Those who are, like Glen, dissatisfied with the scene must first put their struggle with society into perspective. They must, in other words, define for themselves the meaning of homosexuality, and determine whether the world's view of them is consistent with the sort of people that they wish to be.

It may take a person a long time to accept the idea that such a choice exists. But it does. To begin with, one must understand something about one's basic worth, capacity, and value. The job of counsellors—perhaps their most important task—is to be of help to gays in this process of self-identification. The basic work will be done by gays. But this is not to say that counsellors cannot be of assistance in helping gays create the sort of 'inner space' which might allow for relationships to grow and develop. Developing in life is a difficult task, as people are always up against problems they have had in the past. Somebody must be there to interpret what is happening so that the troubled individual is not overwhelmed by the fact that he or she has stepped out into a bigger world where some of the same or a different set of problems exist.

Learning how to support another person is really quite difficult to do with the kind of responsibility that implies you're somehow going to drastically alter somebody's situation. But learning how to do that is what counselling is all about. People want to be happy. Usually, too, they want to trust someone. They want someone in their lives who really cares; someone who can be relied upon; someone who will be important to them. Although not everyone feels the need for a steady relationship, many of us express a desire for the companionship of another person to love and trust. Whether or not these partnerships survive depends on such factors as personality, maturity, sexual adjustment, outside commitments, and common interests. And for the gay couple one additional factor is often of crucial importance: environmental support. Gays must contend with all those social pressures which militate against the growth and development of stable relationships. The very powerful social forces which promote the stability of heterosexual unions are unfortunately nowhere present in encouraging the same stability on behalf of gay partnerships.

Jean and **Enid** are both in their early forties. Speaking of the obstacles which beset gay relationships, Jean says:

The basic problem of *any* gay relationship is learning to live with another person *as an equal*. When heterosexuals undertake to marry, each of the partners understands and accepts the role of the husband or wife. You know, the husband is the doer and breadwinner—the *active* partner; while the wife is maternal and domestic—the *passive* partner.

In the beginning Enid and I emulated these roles. Of course, they didn't work. We're both very independent ladies! But we thought, you know, one of us *has to be* the 'male' and the other the 'female'. There didn't seem to be any other alternatives. So when we discovered that these roles didn't suit us, we wondered whether perhaps we were wrong for one another. . . .

Our primary problem was trying to de-condition ourselves, if you like. We had to learn, by trial and error, the best way to live our lives together *as equals*.

Enid agrees with Jean's assessment of the problems confronting gay relationships, but suggests a further difficulty confronting lesbian partnerships:

I think that a major obstacle to lesbian relationships is having to deal with this terribly oversimplified view that people have about human sexuality. It's true that, deep down, people think that it's *irresponsible* for women to satisfy their sexual needs without any accompanying desire to have a child. I find this a very warped view of human sexuality, but it's a view that women are always confronted with. People don't tell you this *to your face*, but that only makes the matter worse. . . . Unless gay women can resolve the problem of relating to their own needs as lesbian women—not as society defines these needs, but as each gay woman defines them for herself—then the relationship is really headed for trouble.

Keith, twenty-seven, and Charles, thirty-one, have been living together for the past four years. They see the problem of establishing and maintaining a relationship from a somewhat different perspective. As Keith explains:

I think that the main reason a lot of gay men find it difficult to get a relationship going is that they haven't learned how to break out of what I call 'the man's mould'. I forget who it was that said that the woman most desperately in need of liberation is the woman every man keeps locked up in the closet of his own psyche. And I agree with that.

I know that this certainly fits in with my own experience. I've been learning how to 'be a man' ever since the cradle. I learned how to be hard and forceful, competitive and ambitious.

Most of all, though I learned that I wasn't supposed to express any feelings of affection for other men. I shouldn't be tender or warm towards them. This was 'cissy'; it was 'queer'. It's this kind of learning that makes it difficult for two men to live together in a loving relationship. I know that for Charles and me this has been the biggest hurdle of all—trying to unlearn what it means to be a man. It hasn't been easy, and I don't know what will happen to us in future. Basically, I'm an optimistic person, so I think it will all come out right in the end. And if it doesn't, well, it's because you just can't change overnight; old habits die hard.

As we have discovered from the interviews in this chapter (and throughout the book), most of the gay person's problems are due to society's view of human sexuality. One problem which is rarely explored in the literature of homosexuality is the formation of 'stable relationships'. Such relationships do exist, despite society's determined efforts to put obstacles in their way, and the desire to create them is even greater with the advent of AIDS. Some of these, as we have seen, are modelled after traditional marriage. But the majority are not so rigidly defined. In the eyes of the world these are often thought to be shamefully promiscuous. But such a charge is hypocritical since, in a society where passing for straight is, for many, of crucial importance, casual affairs and anonymous encounters will be easier to sustain than stable relationships. And in the absence of social supports, rules and guidelines governing homosexual relationships, there is a strong possibility that the same stresses and strains which plague but are generally resolved in heterosexual marriage may quickly end a potentially stable gay partnership.

Jealousy is one of the most frequently cited factors in the break-up of gay relationships. In view of much current thinking on the matter which tends to identify all manifestations of jealousy with a neurotic, possessive, and insecure personality, it is important for counsellors to distinguish between those jealous feelings which spring from legitimate fears concerning the stability of a relationship, and those which might be characterized as a reflex of insecurity. It is this latter form which **Henry**, thirty-nine, discusses here:

As they say in some song or other, I was in love with love. From the moment I came out, I seemed to live in a continual state of romantic tension. I was always searching for a lifetime partner.

When I found Peter, I thought, this is IT! This is the person to complete my life! Feeling that way about him, I wouldn't let him out of my sight. If it hadn't been for the fact that he worked on the other side of London from me, I'd have met him every day for lunch. That's how possessive I was. I was always worrying that he'd meet someone else. '*Who* did you say you ate with today?' I'd ask.

Peter didn't mind at first; I think he liked the idea of my caring about him so much. But after a while, he began to feel stifled. At least that's what he told me. . . .

I suppose my problem was that I never believed anyone could *really* love me. I was always selling myself short, measuring myself against erstwhile or imaginary competitors. . . .

What I wanted was a relationship that would last a lifetime. I was so concerned that Peter and I should remain together for always that I guess, in time, I had become his jailer. . . .

In the end my constant suspicions killed the relationship. It was all my doing. . . . I hope I've learned at least one thing from all this, though—you can't protect yourself against losing the one you love. I know, because the more I tried to hold on to Peter, the less he seemed to like me. And finally I lost him altogether.

It is often jealousy which warns us that a loving relationship is no substitute for a lack of inner identity. Relationships can only sustain something of their original intensity if firmly grounded on an acceptance by both partners of the need for shared growth. This is absolutely essential. Since the conventional social supports inherent in the institution of marriage are unavailable to gays, stressing the importance of independence is crucial. It is true, of course, that independence is an intrinsically unstable force, and it is quite possible that by growing as individuals we may grow away from those we love. Yet in the final analysis there is little choice but to allow for spaces in a loving relationship—spaces in which each can help the other to explore his or her individuality. It is out of this process of shared growth, a sort of mutual therapy, that there develops a stability far stronger than any externally imposed supports.

Paradoxical though it may seem, one result of deepening emotional ties is sometimes that of sexual boredom—a waning interest in sexual activity between the two partners in a relationship. Assuming the continuing reality of love, this situation is often temporary, so that genital sex is eventually resumed. In other cases, physical affection continues in the absence of sexual acts. To assume that this is indicative of a failed relationship is, I feel, a mistake. Loving someone involves a respect for the loved one's individuality, and this includes his or her emotional and sexual requirements. Thus, if mutual consent can be reached regarding the sexual parameters of a partnership, there would then be little reason to fear for its future on this account.

Those who condemn multiple relationships should not forget the conflicts inherent in the institution of monogamous marriage. According to psychologist Clarence Tripp:[6]

Of the thousand or more different societies that have been carefully studied, less than five per cent claim to expect monogamy. Ours is one of them. There are no societies on record, including ours, that can demonstrate working monogamy. Where both parties, for moral or any other reasons, practise real monogamy, it kills the spontaneity. The quantity goes down, the quality goes down, and sex becomes routine. The non-sexual parts of the relationship suffer as well.

Whether gays choose multiple or monogamous relationships, the important thing is that the choice be made in the best interests of the relationship. Although no two relationships will ever be the same, counsellors will bear in mind that gays are attempting to develop creative alternatives to the socially reinforced institution of heterosexual marriage. New definitions of loyalty are being formulated which stress mutual commitment to an emotional sense of responsibility rather than simple pledges of erotic fidelity. Counsellors must therefore encourage affirmation rather than apology, thus helping to ensure that gays will no longer judge themselves according to heterosexual standards of what constitutes a socially 'healthy' pattern in their sex lives. The most important task for the counsellor, therefore, is to help gays towards a new level of consciousness where self-pride and social concern are united, and where one's potential for love and human relationship can be fully realized.

Summary

Once gays have freed themselves from the tyranny of conventional social roles, they are confronted with the problems of readjustment. Part of the creative process of homosexuality consists of evolving a new basis for relationships. But gays, unlike heterosexuals, cannot expect to meet a prospective partner in the course of their everyday activities. This fact, which springs from society's disapproval of homosexuality, explains the existence of a 'gay scene' providing homosexuals with certain of their social, sexual, and psychological needs.

The key fact of this gay scene, whose principal institutions are the pub, club, and disco, is that many of those who inhabit it feel the need to lead a double life. Obstacles to the development of personal relationships on the scene include the often tense and competitive atmosphere of pubs and clubs (**Ernie**), the uncertainty caused by the vagaries of licensing laws (**Guy**), and the rigidly prescribed roles that are frequently acted out here (**Ursula**).

Gay liberation has resulted in a reassessment of the gay scene, particularly in relation to those oppressive features which prevent gays from coming together (**Glen**). Although not everyone feels the need for a steady relationship, many do express a desire for the companionship of another person to love and trust. **Jean**, **Enid**, and **Keith** speak of the obstacles which frequently beset gay partnerships, e.g. the difficulties of two individuals living together as equals, and the pressures of society to make us all conform to pre-defined roles.

In the absence of the usual social supports, rules, and guidelines governing stable relationships, jealousy and promiscuity may operate as powerful factors in the breaking-up of gay relationships. It is therefore important for counsellors to distinguish between those jealous feelings which spring from legitimate fears concerning the stability of a relationship and those which might be characterized as a reflex of insecurity (**Henry**). It is often jealousy which warns us, first, that a loving relationship is no substitute for a lack of inner identity and, second, that the best formula for success in any relationship is the acceptance by both partners of the need for shared growth. The most important task of the counsellor, therefore, is to be of supportive help to gays in their effort to reach a greater degree of self-realization, so that each person's capacity for love and human relationship can be fully realized.

8

Gays and Aids

'A Virus Knows No Morals'
Title of a 1986 film by Rosa von Praunheim

A Gay Backlash

From the mid 1980s, a quite perceptible change of attitude developed in Britain towards homosexuals. Articles appeared in the national press which told of a 'gay backlash', a 'big increase in attacks on homosexuals' and a call by the 'Moral Majority' to 'treat these perverts [i.e. gay men] with the contempt they deserve'.[1] Then, on 14 March 1987, an editorial entitled 'Decent and Indecent' appeared in the *Spectator* which condemned homosexuality and called for an end of tolerance towards homosexuals. Lamenting the fact that 'exponents of post-Sixties morality' were defending 'any sexual habit' carried on with the consent of both parties, the *Spectator* insisted that such toleration should be resisted, arguing that:

> The belief that some sexual acts are perverted accords with the emphasis—essential in a civilized society—on the dignity of man. Acts which stray from those for which the human body is designed and which defy the chief purpose of sexual intercourse impair that dignity. Homosexuality is morally . . . a dead end . . . Homosexual acts . . . are beneath human dignity . . . What is needed is a repudiation of homosexuality.[2]

In short, homosexuality, in addition to being a 'habit' (and therefore subject to conscious change, like any 'addiction'), is also perverted, uncivilized, undignified, abnormal, unnatural and immoral.

The *Spectator* editorial is indicative of a mounting level of intolerance towards homosexuals in Britain.[3] Much was made in the media in the autumn of 1986 of a South Staffordshire District Councillor's expressed wish that 'ninety per cent of queers should be gassed'. But despite being widely reported, the plea for a final solution to the homosexual 'problem' was met with scarcely a note of indignation, far less rebuke (except from the gay press). Had such an incendiary statement been directed against, say, a racial minority, the councillor would have received just and, probably, legal reprimand. In the event, the only party to be censured was a small group of gays arrested for staging a peaceful protest against the councillor's intemperate remarks.

Even the politicians have taken up their cudgels. During the general election campaign of 1987, Conservative Party Chairman Norman Tebbit ridiculed lesbian and gay rights in a party political broadcast on television, attacking sex equality policies and the idea of employing gay teachers. 'It all sounds like an Ealing comedy,' he mused. What is certainly not amusing, but hardly surprising in view of the sentiments expressed above, is the fact that attacks on gay men have increased tenfold since 1985, with, it is estimated, many more cases unreported.[4] Such harassment takes place at the same time as parliamentary calls increase for changes in the 1967 law which permits homosexual acts in private. Indeed, the Conservative Family Campaign is working actively to repeal the law, with MP Geoffrey Dickens pressing for legislation which will once again make a crime of consensual sex between two men in private. In addition, MP David Wilshire has recently introduced a clause into a new Local Government Bill which would, if passed by Parliament, ban the 'promotion of homosexuality' and 'the teaching in any maintained school of the acceptability of homosexuality'. Such legislation could very easily, thanks to the looseness and inaccuracy of the clause's wording, encourage the sort of intolerance and prejudice with which many lesbians and gays are already acquainted.[5]

One could cite numerous other instances that tell of prejudice, discrimination and violence against gays. The provocation for this overt antipathy is, of course, AIDS, the impact of which in Britain is felt most by the group presently at highest risk—homosexual men. It is the phenomenon of AIDS that has given many people the necessary excuse to drop their masks of tolerance and concern. AIDS has created a climate in which people are able to feel secure in voicing and practising discrimination and prejudice against the gay community. In fact it has provided a justification for releasing barely suppressed feelings of hatred in certain quarters. In short, what we are experiencing in the 1980s is an eruption of homophobia which condemns homosexuals for the spread of AIDS: PERVERTS ARE TO BLAME FOR KILLER DISEASE!, as a newspaper headline informed its readers, paraphrasing a remark made by police chief James Anderton, who argued that AIDS was a 'self-inflicted scourge' resulting from 'degenerate conduct'.[6]

The real significance of such chilling judgements is the devastating toll they take on the psychological well-being and social position of the gay community: homosexual men in general; lesbians, who have also felt the backlash; and, in particular, those exposed to the virus or who are suffering from the disease. Such lack of compassion and uninformed discussion of AIDS create irrational fears that will further encourage discrimination against and oppression of gays. At the very moment in time when society appeared to be moving gradually away from the notion that homosexuality is an illness, AIDS appears as a metaphor linking homosexuality with disease. Once regarded by some as recruiters and corrupters of innocents, gay men are now viewed by many as wilful agents of a 'plague'.

An ABC of AIDS

Before exploring further the extent and psychosocial consequences of such attitudes, we need to look briefly at the nature of this disease, AIDS.[7] (The reader will refer to the Critical Bibliography for books which aim at comprehensiveness and the provision of detailed or technical information.) As almost everyone now knows, AIDS (Acquired Immune Deficiency Syndrome) is caused by a virus known as HIV (Human Immunodeficiency Virus) which leads to a partial or complete breakdown of the body's natural ability to fight off diseases, thus leaving the afflicted individual susceptible to rare cancers and serious infections.[8] Strictly speaking, no one has ever died from AIDS but, rather, from the other (opportunistic) infections that develop when the body's defences are weak.

The illnesses comprising AIDS can attack different parts of the body. Lung disease is the commonest form by which AIDS is diagnosed in the UK. This usually starts with a gradually progressive shortness of breath over the course of several weeks, generally accompanied by a non-productive cough and fevers. The organisms usually involved are pneumocystis carinii and cytomegalovirus (CMV). Skin disease is the next commonest form by which AIDS is diagnosed in gay men, though this appears to be rare in other risk groups. The problem here is a rare form of cancer known as Kaposi's Sarcoma, usually appearing on the skin or in the mouth, but also affecting the intestines and lymph nodes. It often appears as a firm red or purplish mark, flat or raised, which may enlarge and then appear in other places. It shouldn't be confused with minor skin problems, birthmarks, or the small blood spots so often found on ageing skin, which may look very similar.

Two other forms by which AIDS is diagnosed in gay men are intestinal disease and disorders of the central nervous system. The former occurs when the upper end of the oesophagus is infected by an exceptionally severe form of candida or thrush (a yeast-like fungal infection) which spreads down from the mouth. This produces chest pains and difficulty in swallowing. Another major intestinal symptom is severe and persistent diarrhoea that is unresponsive to conventional treatment. This is usually caused by cryptosporidiosis or cytomegalovirus (CMV) infection. Lastly, brain disease, which is caused by infections and rare cancers called lymphomas. Problems with the central nervous system can affect either a single area and lead to convulsions, partial paralysis or visual disturbance, or they might affect the brain more generally, causing alterations in personality and impairment of intellectual functions.

HIV is also the cause of two less severe AIDS-linked illnesses: ARC (Aids-Related Complex) and PGL (Persistent Generalized Lymphadenopathy). ARC is a broadly defined term used to describe those people who are known to be HIV positive and who have developed symptoms which indicate a suppressed immune system but which fall short of the case definition of AIDS. Such symptoms include profound fatigue, persistent fevers, unexplained weight loss, persistent diarrhoea and drenching night sweats. Often associated with this condition are unusually severe forms of shingles, herpes and thrush in the mouth. PGL is a relatively minor illness caused by HIV infection. Its principal feature is that the lymph nodes in the neck and armpits remain swollen and sometimes painful for a minimum of three months for no apparent reason other than HIV infection.

The Politics of AIDS

In the UK those at highest risk from AIDS, as already stated, are homosexual and bisexual men. However in the Third World, where

AIDS may reach levels significantly greater than in the West, it is clearly linked to heterosexual transmission. It is far from inconceivable that the pattern established in certain African countries, where the overwhelming majority of AIDS sufferers are heterosexuals, could also emerge in the UK and throughout the Western world.[9] Today, the fastest growing category of AIDS cases in the US is heterosexuals. If we follow the American pattern closely, the picture of AIDS as something confined to a few high-risk groups will change. It would then no longer be possible to think of AIDS as essentially linked to homosexuality.[10] Once we cease thinking of the disease as the issue of particular (and unpopular) groups and regard it, instead, as a public health problem, we arrive at the conclusion that the only 'high-risk' group is the human race. For in addition to affecting both heterosexuals and homosexuals, AIDS also imperils women as well as men, children as well as adults, rich as well as poor.

Plainly, then, AIDS like any virus knows neither nationality nor sexual orientation. And like every other historically recorded epidemic, it is no respecter of sex, age or wealth. Though the public's perception of AIDS has been shaped in no small part by the fact that the first reported cases in the West were almost exclusively among homosexual men, 'AIDS', as Dennis Altman has pointed out, 'is intrinsically no more gay than Legionnaires' Disease is an illness of ex-soldiers, or than rubella (German Measles) is inherently German.'[11]

(Though the first reported cases in the early 1980s were exclusively among gay men, the World Health Organization reported seven deaths from AIDS in Western Europe prior to 1979. The Center for Disease Control in Atlanta, Georgia, has suggested that Britain had cases of AIDS in the 1960s, while the US had a case as long ago as 1959. And at the International Conference on AIDS in Belgium in 1985, epidemiologists argued that, for more than a century, doctors have been describing an illness in Central Africa that sounds very much like AIDS.)

In view of the backlash against gays referred to above, it is therefore useful to see AIDS from a somewhat wider perspective. We might remind ourselves, for instance, that sexually transmitted diseases have been around for centuries. Prior to the discovery and subsequent use of penicillin in the 1930s, 60,000 people per year (including several thousand children) died from the early or late

132

consequences of syphilis. Looking at the army literature of the First World War we find that twenty-five per cent of British and Allied troops suffered from syphilis or gonorrhoea at any one time. Yet none of these statistics gave rise to calls for legislation against heterosexuality (neither does the recent rise in the number of cases of the genital papilloma virus, which is thought to cause cervical cancer in women). In short, syphilis in no way epitomized heterosexuality as AIDS now appears, for so many, to equate with homosexuality.[12] 'Gay = AIDS', a popular graffiti message reads, an equation that perfectly sums up the traditional fear that homosexuality may, in some mysterious way, be catching—the contagion theory of sexual attraction.

This insistence on the unbiased nature of AIDS is a necessary first step in dealing with the social stigma attached to this disease. Even more than lung cancer or cirrhosis of the liver, both of which are frequently linked to personal behaviour, AIDS has been seen as the fault of the sufferer. 'Homosexual men have only themselves to blame for their terrible plight,' an editorial in the popular press recently announced.[13] Hardly surprising, then, that people with AIDS are so often denied the care and concern readily afforded others with life-threatening diseases.

In this connection, we have noted that the media, and even on occasion the medical profession, have laid stress on 'homosexual promiscuity' as a factor 'explaining' AIDS.[14] The 'culprit', then, is seen as a certain lifestyle, not a specific organism. It is, of course, self-evident that promiscuity increases the risk of exposure to dangerous organisms. But this is a very different matter from creating the impression that promiscuity *as such* causes the disease. This distinction needs to be stressed, not least because there are many who are wedded to the idea that all gay men are sexual athletes having multiple and frequent sexual encounters involving many different partners.[15] What is especially worrying about such thinking is that people then conclude not simply that promiscuity is a risk factor, but that all those afflicted with AIDS have necessarily been promiscuous—which is not the case. It is bad enough to be ill, but to be also thought responsible for one's illness—when one, in fact, is the 'victim' of a virus—is intolerable.

The tendency to link gay men, promiscuity and AIDS in an unholy alliance certainly accords with a long tradition of perceiving epidemics as the consequence of God's displeasure (like the Black

Death) or widespread sin (American cholera in the nineteenth century). AIDS is only the most recent epidemic to conjure up such notions of disease as self-inflicted disorder, an attitude which too easily justifies the relative lack of concern for the present situation of homosexuals.[16]

Fear and ignorance of AIDS have been manipulated to erode concern for those at present most affected. The association of this disease with unpopular minorities (homosexuals and intravenous drug users) virtually guarantees that those most at risk are regarded with a greater degree of negativity, and experience forms of discrimination unknown to any other terminally ill individual. AIDS is not a gay disease, of course. But the power of prejudice can be chillingly greater than that of logic. And the fact remains that at present the majority of AIDS cases in the UK are gay men, so that before constructive self-help or counselling ensues, the morality issue must be separated from the problems of personal and public health. Condemnation is never a useful response to disease, but its prevalence during the present crisis testifies to the emotional turbulence surrounding this issue.

To Test or Not to Test

Faced as they are with public concern and their own understandable anxiety on the subject of AIDS, gay men are confronted with the difficult decision of whether or not to undergo a blood test which would show if they have been exposed to the virus. Since October 1985, hospital clinics have made the HIV test available to people from AIDS 'risk groups' and their sexual partners. This test determines whether or not antibodies to the virus are present. A positive result indicates the existence of antibodies (which are built up by the blood whenever a new virus, e.g. AIDS, enters the bloodstream), and shows that the person concerned has been infected with the virus at some point in the past and that they may still be infectious. It must be stressed that this is *not* a test for AIDS. In fact, at present there is no single definitive test for the disease. There are only procedures which check for opportunistic infections, cancers and immune deficiency. The HIV test, if positive, leaves open the question of whether the virus is still present, or whether it has been destroyed. Neither does it offer any indication of the severity of the infection. And it certainly does not show whether the person will ever develop AIDS.

Despite the unanswered questions raised by a positive result, many people will wish to take the test. It is easy to see why. With the advent of extensive media coverage and government health education, increasing numbers of people are voicing fears about their possible exposure to infection. Often, such fears reveal a misunderstanding of the routes of HIV infection. Anxieties within this group commonly relate to non-sexual modes of spread, like cooking and eating utensils, towels and linen, or non-sexual touching and kissing. People worried about this sort of contact will usually respond positively to clear and rational discussion of the known risks of infection and the absence of risk attached to harmless activities.

More difficult to convince are the 'worried well'. Within this category are those with various physical complaints that are seen as certain signs of HIV infection. Every pimple, rash, cold and cough may be regarded as a suspected symptom. (Not that this reaction is overly surprising, given the scare tactics of much of the present AIDS literature and journalism.) Despite repeated assurances that it is not at all likely that they will test positive (owing to low-risk sexual history, for instance), such people frequently remain unconvinced, the virus perhaps acting as a convenient vehicle for the expression of sexual guilt or existing high levels of anxiety and depression. Sadly, such individuals often fail to be reassured even when a test proves negative, and thus may require further referral for counselling over a long period.

For all others who are thinking of taking the test, it is crucial that they think through the reasons for doing so. It is here that counselling is especially helpful. Preparation for the possibility of a positive result (if this is what one's sexual or other history indicates) is essential in helping to cope with the aftermath of the test. It cannot be stressed enough that the complex issues surrounding the test must be understood before an informed and wise decision can be made. Consider, then, some of the possible arguments in favour of taking the test.

First of all, an advantage might be gained if a doctor who is experienced in dealing with HIV infection considers the test to be a useful part of his or her investigations. In such a situation, the potential value of the results in terms of treatment may be thought to outweigh the risks involved. Testing might also be advisable for those in the process of making decisions regarding the formation or continuation of a relationship. Individuals suspecting that they may have been infected with HIV and who are embarking on a new relationship without always being able to practise 'safe sex' (i.e. practices that prevent semen and blood from entering another person's body; see below for further discussion) might be advised to take the test if this were thought likely to serve as a check against unsafe practices in future.

Of course, one should not forget the difference between *assuming* and *knowing* that one is positive. Often a person assumes themselves infected because of previous 'risky' behaviour (i.e. non-safe sex practices), even though this in itself is insufficient evidence. Nevertheless it is sometimes the case that people are more likely to make constructive changes in their lifestyle if they learn that they are antibody positive. If taking the test serves as a sort of self-confrontation, forcing one to face up to the issue of AIDS and acting as a catalyst for the adoption of safe sex practices, then perhaps it ought to be seriously considered.

Also, some people whose lovers or partners have been diagnosed as having AIDS might understandably be concerned about their own state of health. Perhaps it is only by having the test that such individuals can get on with their lives and face the future. Once again, however, they must prepare themselves for the possibility that the test will be positive, with all that this entails. People given to worry are usually the least able to cope quickly with a positive result. Finally, testing might be thought advisable if an individual needs to know his or her health status in anticipation of future, non-anonymous testing—as might be required for travel purposes or emigration.[17]

If, then, the decision is made to take the test, the individual ought to seek assurance that the principle of confidentiality will be honoured and that only those who really need to know will be given the result. STD clinics, to which one can go without referral by a GP, are obliged by law to make certain that the results stay private. These can only be passed on to other sources with the written permission of the tested individual. It should be borne in mind, however, that if one is sent to other departments within a hospital, the specialists there are told the result, which will then probably enter the individual's general hospital notes. These tend to be less confidential than those kept in the STD clinic.

This matter of confidentiality is stressed because of many blatant cases of discrimination experienced by those whose test results have been made available to others. Although a positive result does not indicate that one has, or ever will have, AIDS, it has nonetheless been used in a discriminatory way. One of the most devastating consequences of the public's perception of AIDS is the large-scale discrimination it has fostered—not just against people with the disease or who are HIV positive, but against gays in general. Many gays have been sacked from their jobs and evicted from their flats. Lesbians also suffer from this misrepresentation, like the two Nottingham librarians dismissed from their jobs because of fears that they might spread the disease, despite lesbians being one of Britain's lowest risk groups (a fact rarely mentioned by the media).

One gay man who has experienced discrimination in both employment and housing is **Martyn**, a twenty-four-year-old clerk from Birkenhead:

Two years ago I was diagnosed as being seropositive [HIV antibody positive]. When I first got the news—the same day, in fact—I told this person at work, someone I regarded as a friend. I suppose I should have waited a bit, maybe not told anyone, especially not at work. But I was so upset I felt I had to talk to someone.

Anyway, by the very next day almost everyone in the office seemed to know. Two days later I received my first hate letter. It was on my desk when I arrived at work. By the end of the first week I had received three letters, all of them saying that I had better quit or things would get very bad for me, calling me a 'sick queer' and saying 'you got what you deserve' . . .

I was a coward about this—I resigned, not wanting to work around people like that and believing, at the time, that I'd quickly find another job. I didn't—not for another ten months.

It was during this period that I thought of committing suicide, that's how low I felt.

Someone—I suspect it was one of the people at work—had actually sent a letter to my landlady, an anonymous letter telling her I was gay and 'an AIDS case', and she threw me out. She couldn't really legally have done this, I don't think, but I didn't want to stay there after that, not after being told that my 'kind of person' wasn't wanted. I got out and found a small room somewhere else—twice as expensive. My savings started to drain away . . .

I felt like a sexual leper. It was as if I had lost total control of my life. I never felt as alone or as helpless as I did then.

Anti-gay abuse and discrimination have greatly increased since AIDS, and one should be aware that the reactions of others (especially employers and landlords) to your taking the test, regardless of the result, can be unpredictable, sometimes leading to unforeseen, adverse consequences. Therefore, though it is important to give vent to one's feelings in the immediate aftermath of the test, it is also wise to think carefully about who (and whether, at this stage) to tell. One is under no obligation to inform others that the test is being taken—far less that the result is positive. Even knowing that you are at risk may cause hostile reactions from others, including family and friends.

An exception might be considered in the case of one's GP. If you become ill, your GP should be told immediately of a positive result to prevent any dangerous delay in diagnosis. Here, again, one would try to make certain that doctors are aware of the need for confidentiality. For though there are no rational or medical grounds for discrimination purely on the basis of a positive test result, it is not so easy to persuade others that this is so. Furthermore, proving discrimination and obtaining legal redress is often extremely difficult and time-consuming.

According to **Daley**, a union representative at a college of printing, discrimination based on the fear of AIDS is more serious in the area of jobs and housing than the public generally realizes:

There's a bit of support for gays on paper—you know, policy documents, DHSS booklets, etc. But it doesn't always get translated into active support. I know three HIV positive gay men who were literally harassed out of their jobs, and one of them as a direct consequence lost his accommodation . . .
I'm worried, too, that if schools are allowed to drop out of local authority control, gay teachers—lesbians and gay men alike—won't be very well protected.
In this climate of ignorance and—let's face it—hatred, anti-gay action at the workplace is a real possibility. I wouldn't be at all surprised if this is just the beginning, that we'll be seeing anti-gay legislation in the next few years. Why not? Even now, discrimination against homosexuals is *still* not illegal. I'm not at all optimistic about the future.

The comments made by Daley and Martyn give added urgency to the need for being well acquainted with the various groups and organizations helpful to gays in situations such as those described. Gay community advice and support groups, as well as social service agencies responsible for home help and housing, can provide much-needed support. As far as counsellors are concerned, they should plan an active liaison with these organizations and agencies as an integral part of their work. (See Guide to Organizations Giving Advice and Help.)

The advent of AIDS has also caused many gays to be refused life and health insurance. Indeed, at present no major insurance company will accept people who are antibody positive for any type of life insurance. As the 1986 annual conference of the local government union NALGO stated, 'AIDS sufferers, those with positive HIV antibody tests, and others in the 'at risk' groups, are being unfairly denied access to life insurance. This is part and parcel of the AIDS panic which has been used to discriminate against, and blame, the largest affected group—gay men.'[18]

In the area of private health care, the policy of BUPA is the clearest sign of the alarm bells sounded by AIDS. For new members BUPA now imposes a five-year period after joining during which benefit for treatment of AIDS and AIDS-related conditions will not be payable. As far as the National Health Service is concerned, Dr Alex Hills of the Terrence Higgins Trust has pointed out that there are many cases of gay men being refused dental and routine medical treatment, while a recent survey showed that sixty per cent of doctors were hostile to AIDS patients and would refuse to treat them—though the General Medical Council has warned that doctors are liable to face charges of serious professional misconduct should they refuse to treat people with AIDS. It is equally unethical, says the GMC, to withhold treatment from a patient on the basis of a moral judgment about the individual's supposed lifestyle. Doctors found guilty of serious professional misconduct can be struck off.[19]

Many homosexuals are also denied mortgages and loans. According to the Banking Information Service, the banks do not generally give mortgages without life insurance. If an applicant is refused life insurance, a mortgage request will also be refused. The same is true for bank loans requiring life cover. Moreover, the most popular mortgages—roughly seventy per cent of all those that are granted— are linked to endowment policies, with applicants often turned down on the grounds of health.[20]

No less disturbing, and a further reason to think very carefully about being tested, is the ominous press speculation on the subject of quarantine. This may seem rather far-fetched, and I suspect it will never happen, but it is worth recalling that in the last century the British Contagious Diseases Act required that prostitutes and 'licentious women' be subject to registration and fortnightly health inspections. But however unlikely quarantine may be, in the present climate of fear and growing intolerance (for instance, the calls in some parliamentary quarters to reintroduce legislation making homosexual acts a criminal offence), it is not at all surprising that some in the gay community wonder whether AIDS is not becoming the latest means of regulating, if not altogether outlawing, gay sexuality.

Apart from such discrimination, one of the principal drawbacks of taking the test is that a negative result may cause a false sense of security, while a positive result can provoke extreme anxiety and long-term depression. I know of no one for whom a positive result has not been accompanied by enormous psychological stress and frustration. Many people, no matter how carefully they may think they have geared themselves to the result, are emotionally unprepared in the event. **Graham Wilkinson** has written in *Gay Times* of the shock he experienced following a positive test result:[21]

> I knew I was at some risk and had experienced some symptoms. However, when I got the result I was in shock, and it wasn't until I had spoken with someone who had also been diagnosed that I really began to accept the situation . . .
>
> That was two years ago. But I think about it every day—when I'm tired, when I go to the toilet, when I cough, when I see someone I fancy.

It cannot be stressed too often that the news of a positive result is usually shocking. One hears again and again of people who were traumatized by the experience, who felt altogether alienated and isolated, withdrawing into themselves and shunning friends and others who, it was feared, might regard them as pariahs. The American writer **Edmund White**, who now lives in Paris, discusses the impact of the test on himself and his lover:

> We took the test and waited two months for interpretation of the results. It was an agonizing period, as in the intervening time his

ex-lover had tested and was antibody positive . . . The results showed that he was 'negative' and I was 'positive', just as I had thought. Well, we then went off for a romantic trip to Vienna which had already been planned. I just wept the whole time. That was all summer.

Since then, I would say we've had real strains on the relationship, but it continues . . . Every gay couple I know is going through something like this. When only one is positive then there is the danger that he may feel like a pariah. This whole thing therefore creates a totally new moralistic atmosphere.[22]

Perhaps the principal argument against taking the test, given the fact that it does not diagnose AIDS and often results in discrimination and anxiety, is the fact that it leads to no constructive action that could not just as well be taken without the test. I refer here not only to safer sex practices, but also to the necessity for developing a sensible regard for the various means of increasing one's physical and psychological strength (good nutrition, adequate sleep, stress reduction, etc.) and thereby limiting immune damage and reducing the risks of illness. If, in future, new drugs or therapies are developed which would definitely assist those who are HIV positive, that fact would doubtless alter the whole nature of the argument. Certainly there are now signs of guarded optimism within the scientific community that additional methods of treatment will become available and that, in combination, they may offer hope of an effective treatment. But this, at present, is not the case.[23]

People with AIDS

We have considered only a few reactions to testing positive. There are others. Indeed, one sees different stages of psychological response to being diagnosed as positive or as having AIDS. Although these stages do not necessarily follow the order listed below, or are all invariably experienced by everyone, certain reactions are characteristic: denial, shock, fear and anxiety, depression, anger and frustration, guilt, acceptance.

The point at which a person is diagnosed as being HIV positive, as we have seen in the cases of Graham Wilkinson and Edmund White, is a point of crisis. Typical initial reactions to discovering symptoms of the disease itself are denial and shock, both of which were experienced and are well-remembered by **Roy**, a twenty-five-year-old social worker:

> It will be two years ago this month that I saw the first lesions. They were these little purplish-red spots, two of them, one above my ankle and the other on the sole of my foot. I don't know how long they were there. Not more than a few days, I suppose. I noticed them at the same time, in the shower. At first I thought they were bruises, or a rash, maybe, and that they'd go away.
>
> I was afraid to look the next day. But I did. They were still there. There seemed to be a third one, too—one that I hadn't noticed. I tried ignoring them, just pretending like they weren't there. For weeks I did this. But it was really all I could think about. Nothing else mattered but those spots. Because deep down, I knew what they were. It was just that, I was so frightened. I kept thinking, 'No, it can't be. I still feel fine.'
>
> When I showed a friend, this friend whose ex-lover had Kaposi's, he took one look and he said, I'll never forget the way he said it, 'That's it!' It was like a death warrant. But still I couldn't believe it. Or didn't want to . . .
>
> Six weeks later I finally got the courage to see a doctor. That's when I had my answer. It was Kaposi's Sarcoma, he said. I had to wait ten days for the results of the biopsy, and I was shocked. I can remember being called in by the doctor, who was very good, very sympathetic. But I didn't hear a word. I was numb with panic. It was like he was a hundred miles away, his voice getting smaller and smaller as he went on, saying one thing and another, and all I could think of was: I've got it. This is it. I've got AIDS. I'm twenty-three years old and I've got AIDS and I'm going to die.

There are many varieties of denial. In some cases it is the principal defence against seeing the extent of a problem and its possible consequences. As such, it prevents a person from seeking confirmation or treatment. Denial might occasionally manifest itself as a disdainful attitude in which certain extreme forms of behaviour act as a means of disproving the truth. A supportive environment is then essential to encourage the development of more positive defences. But denial is also, for some, a lifeline: the only coping mechanism available until one is able to absorb the full implications and meaning of being ill. We shouldn't argue with such denial which, up to a certain point, may be necessary and useful. Time must be allowed for the news to sink in. Shock will mean that, as in the case of the person newly diagnosed, like Roy, very little information or advice will be taken in. This can be a period of emotional 'ventilation', when the individual gives expression to a rush of intense feelings. Fear, anxiety and depression are characteristic at such a juncture, as in the case of **Neil**, a twenty-eight-year-old dancer from Cardiff:

> I was told I had AIDS on a beautiful, sunny morning in July. It was the sort of day that makes you feel good to be alive. Funny, isn't it, because I remember thinking later, as I left the hospital, this is the first day of the end of my life. I *know* it sounds melodramatic and self-pitying, but I don't care. I think I've earned the right to feel just a little sorry for myself . . .
>
> I'll never forget the day or the time or everything that happened *just before*. I draw a blank on what happened after—even though I was with a counsellor for over an hour. All I remember is that I stumbled out of that building and got on a bus and rode around for hours, then finally went to Hyde Park and found a bench in the middle of nowhere and cried my head off.
>
> The next day, I think you could say I started acting a bit crazy, just saying everything that came into my head—mainly a lot of babbling about my so-called future. Like I wondered, 'Will I be disfigured?' 'Will my friends steer clear of me?' 'And what about my lover? Was he infected, too?' 'Were we infecting others?' 'Would we *both* lose our jobs?' I couldn't afford to lose my job. I just don't have that much money saved. 'Was I *certain* to die?' 'What would happen after death?' 'Was the rest of my life to be nothing but constant worry over AIDS—nothing else but wondering whether today was the day, or would tomorrow be even worse?' I went on like that for a month, maybe longer. It was terrible. Like hell on earth.

Fear, anxiety and depression are understandable reactions after being diagnosed with a life-threatening disease. There is fear and anxiety over the course the illness will take, the effects of medication and treatment, the possibility of abandonment, as well as existential concerns. There is depression, too, in the absence of a cure, just as there is at the prospect of limits imposed by ill health and the possibility of social, occupational and emotional rejection. The counsellor's immediate goal, then, is to help people get through this period of crisis—to help them reach out to those they trust for comfort and support and, at least for the first few days following diagnosis, to provide a lifeline (telephone numbers of community agencies concerned with AIDS, for instance) and, if at all possible, to ensure that no one is left alone at a time when extreme reactions are most likely to occur.

Counsellors will face additional challenges during the days and weeks following a diagnosis of AIDS. Not the least of these is the anger and frustration felt by the person with AIDS. This is an emotion which, for **Curt**, thirty-nine, was the strongest he experienced in the first month of being, as he puts it, 'a walking time-bomb':

My first reaction was, 'Why me? Why did this have to happen to *me*? How could God allow this to come about?' My lifestyle had always been moderate. I was never what you'd call promiscuous. I wasn't obsessed with sex, which people assume you *must* be . . .

I met Rob two years after coming out, when I was twenty-nine. We lived together for nine years, until about a year-and-a-half ago when—it was shortly after his mother's death—he returned to New Zealand to look after his father. I was mostly monogamous for the time we lived together. Not exclusively, though. And I suppose I've had maybe four or five sexual encounters since then, which includes one brief but fairly intense affair—someone I met at a church social . . .

I said my lifestyle was moderate, and that includes drugs, or what's called recreational drugs, which I've never, ever used. I don't smoke. I rarely drink. I've never even used poppers! I've got a great job which I love, with a lot of good mates. But then at thirty-nine I discover I've got AIDS. And I ask myself, 'What the hell do I do now? What do I *do* with my life? How much longer am I going to be able to work?' I can't answer. Life goes on, but I don't really feel a part of it. I wish I didn't feel angry, but I do. It's the only thing that's holding me together.

I feel hurt and cheated, and on top of that I don't think the people who could help are helping—certainly not my church, which just doesn't care enough: a case of the disease fitting the patient's character, I think. There are even cranks who think this is all God's wrath on homosexuals. But if it is, he certainly looks kindly on lesbians, doesn't he, the group at lowest risk? . . .

I don't know. I think of a friend of mine who committed suicide after he discovered his first purple spot. Poisoned himself. But before he did that, he telephoned his friends to say goodbye. How many gay men do you suppose are doing that? Where's the public's sympathy? There's not a lot of that around. With AIDS it's like, so long as it's happening to queers, who the hell cares? Sure, let's find a cure. But not too quickly.

Probably the hardest thing to accept is that, in human terms, AIDS is without meaning. There are no innocent or guilty parties when a disease strikes. There are only sufferers, whose search for rational explanation is understandable, if ultimately fruitless. Many, like Curt, express problems with their religious beliefs at such a time. In my own experience I have found that, even prior to AIDS, many gays have already rejected the formal religious structure of organizations, though they have retained a personal set of values. Although the health crisis has motivated some to return to religion, many have found that it does not address their needs, the Church often finding itself caught between concern and condemnation when it comes to homosexual activity. Developing new forms of 'faith' as a response to health issues—a sense of self-worth, a goal or purpose in life, an active participation in fighting the disease, a positive mental attitude—is one way of reinforcing one's self-determination and sense of control: a process leading to a greater self-respect and well-being.

Perhaps the strongest challenge confronting the person with AIDS is holding on to one's self-esteem. For AIDS is a disease that attacks not only the body, but one's sense of identity and self-respect as well. This is not surprising, since many have put the responsibility for the disease on the sufferer. It is often assumed, as we have seen, that gays who are now sick have only themselves to blame. Such heartless judgements can contribute significantly to an individual's sense of isolation, shame and self-blame, possibly reactivating dormant conflicts concerning one's sexual orientation. One of the principal problems causing distress among people with AIDS is this social stigma attached to their disease—a stigma that denies to the sick the caring and concern so spontaneously offered to virtually everyone else suffering a life-threatening illness. This is tragic, for such stigmatization causes additional stress for people with AIDS, possibly putting their lives in further danger.

What is deeply distressing to these people and, indeed, to the entire gay community, is the relative lack of compassion and dignity extended to those most directly affected by this epidemic. Gays with

AIDS, and those who are HIV positive, have too often been un-
feelingly smeared, scapegoated and stereotyped. Even if this tendency subsides as our understanding of the disease grows more
sophisticated, the damage will have been done, as can be seen in
the case of **Dougal**, a bookshop clerk in his early twenties who
speaks of society's negative attitudes having become internalized,
producing painful feelings of guilt and self-blame:

> After the bombshell of finding I was [HIV] positive, I began
> thinking things like, 'Mum and Dad were right to be horrified
> when I first told them I was gay,' and 'The Church was right all
> along.' That sort of thing. I blamed myself completely. I spent all
> my time accusing myself, pointing to the three or four affairs that
> I had had, as if my lifestyle were to blame.
> Throughout this time I had feelings of being a sort of leper—
> diseased, dirty, even deadly . . . I remember as a kid I felt such a
> freak for being gay. I finally learned to deal with it—accept it,
> even, and to like myself. Now I'm back to square one, because I
> feel a freak again—this time for having AIDS. All my former
> arguments about being glad to be gay, about it being a positive
> thing in my life—and really every good feeling about myself—
> were shattered. Just shattered, completely.

Attributing responsibility to oneself for a life-threatening condition
can be extremely stressful, and devastating to one's self-image. It
often leads to isolation, thus seriously impairing one's ability to
cope—both physically and psychologically. A positive attitude about
one's sexual orientation unquestionably results in less stress, less
depression, greater well-being, and a better chance of remaining
healthy. It is therefore crucial that this internalized homophobia is
uncovered and dealt with. Again and again one must emphasize to
AIDS sufferers that they are sick because of exposure to a virus that
knows no morals, a disease that infects both heterosexuals and
homosexuals, men and women, adults and children. To hold that
any single group of 'culprits' is responsible for AIDS is, simply,
ignorant.

Summary
This chapter began by pointing to the 'gay backlash' of the 1980s.
The provocation for the recent upsurge of prejudice, discrimination

and violence against gays is AIDS, whose impact in Britain has been felt most by the group presently at highest risk—homosexual men. Before exploring the extent and psychosocial consequences of such attitudes, we looked at the nature of the disease: its origin, cause, spread, effects on the immune system, and methods of transmission. Much emphasis has been given to the fact that AIDS, like any virus, knows neither nationality nor sexual orientation. Though the public's perception of AIDS has been shaped in no small part by the fact that gays presently form the highest risk group, the disease is intrinsically no more 'gay' than German measles is inherently German.

Fear and ignorance of AIDS have been manipulated to erode concern for those at present most affected. The association of this disease with unpopular minorities virtually guarantees that those most at risk are regarded with a greater degree of negativity, and experience forms of discrimination unknown to any other group whose lives are at risk. Faced as they are with public concern and their own understandable anxiety on the subject of AIDS, gay men are confronted with the difficult decision of whether or not to undergo a blood test that shows if they have been exposed to the virus. For all those thinking of taking the test, it is crucial that they think through the reasons for doing so. Several arguments have been advanced for taking the test: if a doctor experienced in dealing with HIV infection considers it to be a useful part of his or her investigations; if a person is in the process of making decisions regarding the formation or continuation of a relationship; if individuals who suspect that they have been infected with HIV are embarking on a new relationship without always being able to practise safer sex; if taking the test would force one to face up to the issue of AIDS and, therefore, adopt safer sex practices; or if one is overly anxious due to a lover having been diagnosed as having AIDS.

If the decision is made to take the test, assurances of confidentiality must be sought. This is most important due to many cases of blatant discrimination experienced by those whose test results have been made available to others. **Martyn**, for instance, experienced discrimination in both employment and housing, while **Daley** warns that discrimination based on the fear of AIDS is more serious in the area of jobs and housing than the public generally realizes. The advent of AIDS has also caused many gays to be refused life and health insurance, mortgages and loans. Apart from such discrimination as this, many who have taken the test, like **Graham Wilkinson** and **Edmund White**, were emotionally unprepared for the results. But perhaps the principal argument against taking the test is the fact that it leads to no constructive action that could not just as well be taken without the test, i.e. safer sex practices and the development of a sensible regard for the various means of increasing one's physical and psychological strength.

Typical initial reactions to discovering symptoms of AIDS are denial and shock (**Roy**); fear, anxiety and depression (**Neil**); anger and frustration (**Curt**). Perhaps the strongest challenge confronting the person with AIDS is holding on to one's self-respect. For AIDS attacks not only the body, but one's sense of identity as well. **Dougal** discussed the way in which society's negative attitudes had become internalized, producing painful feelings of guilt and self-blame. Thus we must emphasize over and again that AIDS is a virus that knows no morals, and that no group ought to be held responsible for the disease.

9

Surviving AIDS

In the depth of winter, I finally learned that within me lay an invincible summer.

Albert Camus, *La Peste*

Telling Friends and Family

It is the fear and ignorance surrounding the issue of AIDS—the tendency to see AIDS not just as a life-threatening disease but a shameful one—that is so discouraging to gays who might wish to share their health concerns with others. Even when friends are 'sophisticated' there may be problems, as **Des**, a thirty-year-old actor, explains:

> My straight friends, like my gay ones, bless 'em, they're very *Guardian*, terribly broad-minded, very accepting and quite soph-isticated in their understanding of the 'Situation'. Most of them, at any rate. Yet I was still very, very cautious about spilling the beans. And I'm certain that this was right. So long as I was 'only' HIV positive it wasn't necessary to say anything. Only my lover Jim knew, and he's been fine—heroic, in fact, especially now that I've been diagnosed with PCP [Pneumocystis Carinii Pneumonia] . . .
> It's been necessary to tell others recently. People aren't blind! They can see the changes in my appearance—my weight, in particular. And then I've had a lot of worry, and that shows too.
> Most people have been very good, I will say that. But with one or two, well, it's been different. Some have shunned me altogether. A few, especially those with children, tend to keep their distance. It's as if the disease is morally contagious. Some find it depressing to have me around—though they'd never say so. I mean AIDS is identified with death, isn't it? I'm sure my friends don't think I've noticed these reactions but I have, no matter how tactful they've

149

been. You develop a sixth sense about such things when you're sick. I see it, and it hurts.

Despite the difficulties of Des, experience clearly shows that those who are able to be open with at least one or more trusted friends, family members or a counsellor will feel less distress and are better able to cope. This was certainly true in the case of **Edgar**, forty-six, a teacher at a London comprehensive:

From the time I was diagnosed with AIDS in March 1986 till December of that year, I couldn't tell anyone. No one at all. It was the greatest period of depression in my life. I wanted to tell someone, but I was afraid of upsetting them—afraid, too, of their reaction.

Then around Christmas time I decided to tell my sister, who has known for years that I'm gay. I guess I've been closer to her than anyone else. Still, I put it off a number of times. Then finally, a week before Christmas, I rang her and asked if I could come over. Because I couldn't let it all out at once, when I saw her I was beating round the bush; and she listened, sort of picking at the ends of a curl as I was talking, wondering what I had come to say. And when I told her, her fingers suddenly froze in mid-air, and she looked at me without saying a word for about a minute, and then she got up and sat next to me and took my hand and she said, 'Oh, Eddie, I *am* sorry. But you're not alone. You've got me. You've got the family. I'll see to that. We love you for what you are. And we'll stick together. And Eddie, we'll get through it. You'll see.'

That's when I broke down and cried, and so did she, the two of us bent over one another with our arms around each other, each trying to out-blubber the other I think. Later on we laughed. Then we started talking about the future. From that day on everything seemed to improve—even, a little, my health. I'm in pretty good shape at the moment. I've been in remission. I haven't had any visible lesions for, I think it's four, five months. I don't know how long this will last, and I *know* I'm not about to raise any false hopes. But sharing this with others has made life one helluva lot easier.

Although many gays have disclosed their homosexuality to family members, research done in the United States shows that although approximately eighty-one per cent of men desire counselling after discovering that they have AIDS, one-third of these had not discussed their health problems with one or more family members for several months following their diagnosis.[1] For Edgar to have confided in his sister, especially given his earlier anxieties, was a courageous decision. Unquestionably the revelation was made easier by the fact that his sister already knew of his homosexuality. One of the most common reasons for not discussing health concerns with others is not having come out as gay. Imagine, then, the situation of those who, having been diagnosed with a life-threatening illness, must tell their family both that they are ill with AIDS and that they are homosexual. To contemplate self-disclosure at such a time can cause panic and anxiety, and raises understandable fears of rejection just when one is particularly vulnerable. Being forced to come out and then being subjected to condemnation is an all-too-common occurrence, as the story of **Ashley**, a twenty-four-year-old London librarian, reveals:

It was two months after learning that I had AIDS that I decided to tell my parents. They live in a small village in the Midlands, and their views on homosexuality are just so negative that I guess I never had the nerve. You remember when there were all those programmes on AIDS early in 1987, when you couldn't turn on the TV without seeing some AIDS chart or pictures of the AIDS virus? It was on just one of those weekends that I had gone home to tell my parents . . .

I had already developed symptoms, and I was really scared: night sweats and diarrhoea and swollen glands, none of which they knew about. And I looked pretty terrible which, you know—it's funny now, thinking back—they reckoned was due to my living in London. Anyway, just as I was about to say something, my father flicks on this 'Horizon' programme on whether the spread of AIDS could be halted, and says something like, real angry: 'They brought it on themselves, didn't they?' That's why I waited another day, till just a few hours before I left, in fact. You know, I didn't know which was going to be worse, either—to tell them that I'm gay or that I've got AIDS. And I was really feeling bad, being up most of the night, shaking. I kept thinking that I had to get back to London to see someone about the way I felt.

But I told them. God, I'll never forget. 'Mum, Dad,' I said, 'I've got bad news. I just couldn't tell you before.' And my mother, she looked so frightened; she kept asking what it was, and I started trembling. Then I remember taking her hand and saying, 'Mum, I'm so sorry. I'm not at all well. I've got AIDS.' I said it that way, all at once, because I couldn't find the right words. Then I said, 'I'm gay.' I practically shouted it: 'I'm homosexual.'

It was only when I said that that my mother, she suddenly took her hand from mine and stood up, looking at me with such . . . disbelief, and walked out of the room. My father, all he could bring himself to say was, 'Get a grip on yourself. What are you talking about? Why are you upsetting your mother like this?' What he meant was, 'How dare you tell us you're a poof.' It's like, all they heard me tell them was, 'I'm gay.' The fact that I might die, it just didn't register. Later, yes. But not at first. The real shock of that afternoon, the thing that sent them reeling, was that they had a homosexual for a son.

Ashley's experience is one shared by many gay people with AIDS: they are forced to come out as gay when sick, and to deal with rejection and guilt due to their sexual orientation at a time when they are already under enormous stress. The level of denial in the families of such people is probably very high to begin with if the sexual identity of the child is unrevealed prior to discovery of the illness. Parents may need counselling, too, not only in making a double adjustment to a pair of—for them—painful revelations, but because many will seek some 'meaning' in their child's illness or death, and are deeply anguished if unable to find it. This was true in the case of **Curt's Mother** (see p. 144) who spoke to me some months after her son's death:

When Curt told my husband he was sick with AIDS, Paul's reaction was the same as several years previously when Curt told him he was gay. His first reaction was, 'For God's sake, don't tell your mother; it would kill her.' I was shocked when I learned, of course. I won't deny it . . . It's strange, but I had never wanted to talk about this AIDS thing, perhaps because I always feared the worst . . .

I lost my father in World War Two, and it took my mother and me years to deal with that. Yet I found it much easier to explain that sort of loss. And knowing that he died for a reason—I mean, it was a cause we believed in, wasn't it? And that made it easier to cope. You could talk to people about it, too, and they were full of understanding and sympathy.

With AIDS, it's different. People are more horrified than sympathetic. They make you feel, somehow, shamed . . . I keep thinking now that Curt is gone that it's not supposed to happen this way. My son was supposed to bury *me*, and here I am burying him, just like I buried my parents before him. It seems so unjust, so senseless.

There is a widespread spectrum of family response to a gay son's revelations—from rallying round in consolidated support to total rejection. Many people with AIDS feel that, as far as telling their parents is concerned, knowledge is less upsetting than ignorance. Furthermore, the majority of families will wish to be involved during the course of an individual's illness and, as such, can provide comfort and help at a crucially important time.

But it is not only the immediate family who provide comfort for the person with AIDS. Indeed, the concept of 'family' itself has been challenged by the experience of AIDS, with many medical people, social service and mental health professionals experiencing for the first time the 'extended', 'non-traditional' gay family of partners, lovers and friends. Recognizing and respecting the legitimacy of intimate gay relationships is a priority for the counsellor, who should grant this extended family the same consideration and rights as relatives.

Often overlooked in discussions of AIDS are the partners and lovers of those who have died. A great majority of these survivors are young people who have never before experienced the death of a loved one, making their pain all the more confusing. Such people have gone through the most profound emotional experiences—first, in coping with the shock of a loved one's illness and, second, in confronting grief. They also find themselves coping with dramatically changed circumstances upon the death of a partner. **Hugh**, whose lover died of Kaposi's Sarcoma, speaks of a range of reactions doubtless familiar to many:

Frank was afraid of telling me at first. In fact it was several days before he said anything at all. I understand. It was a terrible time for him, and he was worried about my reaction. I still feel sad about that though, because we had been together for ten years and I feel he should have trusted me more. But maybe it's not surprising, because there are so many horror stories about people's bad reactions . . .

Frank was sick for over two years before he died. We went through a real roller-coaster of emotions. All ups and downs, in and out of hospital, and looking so bad once that these two little kids on the street who saw him as he was coming out of the hospital after a painful chemotherapy session, they literally screamed when they saw him. I wasn't with him that day, and so I couldn't shield him from the hurt. I felt guilty for not being there—especially as he was feeling so low and sick.

You feel so inadequate and confused, but especially guilty because, for instance, we would argue over things like Frank refusing to eat or being too exhausted at night to talk. It's just that there was—there was all the nausea, the diarrhoea, the fresh sarcomas. I can't tell you how many times I felt I couldn't cope. There were times, too, when he was jealous of my health, saying he couldn't understand why I was all right and he was so sick, but then he'd feel bad for saying it. So we'd *both* feel guilty, then.

And on top of all this there were practical concerns—legal matters, like what would happen when he died, his will, power of attorney, whether to get in touch again with a sister (which he did) who rejected him years ago when she learned he was gay. God, I could go on and on . . .

Finally, Frank died. I was with him. He was in such a bad way that, in the end, I wanted him to die.

I sat by his bed after he went, and I kissed his cheek. He was so thin, so still. I can't tell you how good it was to see him peaceful like that, after all the pain . . .

For more than two years I had tried to hide my feelings. And when he died I just fell apart. And someone said, a very close friend of ours—and she really meant well—she said, 'I'm really so surprised at you. I thought you were so strong.' And I shouted, 'Well, I'm not! I'm just *not* that strong!' I couldn't control myself. I just wasn't that strong, and I wasn't going to pretend—not any more, not now that he was dead . . .

But the very worst thing that happened after he died wasn't me losing control like that. The worst thing was that after ten years together, ten years of sharing everything, of loving one another like we did, his family just totally rejected me. They had never accepted me, so that when I phoned to tell them that Frank had died, his sister answered, and she just hung up, like I was a murderer, as if I had caused his death.

There is possibly no experience more certain to make one feel inadequate than watching someone you love suffer through a debilitating disease. For the partner of the person with AIDS, the emotional and physical strain can be terrible, and may—as in the case of Hugh—be further compounded by the hostile, rejecting attitudes of a loved one's relatives. For other survivors, like **Leon** who lives in San Francisco, there were further bereavement problems:

> For months after Mikey died it was all I could talk about—Mikey and me. But you know in a city like San Franciso, where AIDS is Topic Number One, people can get tired of hearing about it. Or else they offer advice, like 'Isn't it about time you decorated his room, or gave away his clothes, or started socializing?' . . . I needed to talk, but there's been too much of that in this city. People get tired of hearing you ramble on about your dead lover. Still, it's necessary, and I was lucky in having a mutual friend— an ex-lover of Mikey's—that I could share my feelings with . . .
> One of the things I felt, but could never bring myself to talk about when Mikey was alive, probably because it really only hit me when he died, was the possibility of my catching AIDS from him. And it occurred to me, too, that maybe I had given AIDS to Mikey, and that my time was next. But that this time there'd be no lover to hold my hand.

The difficulties that Leon confronted are fairly characteristic of those experienced by many men whose lovers have died. It is important for such survivors to talk through their feelings, to give vent to pent-up emotions, and to resist the occasional pressure of friends to bury the process of bereavement immediately after the funeral. After the death, the partner may become much more acutely aware of the reality of AIDS, and consequently feel increasing anxiety about his own state of health. This is understandable given the partner's proximity to the disease during the lover's illness. Finally, the survivor may feel stigmatized by his association with the departed. The understanding of others is crucial in countering these intense feelings of alienation and isolation.

It has also proved helpful for the survivors to involve themselves in volunteer activity organized by the gay community—for example at the Terrence Higgins Trust, Body Positive, Gay Switchboard, and Friend. Those who have so involved themselves tend to cope better and recover quicker. Even for those who have not had to face the ordeal experienced by people like Leon, becoming involved in community activities has often proved powerfully therapeutic, both for themselves and for those they assist. This is borne out in the experience of **Merv**, a writer, who is himself in the ARC category and who has for the past year been a 'buddy'—a person who befriends and cares for those who are living with AIDS:

I could have just given up, once I discovered what I had. And I'll tell you, I nearly did. I felt that bad, having come down with just about everything—shingles, herpes, constant diarrhoea, night sweats and, for months, these swollen nodes in the groin. One after the other, and some of them at the same time . . . It took me a long while to go to the clinic. It was a difficult diagnosis to cope with, once the Middlesex told me. But I had heard about Body Positive and I went on one of their counselling courses. Looking back on it I think it was a way of getting out of myself, of feeling less anxious. Still, I don't think it matters what your original motives were. It's what you do . . .

I really came face to face with AIDS for the first time when I met Bill. We hit it off straight away. Bill wasn't in very good shape. He had given up his job, which depleted his bank account and led to a lot of depression and boredom, all of which worsened his health. And he was totally isolated, because he had been very closeted all his life, not telling his family or the people he worked with about being gay. He had always been so concerned about being 'unmasked' as a homosexual (this is the way he put it: being 'unmasked') that he completely separated his social and his sexual life, with not a lot of love in either. So now, when he needed someone more than at any other time in his life I guess, there was no one. It's a miracle he heard about us, or else it would have been a whole lot worse for him, I'm sure . . .

I saw Bill almost every day. When I couldn't go to see him—like on days when *I* wasn't feeling well—there was someone else to see him. I shopped for him, made his meals, read to him, and we listened to music together and talked. We talked a lot. Bill said he had never talked about himself so much, and that it seemed odd that only now, when he was so sick, could he do it, and how much better he felt for it. He said if only he could get well he'd be a different person. He'd be 'out' and 'open' with people. But his health got worse. Every day it seemed to get worse. But he held on. He really *did* hold on because, suddenly, he felt so good about himself. Just as he was dying. This is what having someone around meant to him. A buddy he could talk to . . .

One day, it was last October—the fourteenth—he died. He had felt such pain all that day. It was after we had listened to some of his favourite music and I had gone into the kitchen to get some water. He had been sitting up in bed. When I came back, it was over. At last. I found him with his head to one side and this little smile on his mouth, and his hands across his chest. And so calm . . .

I know it helped Bill to have someone who cared. And I did care, too. But he helped me as well—at least as much as I helped him. Just to see that kind of courage. And his determination to get as much out of life as possible. You see, he was such a different person during the time he was ill. He was able to accept himself for the first time. It's that which really got to me. That's what gave me hope. And pride. Because I'm proud of Bill, and Bill made me proud of myself.

Hope

Preserving self-pride in such trying times is a daunting challenge. And finding hope in the absence of a definitive vaccine or cure will not be an easy task, not least because of the simplified terrors raised by many careless and crude statistics brandished before the general public (for instance, the alleged '100 per cent mortality rate' for AIDS), the effects of which were keenly felt by **Ben**, a twenty-two-year-old trainee pharmacist:

Before I got AIDS, like everyone else I thought of it as the end of the line—the no-hope disease. AIDS equals death. It was that equation which hit me hardest after being diagnosed with PCP. I nearly gave up hope . . . I never kept it a secret that I had AIDS, though there are times when I wish I had. The other weekend at a party, a friend of mine introduced me to a few people, and I overheard one of them say just as I turned to talk to someone else,

'I wonder how long he's got, he looks so well.' Can you imagine? . . .

Okay, maybe I *don't* have that long, but if that's the way I look at
it, that I'm living on borrowed time, I'm done for. It's difficult to
think positive when everyone around you seems agreed that
you're a victim, a statistic, and that there's nothing anyone can
do. You've been given a death sentence . . . There's so much
death around. It's easy to lapse into despair and just give up—
which makes you sicker. I know! I've been around several people
who gave up hope, and most of them aren't here today. Why not?
Because in their mind they were already dead. And the body
simply followed suit.

As Ben points out, finding hope is not an easy task. But it is a
necessary one. People sometimes speak of 'false hope' and its
dangers. But how very much worse a state is hopelessness, where
people are depressed and withdrawn as a consequence of being
bombarded by pessimistic forecasts and negative messages which
induce self-destructive feelings of defeatism and fatalism. The counsellor must find ways of bolstering hope. This in no way means that
we are colluding in false defences. Rather, it signifies support for an
attitude vital to the quality and, very possibly, to the length of the
AIDS-afflicted person's life.

In practice, it is necessary to emphasize that AIDS need not be a
death sentence, though it is best to avoid the trap of attempting
definitive estimates of life expectancy—not only because it encourages chronic depression and undermines the individual's motivation,
but also because one simply doesn't know the answers. It is not
impossible that drugs will be found to prolong life till a cure is
available. There is certainly much encouraging research in progress:
several experimental drugs are being tested to halt the duplication of
the AIDS virus and to prolong life, while other drugs are proving
effective as antiviral agents in the treatment of certain stages of HIV
infection.[2] But perhaps more to the point, perceptions of a disease
that are based on assumptions of certain physical decline and death
may well form a self-fulfilling prophecy. So long as AIDS is regarded
as an invincible predator, and not just a disease, those afflicted will
be greatly demoralized. Moreover, and contrary to popular mythology, AIDS does not invariably result in swift and inevitable death.
There are many with the illness who are leading meaningful and
productive lives several years after their initial diagnosis.

Health practitioners agree that hope and the will to live often determine not only the quality of life but the chances for recovery and survival. It would be a grave mistake for us to automatically interpret a spirit of hopefulness as a form of denial, and therefore takes steps to discourage it. The fact is, those who are able to adopt a positive mental attitude and are willing to undertake an active form of coping are far more likely to experience a high degree of well-being. For many people with AIDS, quality of life becomes a primary goal. One such person is **Allard**, fifty-two, diagnosed with AIDS in 1985, who echoes several of the points made (above) by Ben:

I've met too many people diagnosed with AIDS who give up. They've read everything and heard everything—or they think they have—and it's all been bad news, so they go off into a corner and prepare to die. I knew if I took that course I'd seal my fate. AIDS is a virus, right? But so was polio. Who's dying from polio today? They've licked it, haven't they? And they'll do the same with AIDS. I'm not going to roll over and play dead with this. I want to go on living. I'm really scared of dying, and I won't pretend otherwise. I'm not as strong as I wish I was, but I'm strong enough to know my mind, to know that I won't consent to being a victim. No one who hasn't been in my position—I mean, of being treated as if they were on their death-bed, on the way out—knows what it's like: being patronized, being thought unable to make important decisions, never being asked how you feel because there's no hope anyway, so why the hell bother enquiring?
All around me I hear that there's no cure, or that a cure, if it ever comes, won't help me because it will take three years, five years for the research and the testing, and that no one with AIDS has ever lasted that long. Maybe. And maybe not. Whatever the odds are, I hope to improve them. I feel you've got to be prepared to fight. If they say there's no cure, you've got to start looking and see what you can do for yourself. It's not that I'm saying I *will* recover. I'm only arguing that I *can* recover.

One meets a number of people with AIDS who, like Allard, are not only living long after received opinion argues that they should have succumbed, but who entertain hopes of surviving the disease. Such hope is a better thing by far than the crushing sense of despair which so many experience following their diagnosis. Some, like **Alfred** from New York, 'refuse to wait passively' for science to rescue them:

> I decided I wasn't going to wait for the doctors to heal me. In the thirty-eight months since I was diagnosed with KS I've gone through everything: chemotherapy, Interferon, spot radiation. I think it's helped. But I'm not a very patient person, so I've been trying other forms of treatment, like homeopathy. I'm getting good sleep, I try not to worry or let things get me down. I'm on a macrobiotic diet now which consists primarily of whole grain cereals, beans, sea vegetables, and so on. And I avoid things like meat, eggs, dairy products, sugar, artificially altered foods. I'm also trying very large doses of Vitamin C, and I feel it's working. The best medicine, though, is friends. I'm very fortunate in having friends active in Health Crisis activities who have helped me get out of myself and get involved, and who also, almost without exception, believe in what I'm doing. I need that kind of support to keep me going.

For many people, to suggest alternative therapies or holistic medicine is the sign of a crank. However, for some with AIDS or ARC, dealing with a life-threatening illness requires a shift towards an active programme of self-protection as a means of achieving relief from worry and stress. There are those like Alfred who seek a multidimensional approach: combining several therapies and, at the same time, keeping busy with useful activities designed to enhance self-esteem and prevent one from lapsing into morose introspection and depression. Furthermore, being a follower of holistic medicine doesn't necessarily demand a rejection of traditional treatments. It is not inconsistent to be fully committed to 'scientific' measures and, at the same time, to believe that there resides within each of us further dimensions to healing.

Sex in a Health Crisis

Another means of coping with the crisis of AIDS is through a frank reappraisal of sexual activity. Since AIDS is transmitted chiefly through sex, many sexually active people—of whatever orientation—have been forced into re-examination of their sexual practices. Looking only at the gay community, we find that AIDS has produced a spirit of caution which has led to a dramatic decline in the incidence of sex-linked diseases such as syphilis and gonorrhoea.[3] This indicates both a modification of sexual lifestyles and a much higher awareness of safer sex practices and issues. According to the Terrence Higgins Trust, 'playing safe' in sex means 'having sex that does not involve the exchange of body fluids' which might transmit the virus.[4] In practice, this means preventing semen or blood entering another person's body through certain sexual and other activities, for example anal and vaginal intercourse; oral sex; practices which involve puncturing the skin; sharing sex toys, hypodermic needles, syringes, ear-piercing equipment, tattooing and acupuncture needles.

However, safer sex is not a matter of choosing between abstinence and AIDS. It does not call for celibacy. It requires a concern for safeguarding one's own and other people's health in a time of crisis by establishing guidelines that will minimize or eliminate the risks of infection. It is therefore of utmost importance that one has accurate and *explicit* information about the risks involved in specific sexual practices. David Miller in the *British Medical Journal* has offered the following 'Safer Sex Guidelines':[5]

No Risk
Solo masturbation
Massage away from the genital area

Low Risk
Mutual masturbation
Dry kissing
Body rubbing

Medium Risk
Wet kissing
Fellatio (sucking) may be safe if you stop before climax
Urination (water sports): external only
Anilingus (rimming)

High Risk
Anal and vaginal sex may be safe if a condom is used
Fisting (insertion of hand or fist into rectum)
Sharing sex toys and needles
Any sex act that draws blood

(Further information on safer sex can be obtained from the Terrence Higgins Trust, the Healthline Telephone Service and other resources listed in the Guide to Organizations Giving Advice and Help.)

With regard to the use of condoms, there are those who emphasize the fact that condoms have a substantial failure rate. Dr Janet St Lawrence wrote in *The Lancet* of 7 February 1987 that thirteen to fifteen per cent of women whose male partners use condoms as a sole method of contraception became pregnant within one year . . . Failure rates may be even higher during sexual activity between male homosexuals.' The writer concludes that gay men are better advised to avoid anal intercourse. This letter was followed by an urgent response in the following issue of *The Lancet* of 7 March 1987 from Dr S. J. Tovey of Guy's Hospital, London, who insisted that condoms, while not completely reliable, are better than nothing: 'Sheaths are available fully tested to British Standard BS3704 and thick enough to withstand anal intercourse providing they are put on carefully and a water-based lubricant [such as KY] is used . . . Even if sheaths fail occasionally, their regular use should lower the rate of cross-infection with the virus.' Since these letters have been published, stronger condoms have been developed. Further to this, some health advisers also suggest that gay men should use a spermicidal lubricant which contains a chemical called nonoxynol, which has been shown to inactivate the AIDS virus.

Of course, it is not always easy to alter an established pattern of sexual activity. In calling for a change in sexual behaviour one is asking a great deal of human nature. Throughout history, even in eras of great inhibition, 'sex', as one journalist put it, 'is always the genie that cannot be contained in the bottle'.[6] For many people, making such changes involves a major psychological upheaval. It involves modifying or eliminating behaviour which offers mutual pleasure to oneself and one's partner. Some have had this forced upon them, like **Rudy**, who is in the early stages of AIDS:

AIDS has changed my sex life completely. But it's done more than that. When I discovered I had traces of CMV [Cytomegalovirus] infection, at first I lost my sex drive entirely. I was in shock, and sex was the very last thing I wanted. I felt contaminated . . . My sex drive has returned, but I've done nothing about it.

Once, sex was a very important part of my life. It gave me a feeling of fulfillment—not just physical, either, important as that was. I need—I still need—affection . . . A few months ago, I met this guy at a party and we hit it off. When I mentioned my condition he couldn't get away fast enough . . . At a time when touching, getting physically close, means more to me than ever before, I'm more isolated than at any time in my life.

With AIDS, as we can see in the case of Rudy, a basic aspect of people's lives is often drastically altered: intimacy, affection, sexuality. Feelings of contamination are common, as are altered levels of sexual desire. Not only are many gays now having to deal with a life-threatening disease, they are once again having to cope with issues thought to be long since resolved, such as attitudes towards one's own sexuality. For a substantial section of the gay male community, an awareness of the need for behavioural changes has developed, essentially, into one of two responses. Both insist on safer sex, but while one argues that (in the words of the Terrence Higgins Trust) 'the more men you have sex with, the greater your chance of getting AIDS, [with] anal sex carrying the greatest risk',[7] the other places no restrictions on the number of contacts, though it is still equally insistent on the need for safer sex. **Arnold**, a teacher, basically accepts the first response, pleading for self-constraint on the volume and manner of sexual activity. He also sees the security of a monogamous relationship as the most appropriate response to the health crisis:

As one American gay activist said, 'The brain is your body's biggest sex organ.' By which I think he meant that you can eroticize anything. I used to believe that sex consisted of one or two activities, and that if you weren't engaged in those you weren't having sex. Since AIDS, though, I've met people who've taught me that there are a lot of other things you can do with your body that are really exciting, and they're safe. It just takes a little imagination and a willingness to experiment . . .
Intellectually, I know that it isn't necessary to give up all sex because of AIDS. Emotionally, though, I'm anxious about sex, even when it's safe. That's why there are things which I won't do any more. You have to decide for yourself whether these things are safe or not and whether it's worth it . . .
Before AIDS, I felt I had to live up to a certain standard of sexual

163

activity. Now, I don't feel that pressure. I feel it's important to keep down the number of people you have sex with. Medically, it doesn't make a bit of difference if you get the virus from a lover or a one-night stand, so you've got to take care . . .

I feel that, since AIDS, I've moved on. AIDS has helped me to grow up. I think it's made me more mature, made me understand the value of a lasting relationship.

The second response to the need for behavioural change, and one which strenuously takes issue with several of Rudy's assumptions, is well expressed by **Harding**, a Canadian postgraduate student studying in England:

For me, the decade of the Seventies, before AIDS, was great. I don't see anything to feel ashamed about in having had numbers of sexual partners, so long as it was consensual sex. I don't think we ought to turn our backs on what we did and what we achieved in those years just because the pressure of events has now forced us, quite rightly, to behave differently . . .

All this talk about gay men needing to have more 'meaningful'— meaning monogamous—relationships, it's eyewash. I'm in total disagreement with the view that AIDS has made us see the light and become more 'mature'. These are all value judgments made by people who deplore the liberation of the Seventies. In fact what the AIDS scare has done is to take a very real health problem and use it as an excuse to regulate sexuality, to preach abstinence and instil guilt, not least by throwing around labels like 'sex addicts' and 'sex compulsives'.

I believe that for everyone's sake it's necessary to take care of ourselves. But that's a very far cry from urging monogamy or suggesting monogamy is somehow more mature than having as many sexual partners as you may (or may not) want. That sort of thinking takes us right back to the bad old days—the days before Stonewall. And I hope that there's never any going back to them.

Harding argues that the fear of AIDS has become a pretext for regulating homosexual activity, with the government and public at least as concerned about social control as they are about personal safety. Whether one accepts this line of argument or not, Harding is surely right in asserting that there is nothing to be gained during the current health crisis in preaching abstinence or instilling guilt.

Surviving Aids

Pleasure and danger need not walk hand in hand. The central dilemma
that faces gays while the crisis continues is, as Dennis Altman has
pointed out, 'how to develop safe sex without feeding the traditional
moralism that condemns both homosexuality and sex outside a
committed relationship and which so easily feeds into the heightened
homophobia unleashed by AIDS'.[8]

A New Gay Culture?

It is easier to appreciate the concerns of both Dennis Altman and
Harding if we consider the calls for changes in sexual behaviour from
a historical perspective. Following Stonewall in the summer of 1969,
and the Gay Liberation Movement in the 1970s, many gay men felt it
possible for the very first time to express themselves openly and
honestly. Such openness embraced a belief that gay sexual activity
was not unnatural, abnormal or immoral, but a viable, valid,
pleasurable way of fulfilling oneself. But now, with the appearance
of a life-threatening disease closely identified with homosexuality,
the validity of gay sexuality is being challenged. Fear of AIDS has
emerged as a powerful force determining sexual morality. It is for
this reason, and because a positive attitude towards one's sexuality is
so central to the gay identity, that sexual constraints are regarded by
some, like Harding, as a threat to the legitimacy of the homosexual
identity.

This is why the key to AIDS prevention is credibility. In other
words, it must be emphasized that gays have the right to acknowledge their sexuality. The fact that gay men are taking seriously the
issue of safe sex need not equate with support for the strong anti-sex
lobby gathering momentum both within and outside the gay
community. A prerequisite to behavioural change is self-determination. This is not a political agenda. It is simply advice
crucial to the pursuit of safer sex. Gays, having made a start at
emerging in the 1970s from a long dark age of social and legal
repression, are hesitant about relinquishing hard-won freedoms. To
some, the call for monogamy and reductions in the number of sexual
partners seem like a return to the old homophobia.

For all too many, then, sex today is fraught with uncertainty and
fear. Indeed, it sometimes seems as if the only acceptable way of
discussing the subject is in the language of crisis and panic. What
once brought pleasure is now a source of anxiety and confusion.

165

There needs to be much more thought given, as Ken Plummer has pointed out, to 'the creation of an alternative sex-positive, but healthy, gay culture'.[9] In so far as AIDS blights the image of homosexuality, it increases the traumas associated with self-acceptance and coming out as gay. It has doubtless caused some to deny, rather than affirm, their homosexuality. Indeed, AIDS now helps shape the gay consciousness, and there are many men in their teens and early twenties for whom the health crisis is the most significant historical event in the shaping of their gay identity. The most dramatic difference between young gays coming out in the 1980s and their counterparts in the 1970s is that today's world is dominated by the fearful spectre of the health crisis. A typical reaction to this situation is described by **Victor**, an eighteen-year-old first-year London polytechnic student:

> My self-awareness as a gay person coincided, I think, with the first reports of the 'gay cancer' back in the early Eighties. I thought 'My God, what am I getting into?' I hadn't yet made contact of any sort with other gays. This was at the stage of my thinking where I thought I was the 'only one'. Only me, that is, and all these 'carriers of the plague'.
>
> Growing up into my teens with the popular media as my principal source of information, I felt pretty despondent. Not to mention ignorant. AIDS puts a big pall over everything. You certainly couldn't find many role models in the face of bias like that. There was Rock Hudson, whose death of AIDS came as a real shock. But here was someone forced to go public as he was sick and dying, and it scared the hell out of me . . . I knew very little about the disease, other than what I read in the papers, where the information seemed more calculated to frighten than educate . . .
>
> I think coming out has to be the toughest thing I've ever had to do. And if it hadn't been for people in one or two gay organizations who patiently answered my questions, I might not have had the courage to take the step.

Since the time in the early 1980s when AIDS first came to the public's attention, the difficulties of coming out, of identifying oneself as homosexual, have become increasingly problematic. It is partly to combat the present climate of fear and prejudice, which further stigmatizes homosexuality, complicates the process of coming out and threatens self-esteem, that a new gay culture is evolving in Britain, one which has mobilised and involved individuals who had previously seen themselves as apart from community concerns. Many more gays are now finding comfort, strength and a greater sense of self-worth in joining with others to fight for their own and other people's lives, confronting ignorance through education, and thereby helping refashion a sense of community.

Because the government was slow to act and the public remained apathetic while AIDS appeared largely confined to 'undesirable' minorities, gays have had to take the initiative, giving new life to dormant organizations and revitalizing gay community life. This has been especially true in the United States but also, and increasingly so, in Britain. The efforts of people—many themselves HIV positive or surviving AIDS—combined with a growing awareness that this disease cannot for long be confined to any single group, has led to greater efforts on the part of the government to spend more on research, care and education. Much more needs to be done, and governments throughout the world must be constantly reminded of their principal duty: the protection of human life. To do too little, or to do it too late, will have the most ominous consequences.

We must all prepare for the day—hopefully in the not too distant future—when AIDS has been eliminated. And so it is necessary to be vigilant in the present lest the public is further infected by successive waves of fear, panic and hatred. For there is, as yet, no effective vaccine for the syndrome of social intolerance and repressive conformity, which threaten to do lasting damage to society long after effective medical therapies are found to eradicate this terrible disease.

Summary

This chapter began with an acknowledgement of the difficulties people with AIDS confront in sharing their health problems with others (**Des**); but it has also attempted to demonstrate that those who are able to be open to a trusted friend or family member are better able to cope (**Edgar**). One of the most common reasons for not discussing health concerns with others is due to not having come out as gay. To contemplate self-disclosure at such a time can raise understandable fears of rejection (**Ashley**). The level of denial in the families of some people with AIDS is very high, and some will seek counselling (**Curt's Mother**).

It is not only the immediate family that can provide comfort for the person with AIDS. There is also the 'extended family' of partners, lovers and friends, who should be granted the same consideration and rights as relatives. Often overlooked in discussion of AIDS are the partners and lovers of those who have died, many of whom speak of their grief, feelings of inadequacy and guilt (**Hugh**), while others are faced with hostility from the dead partner's family (**Leon**). Survivors may also feel stigmatized by their association with the departed, and it has proved helpful for such people, and many others, to involve themselves in volunteer activity organized by the gay community (**Merv**, a 'Buddy').

Preserving self-pride in the present health crisis is a daunting challenge. Finding hope is not an easy task either, especially as the media so often distorts information on AIDS, thus causing distress to many in the gay community (**Ben**). In practice, it is necessary to emphasize that AIDS need not be a death sentence. Furthermore, perceptions of a disease that are based on assumptions of certain physical decline and death may well form a self-fulfilling prophecy. Health practitioners agree that hope and the will to live often determine not only the quality of life, but the chances of recovery and survival. Thus for many people with AIDS, quality of life becomes a primary goal (**Allard**). Others, like **Alfred**, have undertaken an active programme of self-protection as a means of achieving relief from worry and stress.

Another means of coping with the crisis of AIDS is through a frank reappraisal of sexual activity. Many people, of whatever sexual orientation, have been forced into a painful re-examination of their sexual practices. It is not always easy to alter an established pattern of sexual activity, which may involve modifying or eliminating behaviour which offers mutual pleasure to oneself and one's partner (**Rudy**). An awareness of the need for safer sex practices has developed into a number of responses, one of which sees security in a monogamous relationship (**Arnold**); another arguing that there is nothing to be gained by preaching abstinence or instilling guilt, AIDS being perceived as a pretext for regulating homosexual activity (**Harding**).

Harding is not alone in seeing sexual constraints as a threat to the legitimacy of the homosexual identity, a conclusion easier to appreciate if we consider the calls for changes in sexual behaviour from a historical perspective. In any case, sex today is fraught with uncertainty and fear, with many gays in the 1980s coming out into a world dominated by the fearful spectre of a health crisis (**Victor**). It is partly to combat the present climate of fear and prejudice, which further stigmatizes homosexuality and complicates the process of coming out, that a new gay culture is evolving in Britain—one in which many gays are finding comfort, strength, and a greater sense of self-worth in joining with others to fight for their own and other people's lives.

Notes

Chapter 1

1. Alfred C. Kinsey, Wardell B. Pomeroy, and Clyde E. Martin, *Sexual Behavior in the Human Male* (Philadelphia and London, W. B. Saunders Company, 1948), pp. 610–66.
   Alfred C. Kinsey, Wardell B. Pomeroy, Clyde E. Martin, and Paul H. Gebhard, *Sexual Behavior in the Human Female* (Philadelphia and London, W. B. Saunders Company, 1953), pp. 452–74.
2. Martin S. Weinberg and Colin J. Williams, *Male Homosexuals: Their Problems and Adaptations* (New York and London, Oxford University Press, 1974), pp. 3–13.
3. Christopher Z. Hobson, 'Surviving Psychotherapy', in *Rough Times*, ed. Jerome Agel (New York, Ballantine Books, 1973), p. 173.
4. David Blamires, *Homosexuality from the Inside* (London, Social Responsibility Council of the Religious Society of Friends, 1973), p. 22.
5. Carl R. Rogers, 'Psychotherapy Today or Where Do We Go From Here?', *American Journal of Psychotherapy* (January 1963), pp. 5–7.
6. Peter Wildeblood, *Against the Law* (New York, Julian Messner, 1959), p. 32.
7. Eric Hoffer, *The Passionate State of Mind* (London, Secker & Warburg, 1956), p. 65.
8. Jess Stearn, *The Sixth Man* (New York, Macfadden Publishers, 1961), p. 202.
9. Weinberg and Williams, op. cit., p. 217.
10. 'Comments on *Manifesto* 7', Report prepared by the London West End Group of the Campaign for Homosexual Equality (London, 22 Great Windmill Street, 1974), p. 18.

Chapter 2

1. Friedrich Nietzsche, *The Will to Power*, tr. Anthony M. Ludovici, in *The Complete Works*, ed. Oscar Levy, vol. 15 (Edinburgh and London, J. N. Foulis, 1910), p. 76.
2. Kinsey, *et al.*, *Human Male*, pp. 638–9; see also Kinsey, *et al.*, *Human Female*, pp. 468–9.
3. ibid., pp. 474–5; see also Kinsey, *et al.*, *Human Male*, p. 663.
4. Charles Virginia Prince, *The Transvestite and His Wife* (Los Angeles, Argyle Books, 1967), p. 8.
5. Quoted in Arno Karlen, *Sexuality and Homosexuality* (New York, W. W. Norton & Co., 1971), p. 367.

Notes

6. See, in particular, C. S. Ford and F. A. Beach, *Patterns of Sexual Behaviour* (London, Methuen University Paperbacks, 1965), p. 202. See also Karl William Kapp, *Toward a Science of Man in Society* (The Hague, Nijhoff, 1961), p. 155.
7. See chapter 5, 'The Acquirement of Sexual Preferences', in Wainwright Churchill, *Homosexual Behavior Among Males: A Cross-Cultural and Cross-Species Investigation* (Englewood Cliffs, New Jersey, Prentice-Hall, 1971), pp. 100–20.
8. Kinsey, *et al.*, *Human Female*, p. 447.
9. George Weinberg, *Society and the Healthy Homosexual* (New York, Doubleday, 1973), p. 116.

Chapter 3

1. A discussion of 'passing' in relation to group cohesiveness can be found in Weinberg and Williams, *Male Homosexuals*, chapter 13, 'Passing and Being Known About'. Also useful here is Erving Goffman, *Stigma: The Management of Spoiled Identity* (Harmondsworth, Middlesex, Penguin Books, 1968).
2. Laud Humphreys, *Tearoom Trade: A Study of Homosexual Encounters in Public Places* (London, Duckworth, 1974).
3. Laud Humphreys, *Out of the Closets. The Sociology of Homosexual Liberation* (New York, Prentice-Hall, 1972).
4. Robin Maugham, *Escape from the Shadows* (London, Hodder & Stoughton, 1972).
5. Humphreys, *Closets*.
6. Goffman discusses this passing strategy at some length in *Stigma*.
7. Humphreys, *Closets*, p. 70.
8. Dennis Altman, *Homosexual: Oppression and Liberation* (Sydney, Angus and Robertson, 1973), pp. 58–95.
9. Ian Harvey, *To Fall Like Lucifer* (London, Sidgwick & Jackson, 1971), p. 25.
10. T. C. Worsley, *Flannelled Fool: A Slice of Life in the Thirties* (London, A Ross, 1967).
11. William Aaron, *Straight: A Heterosexual Talks About His Homosexual Past* (New York and London, Bantam Books, 1973), p. 190.
12. An excellent summary of laws which discriminate against gays, as well as the assumptions on which they are based, and practical suggestions for reform, can be found in Bob Sturgess, *No Offence: The Case for Homosexual Equality at Law*, published by CHE, SMG and USFI, 1975.
13. *Report of the Committee on Homosexual Offences and Prostitution* (The Wolfenden Report), Cmnd. 247 (London, HMSO, 1957).
14. These comments were made by Lord Devlin in a BBC 'Heart of the Matter' programme broadcast in the spring of 1987.
15. The term 'disgraceful conduct of an indecent kind' includes not only all sexual contact between two lesbians or two gay men, but also any conversation which, according to the Ministry of Defence's *Manual of Military Law*, 'does not amount to an attempt in law but only to a

preparation to commit an offence'. Between 1976 and 1980 nearly two-thirds of those convicted for 'homosexual misconduct' were sentenced to prison, with sentences of up to six or nine months being given by courts martial.

16. European States vary in their laws regarding the minimum age for homosexual relationships. There appears to be no specific legislation restricting lesbianism; but as far as gay men are concerned, the legal status of homosexuality is as low as ten years old in Hungary, fifteen years old in Denmark, France and Poland, sixteen in Holland and Switzerland, seventeen in Greece, and eighteen in most other countries, except in the UK where it is twenty-one. Male homosexuality is subject to complete prohibition in Cyprus, Ireland, Romania and the USSR.

17. Further comment on the anomalies of the 1967 Bill can be found in *Homosexuality: Some Questions and Answers*, published by the Albany Trust, 1975.

18. These figures are taken from the annual Home Office statistics.

19. Sturgess, op. ct., p. 23.

20. ibid.

21. See Anna Coote and Lawrence Grant, *The NCCL Guide* (Harmondsworth, Middlesex, Penguin Books, 1973), pp. 165–9.

22. See, for instance, a report in *Gay Times* (issue 106, July 1987, p. 10) which says that 'at least thirty-five men have appeared in court in Oxted in Surrey charged with "gross indecency" as part of a police purge on two public toilets near the town. In the whole of Surrey in the previous year, 1986, there were only four reported cases of "indecency between males". In 1985 there were six cases.'

23. *Questions and Answers* (unpaginated).

24. For a report on police attitudes on cottaging see Jack Babuscio, 'Cops and Gays', in *Gay News* no. 44 (11–24 April 1974), p. 5

25. Humphreys, *Tearoom Trade*, p. 160.

26. Jon J. Gallo, *et al.*, 'The Consenting Adult Homosexual and the Law: An Empirical Study of Enforcement and Administration in Los Angeles County', in *UCLA Law Review* (13 March 1966), p. 796.

27. See chapter 13, 'Censorship', in the *NCCL Guide* for further information on the changing interpretation of the 'public good' under the law.

28. The *Guardian*, 22 August 1975, p. 9.

29. Antony Grey, 'Homosexuals: New Law but No New Deal', reprinted from *New Society* (27 March 1969), pp. 476–9.

30. See, for example, the case of *Buck v. The Letchworth Palace Limited (1987)*, cited in *New Law Journal* vol. 137, no. 6318 (14 August, 1987), p. 754, which regarded as fair the dismissal of a cinema projectionist whose fellow workers refused to work with him 'because they viewed his behaviour with disgust and they also feared that their shared toilet facilities might become contaminated with the AIDS virus'—though there was no reason to believe that the employee had AIDS, nor was it ever proved that he did. Although there are, to date, no fully reported tribunal cases of persons being dismissed because of

the fact that they have AIDS, the Terrence Higgins Trust argues that few cases of unfair dismissal are brought by people with AIDS because they fear adverse publicity.

31. Altman, op. cit., pp. 35–7.

Chapter 4

1. See, for example, Marcel T. Saghir, MD, and Eli Robins, MD, *Male and Female Homosexuality: A Comprehensive Investigation* (Baltimore, the Williams and Wilkins Company, 1973); Weinberg and Williams, *Male Homosexuals*; Humphreys, *Tearoom Trade*; H. Laurence Ross, 'Modes of Adjustment of Married Homosexuals', in *Social Problems* (Winter 1971), Vol. 18, no. 3; F. E. Kenyon, 'Studies in Female Homosexuality: Psychological Test Results', in *Journal Consult. Clin. Psychology* 32 (1968), p. 510; F. E. Kenyon, 'Studies in Female Homosexuality: VI—The Exclusively Homosexual Group', in *Acta Psychiatr. Scand.*, 44 (1968), pp. 224–37; F. E. Kenyon, 'Studies in Female Homosexuality; IV—Social and Psychiatric Aspects', in *British Journal of Psychiatry*, 14 (1968), pp. 1337–50; R. Grundlach, 'Research Project Report', in *The Ladder*, 11 (1967), pp. 2–9.
2. Goffman, *Stigma*.
3. The GLC Women's Committee, *Tackling Heterosexism* (1987), p. 26.
4. The *Guardian*, 7 August 1975, p. 11.
5. ibid.

Chapter 5

1. It should be borne in mind, however, that homosexuality was far from universally condemned in ancient times. For example, prior to the Babylonian Exile (*c.* 700 BC) the Hebrews, as well as their neighbours, accepted homosexual activities. So also did such divergent peoples as the Egyptians, Greeks, Scandinavians, Sumerians, Carthaginians, Celts, and Cretans. 'In fact,' as Wainwright Churchill reminds us, 'certain forms of homosexuality seem to have received approval among the earliest peoples of civilization. It is precisely in the so-called cradle of civilization—the Tigris–Euphrates Valley, the Nile Valley, and the Mediterranean Basin—that homosexuality received the greatest approval during very ancient times and largely still enjoys such approval today in spite of the rise of Judaism, Christianity, and Mohammedanism.' *Homosexual Behavior Among Males. A Cross-Cultural and Cross-Species Investigation* (Englewood Cliffs, New Jersey, Prentice-Hall, 1967; Prism Paperback edn., 1971), pp. 75–6.
2. This point is further developed by D. Lloyd (pseud.), *Christian Renewal*, no. 10 (Summer 1973), pp. 5–7.
3. *The Civil Law (Corpus Juris Civilis)*, ed. S. P. Scott, vol. XVI (Cincinnati 1932), p. 288.
4. This quote, along with a stimulating discussion of the Sodom and Gomorrah story and its impact on homosexuals, can be found in Lewis

Williams, 'Walls of Ice—Theology and Social Policy', in *Is Gay Good? Ethics, Theology and Homosexuality*, ed. W. Dwight Oberholtzer (Philadelphia, Penn., The Westminster Press, 1971), pp. 163–84.

5. It should be noted that in the Revised Standard Version (London, Thomas Nelson & Sons Ltd., 1959) the word 'effeminate' is translated as 'homosexual'. It should also be noted that the word 'effeminate' as well as the word 'homosexual' in 1 Corinthians 6.9,10 have been used in place of the term 'catamite', i.e. a prostitute cupbearer in the temple of the gods. We learn from *Strong's Concordance*, however, that catamites were not necessarily 'effeminate' or 'homosexual'. As for the phrase 'abusers of themselves with mankind', in the same passage, this is translated from the word meaning 'sodomite', which, contrary to present dictionary definitions, meant 'one who forcibly rapes another', a category which would include heterosexuals as well as homosexuals.

6. Derrick Sherwin Bailey, *Homosexuality and the Western Christian Tradition* (London, Longmans, Green & Co. Ltd., 1955), p. 60.

7. Helmut Thielicke, the German theologian, argues that Paul was particularly outraged by lust, and that he did not single out same-sex relations as being any more heinous than other 'sins'; see 'The Problem of Homosexuality', in *The Ethics of Sex*, tr. from the German by John W. Doberstein (New York, Harper & Row Publishers Inc., 1964), pp. 269–92. H. Kimball Jones, author of *Towards a Christian Understanding of the Homosexual* (London, Association Press, 1966), argues that the problem for Paul was one of 'sex as a depersonalizing force versus sex as the fulfilment of human relationship' (p. 76).

8. 'Historical and Mythological Aspects of Homosexuality', pp. 140–64, in Judd Marmor, ed., *Sexual Inversion: The Multiple Roots of Homosexuality* (New York and London, Basic Books Inc., 1965), pp. 145–6.

9. These and other points are admirably argued in The Gay Activists Alliance's *20 Questions About Homosexuality: A Political Primer* (New York n.d.).

10. *Encyclopedia Judaica*, vol. 8 (Jerusalem 1971), pp. 961–2.

11. 'Morality of Homosexuality', in *New Catholic Encyclopaedia*, vol. VII (New York, McGraw-Hill Book Co., 1967), pp. 117–18.

12. See John Kane, *What is Homosexuality?* (London, Clarentian Publications, 1966).

13. *The Guardian* 29 January 1987.

14. The Congregation for the Doctrine of the Faith, *Letter to the Bishops of the Catholic Church on the Pastoral Care of Homosexual Persons* (London, Catholic Truth Society, 1986), n.7.

15. *The Guardian* 29 January 1987.

16. Father John F. Harvey, 'Pastoral Responses to Gay World Questions', in Oberholtzer, *Is Gay Good?*, pp. 134–5.

17. Quoted from a report in *The Times* (16 January 1976), p. 8: 'Pre-Marital Sex, Homosexuality and Masturbation Condemned in Vatican Attack on Permissiveness'.

18. In the March 1987 issue of *Gen*, entitled 'Challenging Racism and Sexism in Education', the editors wrote to the Archbishop of Canter-

bury opposing the Church of England's use of the word 'handicapped' to describe *any* human beings, and asked if there was now a debate in the Church about homosexuality. Keith Cawdron, the Archbishop of Canterbury's Administrative and Research Officer, writing on behalf of the Archbishop, replied by saying that 'the text of the Archbishop's speech in a General Synod debate on a report on the Church's attitude to homosexuality remains the full statement of his views'. Both Mr Cawdron's letter and the statement in the debate on homosexual relationships are included in this issue of *Gen* (published by the Women's Education Group, Princeton Street, London WC1).

19. *The Guardian* 12 November 1987; see also report in *Gay Times* December 1987, p. 6.
20. *The Guardian* 29 January 1987.
21. ibid.
22. *The Guardian* 12 November 1987
23. Father Neil Gray's comments first appeared in *Gay Times*, issue 104 (May 1987), p. 58.
24. Lewis Williams, 'Walls of Ice', in Oberholtzer, *Is Gay Good?*, p. 182.
25. Thomas Maurer, 'Towards a Theology of Homosexuality—Tried and Found Trite and Tragic', in Oberholtzer, *Is Gay Good?*, p. 100.
26. Alastair Heron, ed., *Towards a Quaker View of Sex* (London, Friends Home Service Committee, 1963; rev. edn. 1964).
27. Wainwright Churchill, *Homosexual Behavior*, p. 295.

Chapter 6

1. *Saunders v. Scottish National Camp Association Ltd.* (1980) IRLR 174, (1981) IRLR 277.
2. Quoted in *Gay Times*, May 1987, p. 13.
3. See the report in *Gay Times* (May 1987), p. 13.
4. *Wiseman v. Salford C.C.* (1981) IRLR 208.
5. Statistics published in *Gen*, March 1987.
6. Anna Dunig, Nettie Pollard, Guy Thornton, *Homosexuality and the Teaching Profession*, National Council for Civil Liberties Report No. 8 (London, National Council for Civil Liberties, 1975), p. 2.
7. ibid., pp. 4, 7.
8. Howard J. Brown, 'Coming Out', in *The Universities and the Gay Experience. A Conference Sponsored by the Women and Men of the Gay Academic Union*, 23 and 24 November 1973 (New York, Gay Academics Union Inc., 1974), pp. 59–63.

Chapter 7

1. Sidney Abbott and Barbara Love, *Sappho was a Right-On Woman: A Liberated View of Lesbianism* (New York, Stein and Day, 1973), pp. 94–5.
2. C. S. Ford and F. A. Beach, *Patterns of Sexual Behaviour* (London, Methuen University Paperbacks, 1965), p. 114.

3. Kinsey, *Human Female*, pp. 682ff.
4. Humphreys, *Tearoom Trade*, pp. 104–17.
5. Blamires, *Homosexuality*, p. 35.
6. Clarence Tripp, quoted in 'Can Homosexuals Change with Psychotherapy?', in *Sexual Behaviour* (July 1971), pp. 42–9.

Chapter 8

1. See for example the *Sun*, 12 December 1986, and the *Daily Express*, 13 December 1986.
2. Quoted from an editorial in the *Spectator*, (14 March 1987), p. 5.
3. These changing attitudes to homosexuality and their implications were explored with some sensitivity by Helena Kennedy in a 'Heart of the Matter' programme on BBC in March 1987.
4. These statistics were calculated for London only by GALOP, a police monitoring group.
5. A full report of the Local Government Bill can be found in *Gay Times* January 1988, p. 5.
6. James Anderton's remarks were quoted in the *Sun* 12 December 1986. Regrettably the Prime Minister, Margaret Thatcher, appeared to support these views, arguing that she was 'very glad that some people have spoken out'.
7. I would like to acknowledge my indebtedness to the Terrence Higgins Trust for information on AIDS provided in their excellent pamphlets on the subject.
8. HIV was identified by Luc Montagnier (1983) and by Robert Gallo (1984). It is important to note that it is now known as HIV 1, as HIV 2 has been identified in Africa by Montagnier. Several cases of HIV 2 carriers have already been identified in Europe.
9. The African countries referred to here include Burundi, the Central African Republic, Kenya, Rwanda, Tanzania, Uganda, Zaire and Zambia.
10. In the Western world at present, the spread of AIDS into the heterosexual population has been mainly through infected needles. This method of spread could change, however, once there is a large enough pool of infected heterosexuals. Heterosexuals have a distinct advantage, however, as they at least know about HIV and its effects, and can take precautions. Unfortunately, the gay community was attacked at a time of complete ignorance about this disease.
11. Dennis Altman *AIDS and the New Puritanism* (London and Sydney, Pluto Press, 1986), pp. 175–6.
12. This equation of AIDS and homosexuality is seen at its clearest in a remark made by the Earl of Halsbury in the House of Lords on 18 December 1986, during a debate on a local government Bill seeking to outlaw local authorities funding projects 'promoting homosexuality'. According to the Earl, 'Syphilis, gonorrhoea, genital herpes and now AIDS are characteristically infections of homosexuals.'
13. Quoted from an editorial in the *Sun*, 11 April 1987. As many readers may already know, a large part of the British popular press, with the

Sun leading the way, has been relentlessly persistent in what appears at times to be a settled, co-ordinated, anti-gay campaign. Such a 'policy' not only causes terrible distress to gay people, especially those who are sick, but helps create a climate of fear and hatred in which ignorance and intolerance thrive.

14. This conclusion also leads to pathologizing promiscuity as a sign of homosexual self-hate and immaturity, with gay men being accused of 'an incapacity to sustain love relationships'. This line of argument, and the above quote, can be found in Donald Symons, *The Evolution of Human Sexuality* (New York, Oxford University Press, 1979).

15. See, for instance, a press report in *The New York Times*, 3 July 1981, in which Dr Friedman-Kien was quoted as saying that the reporting doctors 'believed that most cases of the disease involved homosexual men who have had multiple and frequent sexual encounters with different partners'.

16. Perhaps the most extraordinary and saddest example of this sort of thinking comes from Dr Helen Singer Kaplan, the head of the Human Sexuality Program at the New York Hospital–Cornell Medical Center, who argued that 'we could stop the spread of AIDS today if these high risk people, these Typhoid Marys, would stop spreading the disease'. Quoted in *The Advocate* (13 May 1986), p. 45.

17. In future, the decision on whether or not to test may be altogether out of the patient's hands. At the British Medical Association's annual meeting in Bristol on 2 July 1987, it was voted 183 to 140 to carry out secret AIDS tests without obtaining the consent of patients. The decision, if upheld, would overturn the policy of the Department of Health, the World Health Organization, and the BMA's own council.

18. Gay men who are applying for insurance are advised to read the small print very carefully. Dai Harris, legal advisor to the Terrence Higgins Trust, stresses that gay men who want life insurance should not take an HIV antibody test, as a positive result means one will not be insured. Also, problems could arise if a gay man died within months of taking out an insurance policy. Dai Harris is quoted in *Gay Times* as saying that 'if they found from the death certificate that the man had died from pneumonia, the insurance company might well ask for more information. Under normal circumstances they could not get access to medical records; those files are confidential. But the company could demand more information from the dead man's executors and could decline to pay out on the policy until they had that information.' (Quoted in *Gay Times* [July 1986], p. 25.) Proposal forms always include a clause which states that contracts may be invalidated if the applicant fails to disclose information which might influence the assessment of the proposal. Advice on how to approach applications for insurance and mortgages can be obtained from the Terrence Higgins Trust, Body Positive, and from gay financial advisors advertising in *Gay Times*, *Capital Gay*, and elsewhere in the gay press.

19. See reports in *Gay Times* (April 1987), p. 9, and *Gay Times* (July 1987), p. 11.

20. Further information on the difficulties confronting gays in obtaining

mortgages and loans can be found in *The Sunday Times Magazine* (21 June 1987), p. 71, and Paul Crane, *Gays and the Law* (London, Pluto Press, 1982).
21. Quoted in *Gay Times* (February 1987), p. 34.
22. Quoted in *Gay Times* (June 1986), pp. 41–2.
23. At the time of this book going to press, the use of anti-viral drugs has been confined to those with advanced infection. It is very likely, however, that as new anti-viral agents and methods of immunological manipulation are developed, treatment will be started soon after seroconversion. It is for this reason that the *New Scientist*, in its issue of 11 June 1987, spoke of 'restrained but real optimism' at a recent international meeting on AIDS.

Chapter 9

1. See Jeffrey S. Mandel, 'Psychosocial Challenges of AIDS and ARC: Clinical and Research Observations'. in Leon McKusick, ed., *What to do About AIDS* (Berkeley and Los Angeles, University of California, 1986), pp. 75–86.
2. In particular, AZT and Ribavirin have been shown to be effective antiviral agents useful in the treatment of certain stages of HIV infection. It is also worth pointing out that, because the HIV virus is itself a retrovirus (meaning it uses certain unusual enzymes to reproduce itself), it may well be possible to find a drug that will stop the virus multiplying without hurting the infected person. I wish to warn the reader, however, that by the time this book is published further progress will doubtless have been made in this area of AIDS research, and much of the above information may be out of date.
3. *Capital Gay*, 17 April 1987, published statistics gathered by the Middlesex Hospital showing a dramatic fall in sexually transmitted diseases among gays and bisexuals since 1985. According to *The Lancet* (March 1987), STD infection rose at a rate of 7% a year between 1982–1984, but fell to 1.8% after that.
4. See the following pamphlets published by the Terrence Higgins Trust: 'AIDS: The Facts', 'AIDS: More Facts for Gay Men', and 'Facts about AIDS for Drug Users'.
5. See the *British Medical Journal*, vol. 294 (27 June 1987), p. 1673.
6. See *Time* magazine (16 February 1987), p. 26.
7. See the Terrence Higgins Trust pamphlet 'AIDS: More Facts for Gay Men'.
8. Dennis Altman, *ibid* p. 156.
9. See Ken Plummer's excellent articles on AIDS in *Gay Times*: May 1985, pp. 26–9; October 1985, pp. 50–3; and February 1986, pp. 50–3.

Guide to Organizations Giving Advice and Help

The following listings should be of help to those requiring information on AIDS; the gay scene (pubs, clubs, discos, coffee bars, restaurants, etc.); national and local organizations and social groups; counselling and befriending organizations; social activities, meetings and conferences, etc. An up-to-date, comprehensive UK guide can be found each month in *Gay Times* (see Critical Bibliography for further details). The listings below are arranged under the following headings: AIDS HELPLINES–GAY SWITCHBOARDS, CAMPAIGNING, CENTRES, COUNSELLING, DISABLED, EMPLOYMENT, HEALTH, HOUSING, LEGAL, MEDIA, OLDER LESBIANS AND GAY MEN, RELIGIOUS, YOUTH.

AIDS HELPLINES/GAY SWITCHBOARDS

Action Against AIDS Limited
34 South Molton Street, London W1Y 2BP. This was formed to help raise funds for the Terrence Higgins Trust.

AIDS Healthline
College of Health pre-recorded health tapes, 2–10 p.m. 01-980 4848. 24-hour AIDS service: 01-980 7222 or 01-981 2717. There is a number outside London; only the cost of a local call will be charged; 0345 581151.

AIDS Information Service (Department of Health and Social Security)
For information phone (free) 0800-555 777.

AVERT
PO Box 91, Horsham, West Sussex RH13 7YR. The acronym AVERT stands for AIDS Virus Education and Research Trust.

Belfast AIDS Helpline
0232 326117, Mon–Fri, 7.30–10 p.m.

Body Positive
Phone 01 373 9124, Daily, 7–10 p.m. for details of meetings, discos and other activities sponsored by this self-help and mutual support group for people who are HIV antibody positive.

179

Bournemouth AIDS Support Group
0202 424442, Mon–Fri, 8–10 p.m.

Brighton Gay Switchboard
0273 690825, Sat 6–10 p.m., other nights 8–10 p.m.

Brighton Lesbian Line
0273 603298, Tue/Fri, 8–10 p.m.

Bristol: Aled Richards Trust
0272 273436, Mon–Fri, 7–9 p.m.

Bristol Lesbian and Gay Switchboard,
0272 425927, lesbians ring Wed 8–10 p.m., gays ring any night 8–10 p.m.

Calm (South Coast Area),
0243 776998, Mon/Wed/Fri, 7.30–10 p.m.

Cambridge AIDS Helpline
0223 69765, Tues/Wed, 7.30–10.30 p.m.

Cambridge Friend
0223 311791, Wed, 6–9.30 p.m.

Cardiff AIDS Helpline
0222 223443, Mon–Fri, 7–10 p.m.

Cardiff Friend
0222 40101, Tue/Thur/Sat, 8–10 p.m.

Colchester AIDS Helpline
0206 42980, Tues/Fri, 7.30–10 p.m.

Colchester Lesbian Line
0206 870051, Wed, 8–10 p.m.

Coventry CHE AIDS Helpline
0203 714144, Daily, to 10 p.m.

Coventry Lesbian Line
0203 77105, Wed, 7–10 p.m.

Edinburgh Gay Switchboard
031-556 4049, Mon–Sat 8–10 p.m.

Edinburgh Lesbian Line
031-556 4049, Thur, 7.30–10 p.m.

Essex AIDS Line (Southend)
0702 460380, Daily, 6–10 p.m.

Fife Gay Switchboard
0592 759384, Tue/Thur, 7–10 p.m.

Glasgow AIDS Line
041-221 7467, Tue–Fri, 7–10 p.m.

Glasgow Gay Switchboard
041-221 8372, every night, 7–10 p.m.

Grampian AIDS Line (Aberdeen)
0224 574000, Tue/Fri, 7–9 p.m.

Guide to Organizations

Gwent AIDS Helplines
Caerleon 0633 422532, Tues, 6–8 p.m.;
Newport 0633 841 901, Mon–Fri, 8.30–4.30 p.m.

Health Education Council
78 New Oxford Street, London WC1 1AH. The Council is responsible for educating
the community about the nature of AIDS and its related conditions, and the ways and
means of preventing further spread of the virus. In close conjunction with the medical
group of the Terrence Higgins Trust, it produces leaflets on AIDS and the issues
AIDS presents. The Council has devised a workshop on safer sex and also makes
speakers available to other organizations around the country to inform them about
AIDS.

Lancaster AIDS Line
0524 841011, Mon, 7–10 p.m.

Lancaster Gay Info
0524 63021, Thur/Fri, 6–8 p.m.

Leeds AIDS Advice
0532 444209, Mon/Thur, 7–9 p.m.

Leeds AIDS Line
0532 441661, Tue, 7–9 p.m.

Leeds Gay Switchboard
0532 453588, Wed–Mon, 7.30–9.30 p.m.

Leeds Lesbian Line
0532 453588, Tue, 7.30–9.30 p.m.

Lincoln AIDS Helpline
0522 45371, Mon/Wed 5–7 p.m.

Liverpool AIDS Line
051-521 8819, Mon–Fri, 10 a.m.–10 p.m.

London Lesbian and Gay Centre
67–69 Cowcross Street, London EC1M 6BP; 01-608 1417. Open daily. A relaxed
place to meet for a meal or drink.

London Lesbian and Gay Switchboard
01-837 7324 (24 hours). An information service for lesbians and gay men. Lines are
often busy, so keep trying. The LLGS can answer general queries about AIDS, can
put you in touch with local gay support groups and can tell you where your local STD
clinic is located.

London Lesbian Line
BM Box 1514, London WC1N 3XX; 01-251 6911, Mon–Fri, 7–10 p.m. A women-
only information service.

London Lighthouse
178 Lancaster Road, London W11 1QU; 01-727 2018. The first residential and day
care centre established in Britain to care for people with AIDS.

Manchester AIDS Line
061-228 1617, Mon–Fri, 7–10 p.m.

Manchester Gay Info
061-236 5986, every night, 7–10 p.m.

Manchester Lesbian Link
061-236 6205, Mon–Thur, 7–10 p.m.

Medway and Maidstone Gay Switchboard
0634 826925, Thur/Fri, 8–9.30 p.m.

Merseyside AIDS Helpline
051-708 0234, Wed, 7–10 p.m.

Merseyside Gay Switchboard
051-708 9552, every night 7–10 p.m.

Midlands AIDS Concern
021-622 1511, Tue, 7.30–9.30 p.m.

Milton Keynes Gay Switchboard
0908 312196, Mon, 7–9 p.m.

National AIDS Helpline
Freefone 0800 567123, 24 hours, 7 days a week.

North Staffs Gay Switchboard
0782 266998, Mon, 8–10 p.m.

North Staffs Lesbian Support
0782 266998, Fri, 7–10 p.m.

Norwich AIDS Helpline
0603 615816, Thur, 8–10 p.m.

Nottingham AIDS Helpline
0602 585526, Mon/Tue, 7–10 p.m.

Nottingham Gay Switchboard
0602 411454, Mon/Wed/Thur, 7–10 p.m.

Nottingham AIDS Information Project
0602 58556, Mon/Wed, 7–9.30 p.m.

Oxaids (Oxford)
0865 728817, Mon/Wed/Sun, 6–8 p.m.

Peterborough Lesbian Line
0733 238005, open every night until 10 p.m.

Pennine/W. Yorks AIDSLine
0274 732939, Mon–Fri, 7.30–9.30 p.m.

Plymouth AIDS Support Group
0752 229817.

Plymouth Gay Switchboard
0752 266041, Thur, 8–10 p.m.

Plymouth Lesbian Line
0752 261251, Tue, 7.30–9.30 p.m.

Preston AIDS Line
0772 555556, Mon/Tue/Thur, 7.30–9.30 p.m.

Preston Gay Info
0772 51122, Tue/Thur 8–9.30 p.m., Sat, 2–4 p.m.

Preston Lesbian Line
0772 51122, Mon/Wed, 8–9.30 p.m.

Reading Area AIDS Line
0734 503377, Thur, 8–10 p.m.

Reading Gay Switchboard
0734 597269, Tue/Fri, 8–10 p.m.

The Regent's Park Clinic
184 Gloucester Place, London NW1; 01-402 2208 or 01-723 7485. A private clinic providing a blood testing and counselling service which gives people an opportunity to discuss their problems with fully qualified specialists who will respect their anonymity and guarantee complete confidentiality. A fee is charged. The Regent's Park is the only private clinic to have received official approval.

Scottish Aids Monitor
PO Box 169, Edinburgh, 031-558 1167, Mon–Fri, evenings; Dundee, 0343 25083, office hours.

Sheffield AIDS Support Group
0709 895684, evenings.

Sheffield Lesbian Line
0742 581238, Thur, 7–10 p.m.

Solent AIDS Helpline
0703 37363, Tue/Thur/Sat, 7.30–10 p.m.

Solent Gay Switchboard
0703 37363, Tue/Thur/Sat, 7.30–10 p.m.

Southampton Gay Switchboard
0703 37363, Tue/Thur/Sat, 7.30–10 p.m.

South Lincolnshire
0476 60192, Mon/Fri, 9–10 p.m.

Surrey Gay Switchboard
0252 330366, Mon–Fri, 8–10 p.m.

Sussex AIDS Helpline
0273 571660, Mon–Fri, 8–10 p.m.

Terrence Higgins Trust
(London and National), 01-242 1010, Daily, 3–10 p.m.

West Midlands AIDS Line
021-622 1511, Tue/Thur, 7.30–10 p.m.

West Midlands Gay Switchboard
021-622 6589, every night, 7–10 p.m.

West Sussex/Hampshire
Chichester 776998, Mon/Wed/Fri, 7.30–10 p.m.

Windsor Gay Switchboard
07535 56521, Wed, 8–10 p.m.

Women's Reproductive Rights Information Centre
52–54 Featherstone Street, London EC1; 01-251 6332. Offers information on AIDS for all women and provides 'Safer Sex Guidelines for Women'. The Centre argues that

there have been no documented cases so far of sexual transmission from woman to woman. However, women have died from AIDS. Lesbians, though a low-risk group, are also affected, their biggest risk factor being intravenous drug use. The Centre offers very practical advice to lesbians.

York Gay Switchboard
0904 411399, Thur, 7–9 p.m.

CAMPAIGNING

Campaign Against Sexism and Sexual Oppression in Education (CASSOE)
7 Pickwick Court, London SE9 4SA; 01-857 3793.

The Campaign for Homeless People (CHAR)
5–15 Cromer Street, London WC1H 8LS.

Campaign for Homosexual Equality (CHE)
Room 221, 38 Mount Pleasant, London WC1X OAP; 01-359 3973. National campaign and lobbying group providing information and resource material on lesbian and gay rights, parliamentary action and national issues.

Christian Action on AIDS
PO Box 76, Hereford HR1 1JX; 0432 26816. Organizes conferences and action groups around the country to promote its campaigning and caring activities.

Customers Helping AIDS Relief
c/o London Lesbian and Gay Centre, 67–69 Cowcross Street, EC1M 6BP; 01-381 1731, after 7 p.m. Fund-raising group providing people with AIDS with goods and services.

Gay Humanist Group
34 Spring Lane, Kenilworth CV8 2HB; 0926 58450.

Islington Council Gay and Lesbian Subcommittee
Town Hall, Upper Street, London N1. Contact Chair of subcommittee. Discusses issues relevant to lesbian women and gay men in Islington.

Labour Campaign for Lesbian and Gay Rights
c/o 39 Chippenham Road, London W9.

Legislation for Lesbian and Gay Rights Campaign
Room 221, 38 Mount Pleasant, London WC1X OAT; 01-833 3912.

Northern Ireland Gay Rights Campaign (NIGRA)
PO Box 44, Belfast BT1 1SH.

CENTRES

Local Gay Switchboard. There are many centres throughout the country where lesbians and gay men meet. Phone your local gay switchboard for further information.

London Lesbian and Gay Centre
67–69 Cowcross Street, London EC1; 01-608 1471. Open Tue/Wed 6–12 p.m. Thur 12 noon to 12 midnight. Closed on Mon. Ground floor: lounge, cafe/bar. Hot and cold

meals, licensed 6.30 p.m.–midnight Tue–Sat, 7–11.30 p.m. on Sun. Basement: disco bar, licensed till 2 a.m. Fri/Sat (Fri mixed disco, Sat women-only disco). Bar open lunchtimes 12.30–3 p.m. Sun 12–2 p.m. Discos, theatre, music, etc. First floor: women's lounge—creche, meetings, workshops. Second floor: printing, graphics, darkroom. Membership £15 p.a./£7.50 for under 24s, OAPs, unwaged, disabled. Day membership (30p/15p) available. Farringdon tube. Wheelchair access.

COUNSELLING

Albany Trust
24 Chester Square, London SW1; 01-730 5871. Counselling organization.

Beaumont Society
Beaumont Trust, BM Charity, London WC1N 3XX; 01-730 7453, Tue, 7–11 p.m. Help with transvestite problems. Phone 061-256 2521, Wed, 7–10 p.m. for wives/partners of transvestites.

Body Positive
PO Box 493, London W14 OTF. Counselling, support and campaigning group for those tested HIV antibody positive. 01-833 2971.

Buddy and Support Group
(Terrence Higgins Trust), 01-242 1010. Buddies are volunteers who work on a part-time basis to provide help and support for people with AIDS—from washing dishes and doing the laundry to direct counselling support. They also help, if necessary, to support the family, friends and lovers of people with AIDS.

London Friend
86 Caledonian Road, London N1; 01-837 3337, daily, 7.30–10 p.m. Women only on Thur, 7.30–10 p.m. A gay befriending and counselling organization with branches nationwide. Access to experts, often gay, e.g. doctors, solicitors, clergy.

London Friend Women's Group
33a Seven Sisters Road, London N7 6AX; 01-281 4970. Phone line for support of gay women and women questioning their sexuality. Includes counselling services. Facilities include coffee bar, pool table and library.

Parents and Friends of Lesbians and Gays
01-523 2910, 10 a.m.–10 p.m. Helping sons and daughters to come out to parents, and helping parents to accept and understand their gay children.

Project for Advice, Counselling and Education (PACE)
69 Cowcross Street, London EC1; 01-251 2689, Wed, 6–8 p.m. Based at the London Lesbian and Gay Centre, PACE offers a free professional service by lesbians and gay men with training and experience in counselling. They also offer advice and support groups and can give information on a range of topics, including social security, housing, local authority service and some legal matters. Phone or write to make an appointment.

Terrence Higgins Trust
BM/AIDS, London WC1 3XX; 01-242 1010, Mon–Fri 7–10 p.m. Sat/Sun 3–10 p.m. Offers counselling and help to people with HIV virus or AIDS, their friends and relatives; gives advice and information to people thinking of having the HIV antibody blood test; gives detailed information on what is safer sex.

DISABLED

Brothers and Sisters Club
BM B&S, London WC1N 3XX. Club facilities for lesbians and gay men who are
hearing-impaired.

Feminist Audio Books
(Feminist and Lesbian Books on Tape), c/o A Women's Place, Hungerford House,
Victoria Embankment, London WC2.

Gay Men's Disabled Group
c/o Gay's The Word Bookshop, 66 Marchmont Street, London WC1N 3XX.

Gemma
Contact Elsa Beckett, BM Box 5700, London WC1N 3XX. Exists to lesson the
isolation of disabled lesbians of all ages. The group meets monthly. Write for dates.

Sexual and Personal Relationships of the Disabled (SPOD)
286 Camden Road, London N7; 01-607 8851.

EMPLOYMENT

Gay Rights At Work
7 Pickwick Court. London SE9 4SA; 01-857 3793. Offers advice on gay rights in
employment.

Lesbian and Gay Employment Rights
Room 205, Southbank House, Black Prince Road, London SE1 7SJ; 01-587 1636.
Drop-in every Tuesday afternoon.

Unwaged Fightback Lesbian and Gay Group
355 Holloway Road, London N7. Meets Wed, 11 a.m.–1 p.m.

HEALTH

Alcoholics Anonymous Gay Group
(mixed), 01-834 8202, 10 a.m.–10 p.m. for details, times and addresses of meetings.

The Blenheim Project
c/o 7 Thorpe Close, Ladbroke Grove, London W10 5XL; 01-960 5599/5590,
10 a.m.–5 p.m. Offers counselling, advice, information for male and female drug
users (illicit), their families, friends and lovers.

Gay Bereavement Project
Unitarian Rooms, Hoop Lane, London NW11 8BS. Or phone 01-455 8894 or the
London Lesbian and Gay Switchboard on 01-837 7324 for the phone no. of one of the
group's volunteers. The GBP exists to help bereaved gays in various practical ways.
They can also give advice and support at a time when it is most needed.

Gay Medical Association
BM/GMA, London WC1N 3XX.

Guide to Organizations

Haemophilia Society
PO Box 9, 16 Trinity Street, London SE1 1DE; 01-407 1010.

Healthy Living Group
(Terrence Higgins Trust), 01-242 1010. The Group is concerned with alternative therapies.

Lesbians and Alcohol Group
Women's Alcohol Centre, 254 St Paul's Road, London N1; 01-226 4581, Mon–Fri 10 a.m.–1 p.m., Wed 11.30 a.m.–1 p.m.

Society of Homoeopaths
47 Canada Grove, Bognor Regis, PO21 1DW; 0243 860678. They will give a list of registered homoeopaths.

South London Health Clinic
7a Clapham Common South Side, London SW4; phone Mike Strange 01-720 8817. This alternative medicine clinic is run by Mike Strange, an openly gay, registered homoeopath who is critical of conventional medicine and attempts to 'build up the body to provide an environment in which the virus cannot live'.

Standing Conference on Drug Abuse (SCODA)
1–4 Hatton Place, London EC1N 8ND; 01-430 2341/2. They have a full list of local services for drug users throughout the country.

STD Clinics
(Sexually Transmitted Disease Clinics/Special Clinics/Genito-Urinary Clinics). Phone your nearest main hospital or London Lesbian and Gay Switchboard on 01-837 7324 or the Family Planning Information Service on 01-636 7866. Addresses and tel. numbers are in local tel. directories under VD (Venereal Disease). They can give you general advice about AIDS; they can give you the HIV virus antibody test; and they can give special advice and counselling for people with VD, who are HIV positive, or who have AIDS, as well as their friends and family. STD clinics give free and confidential advice and treatment. You do not need a letter from you own doctor. Simply turn up without an appointment at most clinics, though it is probably best to phone first to check on their arrangements. In London the three main clinics are the **John Hunter Clinic**, St Stephen's Hospital (01-352 8161, ext. 223), the **Praed Street Clinic**, St Mary's Hospital, Paddington (01-725 1697), and **James Pringle House**, the Middlesex Hospital (01-380 9141/2/3).

HOUSING

Blue Moon Housing Co-op (Women only), Lewisham: 132b Evelyn Street, London SE8; Southwark: 25 Brook Drive, London SE11; Lambeth: 26 Nursery Road, London SW9, 01-621 5089.

Flatshare List
Lesbian and Gay Switchboard, 01-837 7324.

Gay Housing Group
c/o London Friend, 274 Upper Street, Islington, N1; Gay Switchboard 01-837 7324.

Hackney Short-Life User Group (HSLUG)
Metropolitan Hospital, St Peter's Way, London N1; 01-249 3774. Housing for single young people including lesbian and gay people.

Homeless Action
52/54 Featherstone Street, London EC1; 01-251 6783. For homeless single women.

Housing Advisory Switchboard
01-434 2522. 24 hour switchboard. Housing for childless people in London.

Islington Girls Project
8 Manor Gardens, London N7; 01-263 6270. Short-life housing for young lesbians.

Seagull
36 Cambridge Gardens, London W10; 01-960 4402. Women only.

SHAC
London Housing Aid Centre, 189a Old Brompton Road, London SW5; 01-373 7276.

Stonewall Housing Association
London Lesbian and Gay Centre, 69 Cowcross Street, London EC1; 01-608 1471. Hostel accommodation for young lesbian and gay people.

LEGAL

At Ease
Contact them via **Release**, 1 Elgin Avenue, London W9; 01-289 1123 (or 01-603 8654 in emergencies). A voluntary organization that advises and assists people from the armed forces, British or otherwise, who need help. At Ease can refer people to supportive doctors and lawyers, and advises lesbians or gay men who wish to challenge a court martial or discharge from the service.

Gay Legal Advice (GLAD)
Write c/o London Lesbian and Gay Centre, 67–69 Cowcross Street, London EC1, or phone 01-253 2043, Mon–Fri, 7–10 p.m.

Gay London Police Monitoring Group (GALOP)
BM GALOP, London WC1N 3XX; 01-278 6215.

Guide To Gay Custody: Action for Lesbian Parents
c/o Peaceworks, 58 Wakefield Road, Huddersfield, West Yorkshire. Covers problems of obtaining custody, solicitors and legal procedures.

Legal Services Group
(Terrence Higgins Trust), 01-242 1010. The group was formed to provide legal advice to people who have AIDS, to people who are antibody positive, and to others who are at risk. The group also researches into the legal problems that people with AIDS are confronting so that solutions to them can be found.

Lesbian Custody Group
52/54 Featherstone Street, London EC1; 01-251 6576/7. The project is involved in both advice and campaign work.

Lesbians and Policing Project (LESPOP)
38 Mount Pleasant, London WC1; phone Kris Black on 01-833 4996/4999. Police monitoring group run by lesbians for lesbians. Regular phone in Thur, 2–6 p.m.

National Council for Civil Liberties
Gay Rights Office, 21 Tabard Street, London SE1 4LA; 01-403 3888.

Guide to Organizations

MEDIA

Communications Group (Terrence Higgins Trust), 01-242 1010. The group maintains the communication links both within the THT and with outside organisations. It includes among its volunteers the Press Officer, who surveys all media coverage of AIDS and co-ordinates the Trust's response. The group as a whole arranges media interviews and engagements with relevant Trust volunteers. It also liaises with political parties, unions and other pressure groups, providing them with current information.

The Equality Organizer
National Union of Journalists, Acorn House, 314–320 Grays Inn Road, London WC1X 8DP. These are the people to contact when readers are upset by homophobic comments in the press. The 'Ethics Council' of the NUJ has the power to discipline journalists who overstep the mark. A complaint may not produce immediate results, but it can at least make the journalist take notice of what readers are thinking.

Gay Sweatshop
c/o Drill Hall, 16 Chenies Street, London WC1.

Gays and Broadcasting Project
c/o London Media Project, 237 Pentonville Road, N1 9NJ.

Gays the Word Bookshop
66 Marchmont Street, London WC1N 1AB; 01-278 7654, Mon–Sat 11 a.m.–7 p.m. Sun 2–6 p.m. Gay community bookshop/coffee shop. Also produces bi-monthly *Lesbian and Gay Review*.

Gossip
38 Mount Pleasant, London WC1; 01-837 0596. A journal of lesbian feminist ethics from Onlywomen Press.

Independent Broadcasting Authority
70 Brompton Road, London SW3. For written complaints.

NUJ Equality Council
c/o NUJ, Acorn House, 314 Grays Inn Road, London WC1; 01-278 7916.

Press Council
1 Salisbury Square, London EC4Y 8AE. Considers complaints from newspaper readers. This is a useful means of exerting pressure in the face of biased journalism.

Sheba Feminist Publishers
10a Bradbury Street, London N16; 01-254 1590. Mail order service available. Publishes books by lesbians. Send SAE for catalogue.

OLDER LESBIANS AND GAY MEN

August Trust
42 Tredegar Road, Dartford, Kent; 01-736 6602. Home for elderly lesbians and gay men.

Older Lesbian Network
BM OLN, London WC1N 3XX. Contact: Lorna. Monthly meetings, Bi-monthly newsletter and social gatherings. Group provides strength and support and voices the needs of older lesbians.

Pink Wrinkle Rosa Rimple
Unitarian Library, Palace Gardens, London W8, first Sat every month, 7.30–
9.30 p.m. Social group for mature lesbians and gay men.

RELIGIOUS

Gay Christian Movement
BM 6914, London WC1N 3XX; 01-283 5165 + ansaphone. The GCM offers a
befriending and counselling service. Its aims are to encourage fellowship, friendship
and support among individual gay Christians, to help the whole Church re-examine its
understanding of human sexuality, to work for a positive acceptance of gay
relationships, to encourage members to witness to the Christian faith and experience
within the gay community, and to maintain and strengthen links with other gay
Christian groups both in Britain and elsewhere. The GCM has local groups
throughout the country.

Inter-Faith Group
(Terrence Higgins Trust), 01-242 1010. The IFG was set up to bring together
ministers, rabbis, priests, buddhists and workers in all faiths to advise and help the
Trust. The group's primary aim is to set up a network throughout the country of
people of all faiths. People within the network would then be able to give pastoral care
to people with AIDS, their friends and family, when needed. The group is also
disseminating accurate information about AIDS to the religious community.

Jewish Gay Group
BMJGG, London WC1N 3XX; 01-958 2955, evenings. Support group for Jewish gay
people.

Julian Fellowship
Box 137, Bexleyheath, Kent, DA6 1JF. For Catholic lesbians, although those of other
faiths are welcome. Spiritual growth through prayer, friendship and support.

Metropolitan Community Church
PO Box 99, Smethwick, Warley, West Midlands; 021-565 4378, 24 hours; 01-
435 7507, in North London; 01-677 7020, in South London.

Quest
BM Box 2585, London WC1N 3XX; 01-373 7819, Fri–Sun, 7–10 p.m. A group for
gay Catholics. Masses, discussion, speakers and socials. 'For help and support in
times of calm and crisis.'

YOUTH

Help Starts Here
168 Battersea Park Road, London SW11; 01-720 0753/0582, Mon 2–6 p.m. Wed
10 a.m.–1 p.m., Thur 2–6 p.m. Advice for under 21s, lesbians, gay men.

Lesbian and Gay Youth Movement
BM Gym, London WC1N 3XX; 01-317 9690, Mon/Wed/Fri 6–8.30 p.m., Sat

2–5 p.m. Run by lesbians and gays under 26. There is a phoneline advice service, information and support offered. Also organizes annual spring festival and summer camp.

London Friend
86 Caledonian Road, London N1; 01-837 3337. Telephone counselling service. Youth group meets Fri evenings.

Parents' Enquiry
16 Honley Road, London SE6 2HZ; 01-698 1815. For gay teenagers and their parents.

A Critical Bibliography

The following books are recommended to those readers who wish to explore in depth some of the issues discussed in this book.

ABBOTT, Sidney, and LOVE, Barbara, *Sappho was a Right-On Woman: A Liberated View of Lesbianism* (New York, Stein and Day, 1972)
A rational analysis of lesbianism from an authentic, inside perspective. The book is divided into two parts: Part One, 'What it was Like', focuses on the devastating consequences of guilt on the self-respect of lesbians; and Part Two, 'Living in the Future', reflects the new sense of pride towards which lesbians are striving, but which few, say the authors, have as yet achieved.

AIDS And Employment (Department of Employment and the Health and Safety Executive, The Mailing House, Leeland Road, London W13 9HL)
Very sensible advice to employers on the subject of AIDS. The pamphlet is available free if you write to 'Aids and Employment' and the address above.

ALTMAN, Dennis, *Aids and the New Puritanism* (London, Pluto Press, 1986)
Essential reading for anyone interested in an intelligent, very sensible discussion of the personal, social and political impact of AIDS on the world. Altman argues that because AIDS has been linked to homosexuality in the public's mind, this has become the most politicized of all diseases.

ALTMAN, Dennis, *Homosexual: Oppression and Liberation* (London, Allen Lane, 1974), revised edn.
Perhaps the most stimulating and insightful book to be written on the subject of gay oppression. The author describes the experience of personal liberation through self-affirmation as a homosexual, and his observations and conclusions will have relevance for all readers, regardless of their sexual orientation.

ARNOLD, June, *Sister Gin* (London, Women's Press, 1979)
An American novel about the lives of older lesbians. Vivid, lively and very positive.

BENSON, R. O. D., *What Every Homosexual Knows* (New York, Ace Books, 1965)
A rigorous scrutiny of the four principal arguments against homosexuality ('The Nature Argument', 'The Religious Argument', 'The Psychological Argument', and 'The Non-Rational Argument'), each of which is persuasively demolished by the author.

BERGER, Raymond M., *Gay and Gray: The Older Homosexual Man* (London, Alyson Publications/GMP, 1985)
A sensitive study of homosexuality and ageing.

BLAMIRES, David, *Homosexuality from the Inside: An Essay* (London, Social Responsibility Council of the Religious Society of Friends, 1973)
A brief but comprehensive look at attitudes towards homosexuality, sex roles and social pressures, coming out, and the establishment of relationships. A useful primer for young gays, as well as their parents.

BORHEK, M., *Coming Out to Parents* (New York, Pilgrim, 1983)
A guide for gays and their parents which includes much sound advice on coming out.

BOSWELL, John, *Christianity, Social Tolerance and Homosexuality* (Chicago, University of Chicago Press, 1981)
Professor Boswell of Yale University traces the rise of intolerance towards homosexuals in Western Europe. He aims to prove that the early Church was not especially opposed to homosexuality, and that the rise of intolerance, particularly in the thirteenth and fourteenth centuries, was the product of complex factors. The Church itself would later adopt an intolerant position, the author argues, but this should be seen as reflecting changes that had already occurred in society.

BROWN, Phil, ed., *Radical Psychology* (New York, Harper & Row, 1973)
Essays on the 'myth' of mental illness, antipsychiatry, sex roles, therapeutic encounters, etc., by Thomas Szasz, Erving Goffman, R. D. Laing, *et al.* Also included here are two important gay manifestos: 'Woman-Identified Woman' and 'Gay Liberation Manifesto'.

Capital Gay (Published weekly by Stonewall Press Ltd, 38 Mount Pleasant, London WC1X OAP)
London's best gay newspaper, providing news, the latest information on AIDS research ('Body Matters'), an Arts and Entertainment section, etc.

CHURCHILL, Wainwright, *Homosexual Behaviour Among Males: A Cross-Cultural and Cross-Species Investigation* (New York, Hawthorn Books, 1967)
Churchill presents the topic of homosexual behaviour, which he regards as being within the normal range of human behaviour, in its cross-species and cross-cultural dimensions. The book is of seminal importance in the literature of homosexuality, and the chapters on 'The Acquirement of Sexual Preferences', 'Sex, Sin, and Psychiatry', and 'Sex and Morality' will be of particular interest to readers.

CONN, Philip, *Setting Up Handbook: Guidelines in Organizing Gay and Lesbian Helping/Befriending Services* (National Friend, BM Friend, London WC1N 3XX, 1987)
This is a basic and comprehensive guide to various aspects of setting up 'helpline' and befriending services, with sections on finding volunteers and accommodation, management, finances, fundraising, training, establishing links with other agencies, etc. Thorough and practical.

CRANE, Paul, *Gays and the Law* (London, Pluto Press, 1982)
A comprehensive account of the law on homosexuality in the UK and how it is being used against lesbians and gay men. Combining essential information with passionate but reasoned opposition, Crane deals in some detail with the impact of prejudice on sexual orientation and gender, as well as the effects of the law on personal life, housing, the care of children, etc. Essential reading for counsellors.

CRISP, Quentin, *The Naked Civil Servant* (London, Jonathan Cape, 1968)
Quite possibly the most revealing and witty memoir by a homosexual ever written. No other work so vividly conveys the feelings and attitudes of a 'self-evident' gay, or so provocatively explores the means by which society stigmatizes its sexual non-conformists.

DUFFY, Maureen, *The Microcosm* (London, Hutchinson & Co. Ltd., 1966)
A perceptive and stylishly written novel which portrays a highly credible slice of lesbian life in Sixties England.

ELYOT, Kevin, *Coming Clean* (London, Faber & Faber, 1984)
A wonderfully wise, very funny play about a gay relationship on the verge of breakup.

FAIRCHILD, B., and HAYWARD, N., *Now That you Know: What Every Parent Should Know About Homosexuality* (New York, Harcourt Brace, 1979)
This is mainly for parents of gays and includes much personal narrative on how parents have responded to their child's homosexuality. Much useful and positive information included here.

FISHER, Peter, *The Gay Mystique: The Myth and Reality of Male Homosexuality* (New York, Stein and Day, 1972)
Dozens of answers to all the questions you ever wanted to ask about homosexuals, supplied in non-technical jargon by a gay activist.

FITZPATRICK, Dr Michael, and MILLIGAN, Don, *The Truth About the Aids Panic* (London, Junius, 1987)
Very sober and readable pamphlet that does exactly what the title suggests. The authors argue that AIDS is being used to promote Victorian family values and has allowed prejudice and discrimination to become more publicly manifest.

FRY, Jane (pseud.), *Being Different: The Autobiography of Jane Fry*. Collected, compiled and edited with an introduction and conclusion by Robert Bogdan (New York, Wiley-Interscience, 1974)
An incisive 'history' of a transsexual, told in her own words to Dr Bogdan. This autobiography is one of the most engrossing and highly readable accounts published of what it's like to be different.

GARFIELD, C., ed., *Psychosocial Care of the Dying Patient* (New York, McGraw-Hill, 1978)
A sympathetic study of a very difficult subject, but an area of concern to some counsellors.

Gay Students at School (Advisory Centre for Education, 1985)
A pamphlet which looks at society's attitudes towards homosexuality and what schools can do in terms of curriculum and pastoral care. Available by writing to the Centre at 18 Victoria Park Square, London E2 9PB, or phoning 01-980 4596.

Gay Times (Published monthly by Millivres Ltd, 283 Camden High Street, London NW1 7BX)
Britain's best gay magazine, providing news, articles on gay-related themes, arts reviews, an excellent 'mediawatch' section, and a very comprehensive gay guide to the UK, listing clubs and discos, pubs and bars, restaurants, local groups, local gay switchboards, AIDS helplines, advice and support groups, organizations, special interest groups, religious groups and university/polytechnic lesbian and gay socs.

GREY, Antony, *Christian Society and the Homosexual* (Oxford, Manchester College, 1966)
The author is one who looks at homosexuality from the perspective of Christ's teachings.

HANSCOMBE, Gillian, and FORSTER, Jackie, *Rocking The Cradle: Lesbian Mothers, A Challenge In Family Living* (London, Sheba, 1982)
Discussed here are the different ways in which lesbian mothers conceive and raise their children against the background of a hostile society. The authors write with conviction, passion and reason.

HEGER, Heinz, *The Men With The Pink Triangle* (London, GMP, 1986)
A sobering and very enlightening account of Nazi prosecution of homosexuals by one of its survivors.

HERON, Alastair, ed., *Towards a Quaker View of Sex* (London, Friends Home Service Committee, 1963)
The authors of this pamphlet persuasively argue that certain elements in the Church's attitude to sexuality throughout the centuries appear to be inconsistent with some of the Bible's deepest insights. Relating their observations to homosexuality, the authors conclude that morality must be creative.

HODGES, Andrew, and HUTTER, David, *With Downcast Gays: Aspects of Homosexual Self-Oppression* (London, Pomegranate Press, 1974)
A passionately written and intelligently argued tract which aims to explore the phenomenon of gay self-oppression, i.e. a form of oppression achieved when the gay person has adopted and internalized society's hostile attitudes towards homosexuality.

HOFFMAN, Martin, *The Gay World: Male Homosexuality and the Social Creation of Evil* (New York, Bantam Books, 1969)
The research upon which this book is based was specifically designed to study those homosexuals who do not usually become the objects of scientific attention via the psychiatrist's consulting room or the courts of law. Of particular interest is Chapter 7, 'The Development of Sexual Identity'.

HOFFMAN, William, *As If* (New York, Vintage Books, 1985)
A play that examines the impact of AIDS, especially on the gay community.
Funny and heartbreaking by turns.

HUMPHREYS, Laud, *Out of the Closets: The Sociology of Homosexual
  Liberation* (Englewood Cliffs, New Jersey, Prentice-Hall, 1972)
A sociological analysis and history of the Gay Liberation movement in the
USA.

HUMPHREYS, Laud, *Tearoom Trade: A Study of Homosexual Encounters in
  Public Places* (London, Duckworth, 1974)
A sociological study of casual sexual encounters in public toilets by a former
clergyman, now Professor of Sociology at the University of Southern
Illinois.

ISHERWOOD, Christopher, *A Single Man* (London, Methuen, 1964)
Isherwood's novel focuses on a middle-aged English professor at an American University who is struggling to come to terms with the death of his lover
in a car accident. More than two decades later, this remains a moving and
insightful study of bereavement and one of the best explorations of the gay
sensibility to be found in the English novel. Highly recommended.

JAY, Karla, and YOUNG, Allen, eds., *Out of the Closet: Voices of Gay
  Liberation* (New York, Pyramid Books, 1973)
A collection of personal experiences and critical essays by gays, edited by
two of the contributors, Karla Jay and Allen Young, who regard gay
oppression as a 'class struggle' taking place within a predominantly 'white,
middle-class, male-dominated, heterosexual society'.

JORGENSEN, Christine, *A Personal Autobiography*, with an introduction
  by Harry Benjamin, MD (New York, Bantam Books, 1968)
A fascinating autobiography by a transsexual whose much publicized 1952
sex-change operation awakened the world to the 'transsexual phenomenon'.

KINSEY, Alfred C., POMEROY, Wardell B., and MARTIN, Clyde E.,
  Sexual Behavior in the Human Male (Philadelphia and London, W. B.
  Saunders Company, 1948)
A scientific study of human sexual behavior which, like its companion
volume, *Sexual Behavior in the Human Female*, is unique in terms of scope,
degree of objectivity, methodological skills, and interdisciplinary approach.
Both studies present their evidence without moral bias or prejudice, though
the authors are anxious to emphasize the significance of their conclusions to
education, medicine, government, and the integrity of human conduct
generally. Of special interest is Chapter 21, 'Homosexual Outlets'.

KINSEY, Alfred C., POMEROY, Wardell B., MARTIN, Clyde E., and
  Gebhard, Paul H., *Sexual Behavior in the Human Female* (Philadelphia
  and London, W. B. Saunders Company, 1953)
Of special interest in this companion volume to *Sexual Behavior in the
Human Male* is Chapter 11, 'Homosexual Responses and Contacts'.

LAURITSEN, John, and WILSON, Hank, *Death Rush: Poppers and Aids* (New York, Pagan Press, 1986)
This book's thesis is controversial and not scientifically proven, but well argued: the virus in itself is not a sufficient cause of AIDS; far more crucial to our understanding of the disease are toxic recreational drugs—key co-factors in causing the breakdown of the immune system. The drugs alluded to are alcohol and, especially, nitrate, inhalants or poppers.

London Scene: The Gay Man's Guide (London, GMP, 1987)
The first fully comprehensive gay guide to London. Included here are feature length articles about various aspects of London gay life. There are chapters on art, dance, the cinema, theatre and music, as well as fitness and health (from AIDS to STD clinics). The book concludes with a section on Brighton and Bournemouth.

MACDONALD, Barbara, *Look me in the Eye: Old Women, Ageing And Ageism* (London, Women's Press, 1985)
A sympathetic study of the ageing process and gay life.

MCKUSICK, Leon, *What To Do About AIDS: Physicians and Mental Health Professionals Discuss the Issues* (Berkeley and Los Angeles, University of California Press, 1986)
Papers from a conference convened in San Francisco in September 1985 by a group of experts who provide much insight into different aspects of AIDS and how it affects all those associated with it.

MARS-JONES, Adam, and WHITE, Edmund, *The Darker Proof: Stories From A Crisis* (London, Faber & Faber, 1987)
Six stories by Mars-Jones and White, both of whom are gay, which deal with the physical, intellectual, social and emotional wounds inflicted by AIDS. Some excellent character portrayals throughout by authors who have an eye for telling detail and an abundance of compassion.

MARTIN, Del, and LYON, Phyllis, Lesbian/Woman (New York, Bantam Books, 1972)
The authors, both founder-members of The Daughters of Bilitis, an American gay women's organization, have been actively involved in the homophile movement for well over three decades. Their collective experiences as gay activists, feminists, and counsellors should prove useful to readers, for Martin and Lyon provide us with numerous personal and social histories.

MILLER, David, 'Counselling', in the *British Medical Journal*, Volume 294 (27 June 1987), pp. 1671–4.
This is very useful reading for counsellors, with practical advice on HIV testing, psychological issues in HIV/AIDS counselling, and safer sex.

MILLER, David, WEBER, Jonathan, and GREEN, John, *The Management of Aids Patients* (London, Macmillan, 1986)
This is a medical and technical guide for dealing with AIDS which includes lengthy discussions on clinical management and nursing techniques. Not for the general reader.

MILLER, Merle, *On Being Different: What it Means to be a Homosexual* (New York, Random House, 1971)
A moving and often amusing account, written by a well-known author and journalist, of the consequences to his personal life and career of coming out at the age of fifty.

MURPHY, John *Homosexual Liberation: A Personal View* (New York and London, Praeger Publishers, 1971)
This book is a statement of experiences from a new generation of gays, one which is interested in developing a sense of pride in being gay rather than passing for straight. The author's central thesis is that most of the problems confronting the gay person spring from a lack of self-identity.

PRAKES, C., *Bereavement* (New York, International Universities Press, 1974)
An informative, compassionate, helpful study on the subject of bereavement.

PRATT, Robert J., *AIDS: A Strategy for Nursing Care* (London, Edward Arnold, 1986)
Written specifically for nursing personnel.

Psychiatry and the Homosexual: A Brief Analysis of Oppression (London, Gay Information, 1973)
This pamphlet, the first in a series planned for publication by a collective of gay men, deals with the treatment of homosexuality by mainstream psychiatry.

RICHARDSON, Diane, *Women and the AIDS Crisis* (London, Pandora, 1987)
This very useful book approaches the subject of AIDS from a woman's perspective, offering useful guidelines on high- and low-risk sex, drug use, pregnancy, rape, living with and caring for those with AIDS, etc.

RIGHTON, Peter, comp., *Counselling Homosexuals: A Study of Personal Needs and Public Attitudes* (London, Bedford Square Press of the National Council of Social Services, 1973)
This pamphlet is the published report of working party set up in July 1970 at a national conference on social needs to study counselling services for homosexuals. Section Two is of particular interest for its practical advice on befriending and counselling groups.

ROBERTSON, Roy, *Heroin, AIDS and Society* (London, Hodder & Stoughton, 1987)
The author steps out of line with most of his medical colleagues by drawing attention to the very restricted official information that forms the basis of contemporary attitudes towards drug users. Robertson argues that the high mortality attributed to heroin use is influenced by a number of factors. The major cause of death associated with heroin use is rapidly becoming AIDS, but the dangers come not from the drugs, the author stresses, but from the way they are used.

ROGERS, Carl R., *Client-Centred Therapy* (Boston, Houghton Mifflin Company, 1951)
The client-centredness of the Rogerian position is non-authoritarian. The 'client' is regarded as an equal, and the therapy session is known as an interview. The expression 'client-centred' indicates that the direction of the therapy process is essentially in the hands of the client rather than the counsellor.

ROGERS, Carl R., *Encounter Groups* (Harmondsworth, Middlesex, Pelican Books, 1973)
Practical advice on the formation and conduct of encounter groups by the founder of 'client-centred' therapy.

ROSENFELS, Paul, *Homosexuality: The Psychology of the Creative Process* (New York, Libra Publishers, Inc., 1971)
Rosenfels insists that openness about homosexuality is essential to human creative development. New goals of human devotion to truth and right must emerge so that people can find a way to love and be responsible to one another out of their own human resources rather than conventional social roles.

ROSSMAN, Parker, *Sexual Experience Between Men and Boys* (London, Maurice Temple Smith, 1987)
An important, widely acclaimed work which explores the world of the men who engage in sexual activity with adolescent boys. To gain answers to questions concerning adult motivation, adolescent consent and the role of the law, the author has collected material through questionnaires, personal correspondence and interviews with 1,000 adults and 300 adolescents who have acted as sex partners. Dr Rossman, a Yale professor and an ordained clergyman, is a former dean of the Ecumenical Continuing Education Centre. A very sensible, unusually detached work which is neither a defence nor a condemnation of its subject.

SANDERSON, Terry, *How to be a Happy Homosexual—A Guide for Gay Men* (London, The Other Way Press, 1986)
A book that offers hope and encouragement to gay men while dealing with oppression in a realistic manner.

School's Out: Gay Rights and Education (London, Gay Teachers' Group, 1983)
A collection of accounts and comments by gay teachers and youth workers about their experiences in the area of homosexuality and students, the school curriculum and school policies, youth groups, etc. Very useful.

SONTAG, Susan, *Illness as Metaphor* (New York, Vintage Books, 1979)
A penetrating analysis of social attitudes towards tuberculosis and cancer. The author argues that metaphoric thinking about illness is 'invariably an encouragement to simplify what is complex and an invitation to self-righteousness, if not fanaticism'. A very probing, stimulating book with obvious parallels to much current thinking on AIDS.

SZASZ, Thomas, *Ideology and Insanity: Essays on the Psychiatric Dehumanization of Man* (Harmondsworth, Middlesex, Penguin Books, 1973)
This book has implicit reference to homosexuality, for the author, a psychoanalyst and teacher, warns us of the dangers of avoiding moral conflicts and social problems by defining certain behavioural patterns as forms of mental illness.

TATCHELL, Peter, *AIDS: A Guide to Survival* (London, GMP, 1986)
A useful book which aims to give hope to people throughout the entire AIDS spectrum. Tatchell offers information and practical advice, as indicated by some of the chapter headings: 'Preventing AIDS', 'Fighting Back Against AIDS', 'Living with AIDS' and 'Campaigning to Defeat AIDS'.

WARREN, Hugh, and TRENCHARD, Lorraine, eds., *Something to Tell You* (London, Gay Teenage Group, 1984)
This book critically examines the attitudes of schools, youth services, employers, police and others towards gays, whose home, social and sex lives are described by the young people themselves.

WEBER, Jonathan, and FERRIMAN, Annabel, *AIDS Concerns You* (London, Pagoda Books, 1986)
A basic information text which offers straightforward answers to some complex questions. Like so many books on this subject, however, it is likely to date quite quickly. Until such time, it serves its purpose well.

WEEKS, Jeffrey, *Coming Out: Homosexual Politics in Britain, From the Nineteenth Century to the Present* (London, Quartet Books, 1977)
A very illuminating study of the growth of homosexual law reform from the development of legal and social oppression in the late nineteenth century to the gay liberation movement in the 1970s. Weeks presents a comprehensive study of homosexual reform, but also illuminates wider attitudes towards sexuality in general.

WEEKS, Jeffrey, *Sex, Politics and Society: The Regulation of Sexuality Since 1800* (London, Longman, 1981)
Weeks explores the transformation of attitudes to sexuality in Britain over the last 200 years. The author argues that, in the context of an industrialized, capitalist society, sexuality is shaped and determined by a variety of social forces and has undergone complex historical transformations. The book is full of stimulating, often provocative insights, with much detailed discussion on the significance of the family, changes in the concepts of female sexuality, the development of theories of homosexuality, and changes in the ideologies of sex.

WEEKS, Jeffrey, *Sexuality and its Discontents* (London, GMP, 1985)
The author's principal theme is that we have inherited certain notions about sexuality which dictate the way we now regard it, but which, in fact, are mistaken. Disputing the received idea that sexuality is a natural force, Weeks argues that nature has nothing to do with it; our sexuality, and the attitudes we have developed towards it, are socially constructed. 'Sexuality could be a potentiality for choice, change and diversity', he writes. 'Instead,

we take it as a destiny.' There is also some discussion of AIDS as an emblem of the fear and hostility that sexuality engenders.

WEINBERG, George, *Society and the Healthy Homosexual* (New York, St Martin's Press Inc., 1972; Doubleday, 1973)
Weinberg has written a powerful and persuasive treatise on homophobia, defined as an attitude of revulsion and anger towards all things homosexual.

WEINBERG, Martin S., and WILLIAMS, Colin J., *Male Homosexuals: Their Problems and Adaptations* (New York, Oxford University Press, 1974)
Drawing upon the experiences and feelings of several thousand homosexuals in three countries, the authors examine the male homosexual's problems and adaptations with respect to society's institutions, values and stereotypes.

WILKINSON, Graham, *Working with Gay Men with AIDS* (Sussex AIDS Helpline, P.O. Box 17, Brighton 1987)
This twenty-eight page pamphlet gives advice to those who befriend people with AIDS. The author, who is in the ARC category, helped co-found the Brighton Body Positive Group.